HOW TO REALLY
LOVE YOUR CHILDREN

HOW TO REALLY LOVE YOUR CHILDREN

ROSS CAMPBELL, M.D.

INSPIRATIONAL PRESS

NEW YORK

First Inspirational Press edition published in 1996.

Inspirational Press
A division of Budget Book Service, Inc.
386 Park Avenue South
New York, NY 10016

Inspirational Press is a registered trademark of Budget Book Service, Inc.

Published by arrangement with Victor Books.

Library of Congress Catalog Card Number: 95-81987

ISBN: 0-88486-135-X

Printed in the United States of America.

CONTENTS

I.
HOW TO REALLY LOVE
YOUR CHILD

1

HOW TO REALLY LOVE
YOUR CHILD

CONTENTS

FOREWORD

This book hits us where we live. Yet it does not condemn — but tells us how to be parents in a different and constructive fashion. It is compassionate without being permissive.

Parents have never been trained to be parents. They tend to rear a child without any real fixed standards. Even the successes seem to be primarily by accident; this book is designed to produce successes by intention.

Dr. Ross Campbell has something vitally valuable to say — and says it plainly so we can understand it. This psychiatrist establishes himself in this book as a man of deep personal insight, deep spiritual values, and a great sensitivity both to the children and their parents. He doesn't hesitate to share himself and his own family experiences in illustrating what he has to say.

This is a book you will want to *read* and *reread*. It's that loaded with practical, usable information! Both your mind and your heart will tell you this book is true.

Ben Haden
Speaker, "Changed Lives,"
Chattanooga, Tennessee

This book is for parents of children younger than adolescents. Its intention is to give mothers and fathers an understandable and practical way of approaching their wonderful, yet awesome, task of raising each child. My concerns are the needs of children and how best to meet them.

This whole area of child rearing is in itself a complex venture with which most parents today are having great difficulty. Unfortunately, the outpouring of books, articles, lectures, and seminars regarding children have largely frustrated and bewildered parents despite the fact much of the information has been excellent.

I believe the problem has been that many books, articles, and lectures have homed in on one, or at most, only a few specific aspects of child rearing without covering the subject fully, or without clearly defining the specific area they are covering. Consequently, many conscientious parents have earnestly attempted to apply what they have read or heard as the fundamental way of relating to a child, and often fail. Their failure is not usually due to error in the formation read or heard, nor in the way it is applied.

The problem, as I see it, usually lies in the parents not having a general, balanced perspective on how to relate to a child. Most parents have the essential information per se, but there is confusion about *when* to apply *which* principle under *what* circumstance. This confusion is understandable. Parents have been told what to do, but not when to do it, nor, in many cases, how to do it.

The classic example of this is in the area of discipline. Excellent books and seminars on childhood have addressed the issue of discipline but failed to make clear that discipline is only one way of relating to a child. Many parents, consequently, conclude that discipline is the basic and primary way of treating a child. This is an easy mistake to make especially when one hears the statement, "If you love your child, you must discipline your child." This statement is, of course, true, but the tragedy is that many parents discipline almost *totally* while showing little love which can be felt or bring comfort to a child. Hence, most children doubt that they are genuinely, unconditionally loved. So again, the problem is not whether to discipline; the problem is how to manifest our love to a child through discipline and when to show it in other, more affectionate, ways.

I address these problems in a plain, understandable way, in order to demonstrate how to *generally* approach child rearing. In addition, I hope to provide information which will help parents determine the correct action for each situation. Of course, handling every circumstance correctly is impossible; however, the closer we come to this, the better parents we become, the more gratified we are, and the happier our child becomes.

Much of the material in this book has come from lecture series that I have given over past years at numerous conferences on parent-child relationships.

CHAPTER 1

The Problem

"**A**s Tommy was growing up, he was such a good boy, so well behaved," Esther Smith, her husband, Jim, at her side, began as the grieving parents unfolded their painful story in my counseling room. "Yes, he seemed content and never gave us much trouble. We made sure he had the right experiences—scouts, baseball, church and all. Now he is fourteen and is forever fighting with his brother and sister—but that's just sibling rivalry, isn't it? Other than that, Tom—he's no longer Tommy—has never been a real problem for us," Esther Smith continued. "He is moody sometimes and goes to his room for long periods. But he has never been disrespectful or disobeyed or back-talked. His father saw to that.

"There's one thing we *know* he has gotten plenty of and that's discipline. In fact, that's the most puzzling thing of all. How can a child so well disciplined all his life suddenly begin running around with undisciplined peers and do the things they do? And show such disrespect for his parents and other adults. These kids even lie, steal, and drink alcohol. I can't trust Tom anymore. I can't talk with him. He's so sullen and quiet. He won't even look at me. He doesn't seem to want anything to do with us. And he's doing so poorly in school this year."

"When did you notice these changes in Tom?" I asked.

Jim Smith looked up at the ceiling. "Let me think. He's fourteen now, almost fifteen," he said. "His grades were the first problem we noticed. About two years ago. During the last few months of sixth grade, we noticed he became bored first with school, then with other things. He began to hate going to church. Later Tom even lost interest in his friends and spent more and more time by himself, usually in his room. He talked less and less.

"But things really worsened when he began junior high school. Tom lost interest in his favorite activities — even sports. That's when he completely dropped his old standby friends and began running around with boys who were usually in trouble. Tom's attitude changed and conformed to theirs. He placed little value in grades and wouldn't study. These friends of his often got him in trouble."

"And we've tried everything." Mrs. Smith took up the account. "First we spanked him. Then we took away privileges like television, movies, and so on. One time we grounded him for a solid month. We've tried to reward him for appropriate behavior. I really believe we have tried every recommendation we have heard or read. I really wonder if anyone can help us or help Tom."

"What did we do wrong? Are we bad parents? God knows we've tried hard enough," Jim Smith added. "Maybe it's congenital. Maybe it's something Tom inherited. Could it be physical? But our pediatrician examined him a couple of weeks ago. Should we take him to a gland specialist? Should we get an EEG? We need help. Tom needs help. We love our boy, Dr. Campbell. What can we do to help him? Something's got to be done."

Later, after Mr. and Mrs. Smith departed, Tom entered the counseling room. I was impressed with his naturally likeable ways and handsome appearance. However, his gaze was downcast and when he would make eye contact, it was only for a moment. Although obviously a bright child, Tom spoke only in short, gruff phrases and grunts. Finally, when he felt comfortable enough to share his story, he revealed essentially the same factual material as his parents. Going further, he said, "No one really cares about me except my friends."

"No one?" I asked.

"Naw. Maybe my parents. I don't know. I used to think they cared about me when I was little. I guess it doesn't matter much now anyway. All they really care about are their own friends, jobs, activities, and things.

"They don't need to know what I do, anyway. It's none of their business. I just want to be away from them and lead my own life. Why should they be so concerned about me? They never were before."

As the conversation progressed, it became clear that Tom was quite depressed, never having times when he felt content with himself or his life. He had longed for a close, warm relationship with his parents as long as he could remember, but during the last few months he had slowly given up his dream. He turned to peers who would accept him, but his unhappiness deepened even more.

So here is a common tragic situation today. An early adolescent boy who, by all apparent indications, was doing well during his early years. Until he was around twelve or thirteen years of age, no one guessed that Tom was unhappy. During those years he was a complacent child who made few demands on his parents, teachers, or others. So none suspected he did not feel completely loved and accepted. Despite his having parents who deeply loved him and cared for him, Tom did not *feel* genuinely loved. Yes, he knew of his parents' love and concern for him and never would have told you otherwise. Nonetheless, the incomparable emotional well-being of feeling completely and unconditionally loved and accepted was not his.

This is truly difficult to understand, because Tom's parents are indeed good parents. They love him, and take care of his needs to the best of their knowledge. In raising Tom, Jim and

Esther Smith have applied what they have heard and read and have sought advice from others. And their marriage is definitely above average. They do love and respect each other.

A Familiar Story

Most parents have a difficult time raising their children. With pressures and strains mounting every day upon the American family, it is easy to become confused and discouraged. Rising divorce rates, economic crises, declining quality of education, and loss of trust in leadership all take an emotional toll of everyone. As parents become more physically, emotionally, and spiritually drained, it becomes increasingly difficult to nurture a child. I am convinced that a child takes the greatest brunt of these difficult times. A child is the most needy person in our society, and his greatest need is love.

The story of Tom Smith is familiar today. His parents do love him deeply. They have done their best in rearing him, but something is missing. Did you notice what it was? No, not love, the parents *do* love him. The basic problem is that Tom does not *feel* loved. Should the parents be blamed? Is it their fault? I don't think so. The truth is that Mr. and Mrs. Smith have always loved their son, but never knew how to show it. Like most parents, they believed they were meeting Tom's needs: food, shelter, clothes, education, love, guidance, etc. Yes, they met all these needs but were overlooking his need for love, unconditional love. Although love is within the heart of almost all parents, the challenge is to *convey* this love.

I believe that, despite the problems in today's living, any parents who genuinely desire to give a child what he needs, can be taught to do so. In order to give him everything they can in the short time he is with them, all parents need to know how to truly love their children.

Which Form of Discipline Is Most Appropriate?

"I remember one time when I was six or seven. Even now it makes me unhappy to think about it, and sometimes it makes me mad," Tom continued in a session with me a few days later. "I had accidentally broken a window with a baseball. I felt terrible about it and hid in the woods until Mom came looking for me. I was so sorry and I remember crying because I felt I had been very bad. When Dad came home, Mom told him about the window and he whipped me." Tears had welled up in Tom's eyes.

I asked, "What did you say then?"

"Nothing," he muttered.

This incident illustrates another area of confusion in handling children, that of discipline. In this example, the way Tom was disciplined caused him to have feelings of pain, anger, and resentment toward his parents which he will never forget or forgive without help.

Now years afterward, Tom still hurt from that happening. Why did that particular incident make such an unpleasant imprint on his memory? There were other times when he accepted spankings with no problems, and on occasion was even thankful. Could it have been because he already felt sorry and repentant over his breaking the window? Had he already suffered enough for his mistake without enduring physical pain? Could the spanking have convinced Tom that his parents did not understand him as a person or were not sensitive to his feelings? Could he have needed his parents' warmth and understanding at that particular time rather than harsh punishment? If so, how could Tom's parents know? And, if so, how could they discern which form of discipline was most appropriate at that particular time?

What do you think, fellow parents? Should we decide in advance what action we will routinely take in raising a child? Do you think we should be consistent? How consistent? Should we use punishment each time our child misbehaves? If so, should it always be the same? If not, what are the alternatives? What is discipline? Are discipline and punishment synonymous? Should we study one school of thought, for example, Parent Effectiveness Training, and stick by it? Or should we use some of our own common sense and intuition? Or some of each? How much? When?

These are questions every conscientious parent is struggling with today. We are bombarded with books, articles, seminars, and institutes about how to rear our children. Approaches vary from pinching a child's trapezius muscle to the use of candy as a reward.

In short, how could the parents have handled this situation in a way that would discipline Tom and yet maintain a loving, warm relationship with him? We'll look into this difficult subject later.

I think all parents agree that rearing a child today is especially difficult. One reason is that so much of a child's time is under the control and influence of others; for instance, school, church, neighbors, and peers. Because of this many parents feel no matter how good a job they do, their efforts have little overall effect upon their child.

The Opposite Is True

Just the opposite is true. Every study I've read indicates that the home wins hands down in every case. The influence of parents far outweighs everything else. The home holds the upper hand in determining how happy, secure, and stable a child is; how a child gets along with adults, peers, and different children; how confident a youngster is in himself and his abilities; how affectionate he is or how aloof; how he responds to unfamiliar situations. Yes, the home, despite many distractions for a child, has the greatest influence on him.

But the home is not the only thing that determines what a child becomes. We should not make the mistake of totally blaming the home for every problem or disappointment. For the sake of fairness and completeness, I believe we must take a look at the second greatest influence upon a child.

Congenital Temperament

Actually there are many congenital temperaments. Nine have been identified to date. The research which has given us this knowledge has been done by Dr. Stella Chess and Dr. Alexander Thomas. The data have been reported in their book, *Temperament and Behavior Disorder in Children*, published by University Press, New York.

This book has been acclaimed a classic and is a truly great

contribution to the world of behavioral science. It goes a long way in explaining why children have the individual characteristics they do. It helps explain why some children are easier to raise than others. Why some children are more lovable or easier to handle. Why children raised in the same family or in very similar circumstances can be so different.

Best of all, Chess and Thomas have shown that how a child turns out is determined not only by the home environment, but also by his or her own personal traits. This has had wonderful results in alleviating much unjustified blame toward parents of children with problems. It is an unfortunate habit of many (including professionals) to assume that parents are fully to blame for everything regarding their child. The research of Chess and Thomas proves that some children are more prone to difficulties than others.

Let's look briefly at their research. Nine temperaments that can be identified in a newborn nursery have been described. These temperaments are not only congenital (present at birth) but are basic characteristics of a child that tend to stay with him. These characteristics can be modified by a child's environment; nonetheless, the temperaments are well ingrained in a child's total personality, do *not* change easily, and can persist throughout life. These nine congenital temperaments are:

1. *Activity level* is the degree of motor activity a child inherently possesses and determines how active or passive he is.

2. *Rhythmicity* (regularity versus irregularity) is the predictability of such functions as hunger, feeding pattern, elimination, and sleep-awake cycle.

3. *Approach or withdrawal* is the nature of a child's response to a new stimulus such as a new food, toy, or person.

4. *Adaptability* is the speed and ease with which a current behavior can be modified in response to altered environmental structuring.

5. *Intensity of reaction* is the amount of energy used in mood expression.

6. *Threshhold of responsiveness* is the intensity level of stimulus required to make a response.

7. *Quality of mood* (positive mood versus negative mood):

playful, pleasant, joyful, friendly, as contrasted with unpleasant, crying, unfriendly behavior.

8. *Distractability* identifies the effect of extraneous environment on direction of ongoing behavior.

9. *Attention span and persistence* is the length of time an activity is pursued by a child and the continuation of an activity in face of obstacles.

The third, fourth, fifth, and seventh temperaments are the most crucial in determining whether a child will be easy or difficult to rear. A child with a high degree of reactivity (highly "emotional"); a child who tends to withdraw in a new situation (a "withdrawer"); a child who has difficulty adapting to new situations (cannot tolerate change); or a child who is usually in a bad mood—these children are quite vulnerable to stress, especially to high parental expectations. And unfortunately, they tend to receive less love and affection from adults.

The lesson to learn here is that a child's basic characteristics have much to do with the type of mothering and nurturing he or she receives.

Using these nine temperaments, Chess and Thomas assigned numerical values to evaluate newborn children. From this data they were able to predict clearly which children would be "easy babies," that is, easy to care for, easy to relate to, and easy to raise. The children who were difficult to care for, difficult to relate to, and difficult to raise were called "difficult babies." They would require more from their mothers than would "easy babies."

Then Chess and Thomas compared how the children progress according to the type of mothering they received. Chess and Thomas studied the babies with "nurturing" mothers (mothers who wanted their children and were able to provide a loving atmosphere where the children felt accepted). The two researchers also studied "non-nurturing" mothers (mothers who consciously or subconsciously rejected their babies or were not able to provide an atmosphere where the children felt accepted and loved). The graph on page 19 summarizes their findings.

As you can see, the "easy" babies and "nurturing" mothers were a great combination. These children developed well with almost no negative consequences.

The "nurturing" mothers with "difficult" babies had some problems with their children, but these situations were overwhelmingly positive. Overall, in the loving atmosphere provided by their mothers, these children did well.

The "easy" babies who had "non-nurturing" mothers generally did not do as well. They had more difficulties than the "difficult" babies with nurturing mothers. Their experiences were somewhat more negative than positive.

	Nurturing Mothers	Non-nurturing Mothers
Easy babies	$+$ $+$	$+$ $-$
Difficult babies	$+$ $-$	$-$ $-$

Not surprisingly, the "difficult" babies with the "non-nurturing" mothers were most unfortunate. These children were in such difficult predicaments that they were aptly called "high-risk" children. The situations of these children is heartbreaking. They are in danger of everything imaginable from child-abuse to abandonment. They are indeed our high-risk children.

So, as we put all this invaluable material together, some extremely important facts begin to emerge. First of all, how a child gets along in the world does not depend only on his home environment and parenting. The basic congenital characteristics of each child have a strong effect on how he develops, progresses, and matures.

These traits also affect and often determine how easy or difficult a child is to care for and how frustrating he might be to his parents. This, in turn, influences the parents' handling of a child. It's a two-way street.

Learning these facts has helped many guilt-ridden parents in my daily practice.

Another important lesson for parents to learn is that despite what type of congenital temperaments a child may possess, the type of mothering (and fathering, of course) is more important in determining how a child will do. Study the graph again. Although a "difficult" child is, of course, more difficult to rear, the type of emotional nurturing has more influence in determining the final outcome. Parenting can change these congenital temperaments positively or negatively.

That's what this book is all about. It's a how-to book: how to relate to your child so he will grow to be his best; how to give your child the emotional nurturing he needs so badly. It is impossible to cover every aspect of child rearing here. I have therefore included what I feel is the most basic material for effective parenting.

It is a fact that most parents have a feeling of love toward their children and assume that they convey this love to a child. This is the greatest error today. Most parents are not transmitting their own heartfelt love to their children, and the reason is that they do not know how. Consequently, many children do not feel genuinely, unconditionally loved and accepted.

This, I believe, is true in relation to most problems that develop in children. Unless parents have a basic love-bond relationship with their children, everything else (discipline, peer relationships, school performance) is on a faulty foundation and problems will result.

This book provides the crucial basics in establishing a love-bond relationship.

CHAPTER 2

The Setting

Before we get into the basics of how to genuinely love and discipline a child, it is important to look at the prerequisites of good child rearing. The first and most important of these is the home. We will touch only a few of the essential points.

The most important relationship in the family is the marital relationship. It takes primacy over all others including the parent-child relationship. Both the quality of the parent-child bond and the child's security are largely dependent on the quality of the marital bond. So you can see why it is important to help a husband and wife to have a good relationship before attempting to solve problems they may have in child rearing. The better a marital relationship, the more effective and gratifying will be the application of later information.

However, if you are a single parent, let me assure you that what we discuss in this book applies just as much to you, dear parent. In many ways single parenting is more difficult, yet in some ways easier. But whether two parents or one, the way we relate to our children makes the difference in any home.

We can start by realizing that there is a difference between cognitive (that is, intellectual or rational) communication and emotional (that is, feeling) communication. Persons who communicate primarily on a cognitive level deal mainly with factual data. They talk about such topics as sports, the stock market, money, houses, and jobs, keeping the subject of conversation out of the emotional area. Usually they are quite uncomfortable dealing with issues which elicit feelings, especially unpleasant feelings such as anger. Consequently, they avoid talking about subjects which involve love, fear, and anger. These persons have difficulty, then, being warm and supportive of their spouses.

Others communicate more on the feeling level. They tire easily of purely factual data, and feel a need to share feelings, especially with their spouses. They feel the atmosphere between husband and wife must be as free as possible from such unpleasant feelings as tension, anger, and resentment. Therefore, they want to talk about these emotional things, resolve conflicts with their spouses, clear the air, and keep things pleasant between them.

Of course, no one is completely cognitive or completely emotional. We will all be somewhere on the spectrum this simple graph shows. If a person's personality and communication patterns tended to be almost completely emotional in *manifestation*, this person would appear on the left side of the graph. If a person exhibited a cognitive pattern of communication, he or she would be on the right side of the graph. We all fit somewhere between the two extremes. Where do you fit in?

Emotional   **Cognitive**

Where would you say men and women tend to be on the chart? Right! As a general rule, women tend to be more emotional in their ways of dealing with other persons, especially spouses and children. Men tend to be more cognitive in their ways of communicating.

At this point, you may believe that being on the right side of the graph is more desirable than appearing on the left. This is a common misconception. The truth is that every type of personality has advantages and disadvantages. A person on the left side of the graph, who shares more feelings, is not necessarily less bright or less intellectual. This person is simply aware of his or her feelings and is usually better able to do something about them. On the other hand, a person on the right side of the graph, who does not display feelings, may simply be suppressing feelings and is therefore less aware of them.

A surprising fact is that the so-called cognitive person (on the right) is controlled by his feelings just as is the so-called emotional person, but *he doesn't realize it.* For example, the stiff, formal intellectual generally has deep feelings also, but uses enormous energy to keep them buried so he won't be bothered with them. But unfortunately they *do* bother him. Whenever someone (like an "emotional" wife, or child) is around asking him for affection and warmth, he is not only unable to respond, he is angered that his precious equilibrium has been disturbed.

A Father's Initiative

"My husband, Fred, has been such a good provider and he's so respected," Mary Davis explained to me in her bewilderment, "that I feel terrible about how I feel toward him. I get so angry at him; then I feel so guilty I can't stand myself. I try to talk with him about how I feel about him and about the children. He becomes uncomfortable, clams up, then is mad at me. Then I'm upset and angry and get back at him — I even get frigid and can't make love with him. What can I do? I am so worried about my marriage and my children, but I can't even talk with my husband about it. How can our marriage last?"

There's the old story. Fred Davis is competent in the business world. He knows about his business. He has the facts. He is comfortable in a world where emotional factors are omitted and generally not needed. He is "cognitive" in his communications.

But at home he is like a fish out of water. He's married to a normal wife with normal womanly and wifely needs. Mary needs her husband's warmth and support. She needs him to share in her concerns, fears, and hopes. Mary tends to be "emotional" in her communications. She needs to feel that her husband is willing to assume his responsibility for the family. These needs of hers are normal and do not mean that she is weak, overly sensitive, or that she is not carrying her own responsibilities. I have yet to see a truly happy, warm family where the husband and father did not assume family responsibilities. Again, the wife and mother has her responsibilities, but the husband must be willing to help her and support her in each of these. One reason that this is essential is that a woman has a difficult time initiating love for her husband when she feels her husband is not willing to support her 100 percent in all areas of family life, emotional and otherwise. Of course, the same is true regarding the husband's family responsibilities. He must know that his wife is ready to help and even step in when needed.

Another way to put it is that when a woman must assume responsibilities because her husband simply won't, it is hard for her to feel secure and comfortable in his love. For example, one wife whom I was counseling complained that she felt insecure in her husband's love and had difficulty responding to him lovingly. As it turned out, she was responsible strictly by default for essentially every aspect of the family life, including the yard and handling the finances. This arrangement may be all right if husband and wife both agree and are happy with it; but even then, the husband must assume these overall responsibilities if needed; that is, he must be ready and willing to take over if the spouse is overburdened. A husband's "willingness" to be completely answerable for his family is one of the greatest assets a wife and child can have.

A wife can be wonderful at accepting love initiated by her husband, amplifying it manyfold, and reflecting it to him and the children, filling the home with an inexplicably wonderful climate. But a husband must take the responsibility of initiating love. Husbands who have found this secret are to be envied. The love returned to him by his wife is priceless, in my opinion the most precious commodity in this world. It is difficult to initiate love at first, but as the husband experiences his wife's love in return, he finds it to be multiplied many times, and sees that as this love increases with time, it becomes easier and easier to do.

If there are exceptions, I have yet to find one. The husband who will take full, total, overall responsibility for his family, and take the initiative in conveying his love to his wife and children, will experience unbelievable rewards: a loving, appreciative, helping wife who will be her loveliest for him; children who are safe, secure, content and able to grow to be their best. I personally have never seen marriage fail if these priorities are met. Every failing marriage I have seen has somehow missed these priorities. Fathers, the initiative must be ours.

But, you ask, how can a husband take initiative and responsibility for conveying love in the family when he is essentially cognitive and clumsy in the feelings area, and the wife is more competent in the emotional area? This is one of the most frequent, unrecognized, and difficult problems in marriage today. It is difficult to deal with, because most men, like Fred Davis, are not aware of the problems. Instead of seeing how vital the emotional life of his wife and children is, he sees it as an uncomfortable nuisance which should be avoided. The result, of course, is what we just experienced between Fred and Mary — frustration and bewilderment with a serious breakdown of communication.

It seems that everyone today realizes how crucial communication is in family living. Can you see from Fred and Mary's relationship how communication bogs down when a "cognitive" husband cannot talk on the emotional level, or an "emotional" wife cannot share her innermost feelings and longings? What a dilemma! Husbands, we must face facts. The chances are overwhelming that our wives are more competent in the area of love, caring, and identifying emotional needs in us and our children. And we generally follow the guidance of experts, right? Then, clearly, we men desperately need our wives' help in leading us in this relatively foreign world of feeling.

Not only must a husband be willing to respect and be guided

by his wife's natural know-how in emotional areas, he must encourage his wife and support her daily task of setting the emotional climate in the home. If he is a hindrance to her, insisting on handling matters without regard to her feelings, he will discourage her and eventually break her spirit. Oh, how many wives I have seen in counseling who have been thwarted by their husbands in efforts to feelingly love them and the children. These wives' spirits are broken, and the resulting depression is crippling.

But look at marriages where a husband appreciates his wife's deep feelings and her need to communicate them. He not only listens to her, he learns from her. He learns how rewarding and profoundly fulfilling and satisfying it is to share on the emotional level, whether it is pleasant or unpleasant. This is a marriage that grows over the years. A husband and wife become closer and invaluable to each other. Such a marriage is one of life's greatest gifts.

Is Love Blind?
"See? John doesn't love me anymore. All he does is criticize me," complained pretty Yvonne. She and her husband were seeing me "as a last resort" for marriage counseling. Yvonne continued, "Isn't there anything good you can say about me, John?" Much to my surprise, John actually could think of nothing with which to compliment his wife. Yvonne was attractive, intelligent, articulate, and talented, but John seemed able only to point out discrepancies. They had been married six years. Why the apparent inconsistency?

It's hard to realize, when we think of the astounding divorce rate, that essentially all marriages begin with great hope, expectation, love, and wonderful feelings between the newlyweds. Initially all seems wonderful, the world is perfect. And the marriage of Yvonne and John began that way too. What a startling change! How could it possibly have happened?

One factor is *immaturity*. But what is immaturity? It does correlate somewhat with age, but not necessarily. Within the scope of this particular problem, immaturity can be defined as the inability to tolerate (or cope with) ambivalence on a conscious level. Ambivalence is simply having opposite or conflicting feelings toward the same person.

This explains the saying "love is blind." When we are first in love, and during the first weeks or months of our marriage, we must see our loved one as perfect, and we can tolerate no unpleasant feeling toward her or him. Therefore, we suppress (deny, ignore) anything we might not like in our spouse. We can then be aware of only his or her good points. Then we are oblivious to such things as an imperfect figure or physique, overtalkativeness, quietness, tendency to be fat or thin, overexuberance, withdrawal, moodiness, lack of ability in sports, music, art, sewing, or cooking.

This hiding of our spouse's undesirable aspects from ourselves works beautifully at first. As we live with our loved one day in, day out, month in, month out, there are new discoveries about him or her. Some good and some not so good. Some even revolting. But as long as we keep suppressing the unpleasant into our unconscious, we can continue to see our dear one as a near-perfect model, and everything is fine.

One problem. We cannot keep on suppressing forever. Someday we reach a point of saturation. By that time we may have been married several days or several years. This depends on (1) our capacity to suppress, overlook, and ignore the unpleasant; and (2) our level of maturity, namely, our ability to deal consciously with our mixed feelings.

When we reach this critical point, we cannot continue to suppress the negative any longer. Suddenly we are faced with days/months/years of disagreeable feelings toward our spouse. Again, because of immaturity (inability to deal with ambivalence), we do a flip-flop. We suppress the *good* feelings and accentuate the bad. Now we see our spouse in an almost reversed aspect of being all bad with little or no good — overwhelmingly unpleasant or almost nothing pleasant.

And this can happen quickly. Two months ago John saw Yvonne as the epitome of perfection. Now he can barely tolerate her presence. Yvonne has remained essentially the same. John's perceptions of her have almost completely reversed.

How do we cope with this common problem that is plaguing

our social structure and threatening the strength of our national fiber? As usual, the answer is easy to give, but difficult to carry out. First, we *must realize* that no one is perfect. It's amazing. We hear that statement every day, but we don't believe it. By playing the suppression game, we show that we want and expect perfection from our loved ones.

Second, we must keep ourselves continually aware of our spouse's assets and liabilities. I must realize and not forget that there are things about my wife for which I am grateful and things about her I wish were different—in this way she is like all other women. It's taken me a long time to learn to think of her delightful traits during times when I'm disappointed with her.

Third, we must learn to accept our spouses as they are, including their faults. The likelihood of finding someone or something better through divorce and another marriage, or in an affair, is remote, especially with the overwhelming guilt and other problems such action would produce. Remember that your wife or husband is truly irreplaceable.

Unconditional Love

"Love is very patient and kind, never jealous or envious, never boastful or proud, never haughty or selfish or rude. Love does not demand its own way. It is not irritable or touchy. It does not hold grudges and will hardly even notice when others do it wrong. It is never glad about injustice, but rejoices whenever truth wins out. If you love someone, you will be loyal to him no matter what the cost. You will always believe in him, always expect the best of him, and always stand your ground in defending him" (1 Corinthians 13:4-7, TLB).

This clear statement tells us the foundation of all love relationships. The secret here can be called "unconditional love" that is not dependent on such things as spouse performance, age, weight, mistakes, etc. This kind of love says, "I love my wife, no matter what. No matter what she does, how she looks, or what she says, I will always love her." Yes, unconditional love is an ideal and impossible to attain completely, but the closer I can come to it, the more my wife will be made perfect by God who loves us so. And the more He changes her to His likeness, the more pleasing she will be to me and the more I will be satisfied by her.

This brings us to the end of our discussion on marriage per se. We touched only a few points, but there are many fine books on the subject that one can obtain for further study. Now we want to move on to our primary task of learning how to love a child.

As we explore the world of a child, we must remember that the marital relationship remains unquestionably the most important bond in a family. Its effect on a child throughout his or her life is tremendous.

One example from my experience which bears this out involves a Christian family I saw in counseling. Pam, a fifteen-year-old girl, was brought to me by her parents because of sexual misconduct which resulted in pregnancy. The child was a beautiful girl with a delightful personality. She was talented in several areas. Pam had a strong, warm, healthy relationship with her father—a somewhat scarce commodity these days. Her relationship with her mother also seemed sound. At first I was baffled why Pam chose to become sexually involved in the way she did. She had little feeling or concern about the boy who fathered the child. And she was not of a temperament which would inappropriately seek male attention. Pam had always been a respectful, compliant child who was easy for her parents to manage. Then why did she suddenly become pregnant? I was stumped.

Then I saw the parents together and individually. You guessed it. Pam's parents had marital conflicts that were well hidden from others. These strifes were of a longstanding nature, but the family managed to function for years in a fairly stable way. And Pam had always enjoyed a close relationship with her father. As the child grew older, the mother became increasingly jealous of this bond. But other than this jealousy, the Mother had a fairly supportive relationship with Pam.

Then Pam reached adolescence. As her physical features began changing into those of a woman, the mother's jealousy mushroomed. By various forms of nonverbal communication (which we will get into later), the mother relayed a message to Pam loud and clear. The message was that Pam was now a woman who could hereafter look after her own emotional needs, especially attention from the male population. As many girls of that age do, she attempted to substitute attention from male peers for her daddy's love. She was acting in accordance with her mother's subconscious, nonverbal instructions.

Pam's mother was aware of her own unhappy marital situation which resulted in a poor sexual life with her spouse. She was also aware of the closeness between Pam and her father. She was *not* aware of the intenseness of her jealousy toward Pam. And she was not aware of her role in Pam's sexual acting out.

In cases such as this, it is fruitless and many times harmful to confront each person (especially the mother in this case) with wrongdoing. Though the surface complaint was the child's behavior, the basic problem was in the marital relationship. To help this family in the most supportive, loving, sensitive way, as their therapist, I had to help the parents in their marriage bond and not focus on faultfinding and judging their mistakes. I had to bring them to a point of receiving God's forgiveness in Jesus Christ. As the marital bond is mended in a case of this kind and guilt is resolved, this troubled mother-child relationship can be rectified.

This case illustration should show how important the marital union is in the life of a child. The stronger and healthier this bond is, the fewer problems we will encounter as parents. And the more effective will be the information in this book when it is applied.

Let's look now at the second most important relationship in the family.

CHAPTER 3

The Foundation

Real love is unconditional, and should be evident in all love relationships (see 1 Corinthians 13:4-7). The foundation of a solid relationship with a child is unconditional love. Only that type of love relationship can assure a child's growth to his full and total potential. Only this foundation of unconditional love can assure prevention of such problems as feelings of resentment, being unloved, guilt, fear, insecurity.

We can be confident that a child is correctly disciplined only if our primary relationship with him is one of unconditional love. Without a basis of unconditional love, it is not possible to understand a child, his behavior, or to know how to deal with misbehavior.

Unconditional love can be viewed as a guiding light in child rearing. Without it, we parents operate in the dark with no daily landmarks to tell us where we are and what we should do regarding our child. With it, we have indicators of where we are, where the child is, and what to do in all areas, including discipline. Only with this foundation do we have a cornerstone on which to build our expertise in guiding our child and filling his needs on a daily basis. Without a foundation of unconditional love, parenting becomes a confusing and frustrating burden.

What is unconditional love? Unconditional love is loving a child *no matter what*. No matter what the child looks like. No matter what his assets, liabilities, handicaps. No matter what we expect him to be and most difficult, no matter how he acts. This does not mean, of course, that we always like his behavior. Unconditional love means we love the *child* even when at times we may detest his behavior.

As we mentioned when discussing unconditional love in the marriage relationship, it is an ideal which we will never achieve 100 percent of the time. But again, the closer we get to it, and the more we achieve it, the more satisfied and confident parents we will become. And the more satisfied, pleasant, and happy will be our child.

How I wish I could have said when our children were at home with us, "I love my children all the time regardless of anything else, including their behavior." But like all parents, I could not. Yet I will give myself credit for having tried to arrive at that wonderful goal of loving them unconditionally. I did this by constantly reminding myself of the following:

(1) They are children.

(2) They will tend to act like children.

(3) Much of childish behavior is unpleasant.

(4) If I do my part as a parent and love them despite their childish behavior, they will be able to mature and give up childish ways.

(5) If I love them only when they please me (conditional love), and convey my love them only during those times, they will not feel genuinely loved. This in turn will make them insecure, damage their self-image, and actually *prevent* them from moving on to better self-control and more mature behavior. Therefore, their behavior and its development is *my* responsibility as much as theirs.

(6) If I love them unconditionally, they will feel good about themselves and be comfortable with themselves. They will then be able to control their anxiety and, in turn, their behavior, as they grow into adulthood.

(7) If I love them only when they meet my requirements or expectations, they will feel incompetent. They will believe it is fruitless to do their best because it is never enough. Insecurity, anxiety, and low self-esteem will plague them. They will be constant hindrances in their emotional and behavioral growth. Again, their total growth is as much my responsibility as theirs.

For my sake as a struggling parent in those years, and for the sake of my sons and daughters, I prayed that my love for my children would be as unconditional as I could make it. The future of my children depends on this foundation.

A Child and His Feelings

Remember the simple graph in chapter 2? Where do you think we would find children on it? Right! Way over on the left side. A child comes into the world with an amazing ability to perceive emotionally. An infant is extremely sensitive to the feelings of his mother. What a beautiful thing to see a newborn infant brought to his mother for the first time, if the mother truly wants him. He conforms to the mother's body and the baby's contentment is obvious to all.

But a baby's first meeting with a mother who does not want him presents another picture. This infant is not content and frequently nurses poorly, frets a great deal, and is obviously unhappy. This also occurs when the mother is troubled or depressed, even though there is no discernable difference in the way the mother treats the infant.

So it is important to realize that from birth, children are extremely sensitive emotionally. Since their fund of knowledge is, of course, small, their way of communicating with their world is primarily on the feeling level. This is crucial. Do you see it? A baby's first impressions of the world are through his feelings. This is wonderful yet frightening when we think of the importance of it. An infant's emotional state determines how he sees or senses his world—his parents, his home, himself.

This sets the stage and foundation for almost anything else. For example, if a baby sees his world as rejecting, unloving, uncaring, hostile, then what I consider a growing child's greatest enemy—anxiety—will be harmful later to his speech, behavior, ability to relate and to learn. The point is that a child is not only emotionally supersensitive but also vulnerable.

Almost every study I know indicates that every child wants to know of his parents, "Do you love me?" A child asks this emotional question mostly in his behavior, seldom verbally. The answer to this question is absolutely the most important thing in any child's life.

"Do you love me?" If we love a child unconditionally, he feels the answer to the question is yes. If we love him conditionally, he is unsure, and again, prone to anxiety. The answer we give a child to this all-important question, "Do you love me?" pretty well determines his basic attitude toward life. It's crucial.

Since a child usually asks us this question with his behavior, we usually give him our answer by what we do. By his behavior, a child tells us what he *needs*, whether it's more love, more discipline, more acceptance, or more understanding. (We'll get into this in detail later, but let's concentrate now on the irreplaceable foundation of unconditional love.)

By our behavior, we meet these needs, but we can do this only if our relationship is founded on unconditional love. Note the phrase "by our behavior." The feeling of love for a child in our heart may be strong. But it is not enough. By our behavior a child sees our love for him. Our love for a child is conveyed by our behavior toward that child, by what we *say* and what we *do*. But what we *do* carries more weight. A child is far more affected by our actions than by our words. More about this later.

Another critical concept for parents to understand is that each child has an *emotional tank*. This tank is figurative, of course, but in a sense very real. Each child has certain emotional needs, and whether these emotional needs are met (through love, understanding, discipline, etc.) determines many things. First of all, it determines how a child feels: whether he is content, angry, depressed, or joyful. Second, it affects his behavior: whether he is obedient, disobedient, whiny, perky, playful, or withdrawn. Naturally, the fuller the emotional tank, the more positive the feelings and the better the behavior.

Now here is one of the most important statements in this book: *Only if the emotional tank is full can a child be expected to be at his best or do his best.* And whose responsibility is it to keep that emotional tank full? You guessed it, the responsibility of the parents. A child's behavior indicates the status of the tank. Later we'll talk about how to fill the tank, but now let's understand that this tank has got to be kept full, and only we parents can really accomplish it. Only if the tank is kept full, can a child really be happy, reach his potential, and respond appropriately to discipline. "God, help me meet my child's needs as You do mine." Philippians 4:19 says He will: "And my God will meet all your needs."

Children Reflect Love

Children may be conceptualized as mirrors. As the moon reflects the sun, children basically reflect love, but they do not initiate love. If love is given to them, they return it. If none is given, they have none to return. Unconditional love is reflected unconditionally, and conditional love is returned conditionally.

The love between Tom and his parents (chapter 1) is an example of a conditional relationship. As Tom was growing up, he yearned for a close, warm relationship with his parents. Unfortunately his parents felt that they should continually prompt him to do better by withholding praise, warmth, and affection except for truly outstanding behavior, when he made them feel proud. Otherwise, they were strict, in that they felt too much approval and affection would spoil him and dampen his striving to be better. Their love was given when Tom excelled, but was withheld otherwise. This probably worked well when he was very young; however, as he grew older, he began feeling that his parents didn't really love or appreciate him in his own right, but cared only about their own esteem.

By the time Tom became a teenager, his love for his parents strongly resembled that of his parents for him. He had learned well how to love conditionally. He only behaved in a way which pleased his parents when his parents did something to please him. Of course, with both Tom and his parents playing the game, eventually neither could convey love to the other because each was waiting for the other to do something pleasing. In this situation, each one becomes more and more disappointed, confused, and bewildered. Eventually depression, anger, and resentment set in, prompting the Smiths to seek help.

How would you handle that situation? Some would instruct the parents to demand their rights as parents: respect, obedience, and so on. Some would criticize Tom for his attitude toward his parents and demand that he honor them. Some would recommend severe punishment for Tom. Think about it.

Many children today do not feel genuinely loved by their parents. And yet, I've met few parents who do not love their children dearly. This is not just an academic question to think about and then say, "That's too bad." The situation is alarming. Dozens of religious cults or other devious organizations are capturing the minds of thousands of our precious young people. How can these children so easily be brainwashed, turned against their parents and all other authority, and controlled by such bizarre doctrines? The main reason is that these young people have never felt truly loved and cared for by their parents. They feel that they were deprived of something, that their parents missed giving them something. What is it? Yes, unconditional love. When you consider how few children really feel properly cared for, loved, and comfortable, it is no wonder how far these cultish groups can go.

Why does this terrible situation exist? I do not believe parents per se should be blamed. When I talk with parents, I am gratified to find that most not only love their children, but are genuinely interested in what can be done to help *all* children. I find over and over again that the problem is that parents do not know how to *convey* their love to their children.

I am not pessimistic. As I lecture around the country, I am very heartened that today's parents not only listen, but are willing to expend themselves and their resources on behalf of their children. Many have changed their relationship with their children so that it is founded on scripturally based unconditional love. They have found that once this has been accomplished, their children's emotional tanks are filled for the first time. Parenting quickly becomes fulfilling, exciting, and rewarding. Then these fine parents have guidelines as to when and how to guide and discipline their dear ones.

How to Convey Love

Let's consider how to convey love to a child. As you remember, children are emotional beings who communicate emotionally. In addition, children use behavior to translate their feelings to us, and the younger they are, the more they do this. It's easy to tell how a child is feeling and what frame of mind he's in simply by watching him. Likewise, children have an uncanny ability to recognize their parents' feelings by their behavior, an ability most people lose as they reach adulthood.

On many occasions when my daughter was about sixteen she asked me such questions as, "What are you mad at, Daddy?" when I was not even consciously aware that I was feeling a certain way. But when I thought about it, she was absolutely right.

Children are that way. They can so finely sense how you're feeling by the way you act. So if we want them to know how we feel *about them,* that we love them, *we must act like we love them.* "Dear children, let us not love with words or tongue but with actions and in truth" (1 John 3:18).

As you realize, the purpose of the book is to examine how parents can put their feelings of love into action. Only in this way can they convey their love to their child so that he will feel loved, completely accepted, and respected, and able to love and respect himself. Only then will parents be able to help their children love others unconditionally, especially their future spouses and children.

Before we launch into discoveries of how to love a child, there must be one presupposition. It must be assumed that you are willing to apply what you learn. There is a difference between having a vague feeling of warmth toward a child, and your caring enough about him to sacrifice whatever is needed for his best interest. It is rather pointless to continue reading the book if you are not willing to seriously contemplate what it says, understand it, and apply its contents. Otherwise, it would be easy to read it superficially and conclude the information is simplistic and unrealistic.

Conveying love to a child can be broadly classified into four areas: eye contact, physical contact, focused attention, and discipline. Each area is just as crucial as the other. Many parents (and authorities) will focus on one or two areas and neglect the others. The area most overemphasized today, to the exclusion of the other three, is discipline. I see many children of Christian parents who are well-disciplined but feel unloved. In many of these cases the parents have unfortunately confused discipline with punishment, as though the two are synonymous. This is understandable, since I frequently read or hear authorities tell parents to use the rod and physically pinch a child with no mention of loving him. There is no mention of how to help a child feel good toward himself, his parents, or others, and no mention of how to make a child happy.

Every day I see the results of this approach to childrearing. These children are well-behaved when they are quite young, although usually overly quiet, somewhat sullen, and withdrawn. They lack the spontaneity, curiosity, and childish exuberance of a love-nurtured child. And these children usually become behavior problems as they approach and enter adolescence because they lack a strong emotional bond with their parents.

So we parents must focus on all areas of loving our children. Let's move on and discuss the first one — eye contact.

CHAPTER 4

How to Show Love through Eye Contact

W hen you first think about eye contact, it may seem relatively unimportant in relating to your child. However, as we work with children, observe communications between parent and child, and study research findings, we realize how essential eye contact is. Eye contact is crucial not only in making good communicational contact with a child, but in filling his emotional needs. Without realizing it, we use eye contact as a primary means of conveying love, especially to children. A child uses eye contact with his parents (and others) to feed emotionally. The more a parent makes eye contact with his or her child as a means of expressing love, the more a child is nourished with love and the fuller is his emotional tank.

What is eye contact? Eye contact is looking directly into the eyes of another person. Eye contact is important in many situations. Have you ever tried to have a conversation with someone who keeps looking in another direction, unable to maintain eye contact with you? It's difficult. And our feelings toward that person are very much affected by this. We tend to like people who are able to maintain pleasant eye contact with us. Eye contact is pleasant, of course, when it is accompanied by pleasant words and pleasant facial expressions, such as smiling.

Unfortunately, parents, without realizing it, can use eye contact to give other messages to a child. For instance, parents may give loving eye contact only under certain conditions, as when a child performs especially well and brings pride to his parents. This comes across to a child as conditional love, and as previously mentioned, a child cannot grow and develop well under these circumstances. Even though we may love a child deeply, we must give him appropriate eye contact. Otherwise, he will get the wrong message and not feel genuinely (unconditionally) loved.

It is easy for parents to develop the terrible habit of using eye contact primarily when they want to make a strong point to a child, especially a negative one. We find that a child is most attentive when we look him straight in the eye. We may do this mainly to give instructions or for reprimanding and criticizing. This is a *disastrous* mistake, though using eye contact primarily in the negative sense works well when a child is quite young.

But remember that eye contact is one of the main sources of a child's emotional nurturing. When a parent uses this powerful means of control at his disposal in a primarily negative way, a child cannot but see his parent in a primarily negative way. And though this may seem to have good results when a child is young, this child is obedient and docile because of fear. As he grows older, the fear gives way to anger, resentment, and depression. Reread Tom's statements: this is what he is telling us.

Oh, if his parents had only known! They loved Tom deeply, but they were unaware that they seldom gave him eye contact, and when they did, it was when they wanted to give him explicit instructions or when disciplining him. Tom inherently knew that his parents somehow loved him. But, because of this way of using the critical ingredient of eye contact, Tom grew into his teen years confused and bewildered regarding his parents' true feelings toward him. Remember his statement, "No one cares about me except my friends"? When I replied, "No one?", he said, "My parents, I guess. I don't know." Tom knew he should feel loved, but he did not.

An even worse habit parents may fall into is actually using the avoidance of eye contact as a punishment device. This is cruel, and we often do this to our spouses. (Come on, admit it.) Consciously refusing to make eye contact with a child is usually more painful than corporal punishment. It can be devastating. It can be one of those incidents in a child's life that he will never forget.

There are several types of circumstances between parent and child which can have lifelong effects, happenings that a child, and sometimes a parent, never forgets. The purposeful withdrawing of eye contact from a child as a way to show disapproval can be such a time and is obviously an example of conditional love. A wise parent will do all in his power to avoid it.

Our ways of showing love to a child should not be controlled by our being pleased or displeased. We must show our love consistently, unwaveringly, no matter what the situation. We can take care of misbehavior in other ways — ways which will not interfere with our love-giving. We'll talk about discipline and how to do it without disrupting the love-bond. What we must understand at this point is that parents must use eye contact as a continuous love-giving route, and not merely as a means of discipline.

We Are Patterns

We all know that children learn by role modeling: that is, patterning themselves after us. Children learn the art and use of eye contact this way also. If we give a child continuous, loving, positive eye contact, he will do the same. If we use eye contact as a way to display our annoyances, he will also.

Do you know a child who seems to be unpleasant or even obnoxious? Most likely he will look at you only briefly when he first sees you, and thereafter only when you have something particularly interesting to say or do. Other than that, he avoids looking at you. This fleeting eye contact is annoying, obnoxious, and aggravating. Now observe the way this child's parents use eye contact with him. Is there a similarity?

Imagine the distinct disadvantage this child has and will have throughout his life. Imagine how difficult it will be to develop friendships and other intimate relationships. How rejected and disliked he will be by his peers, not only now but probably indefinitely because the chances of his breaking this pattern of relating are bleak. First of all, he is not aware he's doing it; and second, changing this pattern is extraordinarily difficult, *unless the parents change their own pattern of eye contact before the child becomes too old.* This is a child's best hope.

A striking example of this tragedy was discovered in a research study on a pediatric ward in a general hospital. The researcher was sitting at one end of the corridor recording the number of times the nurses and volunteers entered each child's room. It was noted that some children were visited many times more often than others. The reasons were startling. It had something to do with the type of seriousness of the child's illness, of course, and with the amount of care required by the child. But this did not explain the great differences in the amount of contact with the patients. You've probably guessed it. The more popular children received more attention. Whenever nurses or volunteers had a free moment or a choice between which room to enter, they naturally picked children who could relate in the most pleasant way.

What made the difference in how pleasant these children were? There were several reasons, such as alertness, verbal ability, and spontaneity, but the most consistent factor was eye contact. The least popular children would initially look at the visitor briefly, then immediately look down or away. Subsequently, the children would avoid eye contact, making it difficult to relate to them. The adults would naturally be uncomfortable with these children. The nurses or volunteers, not realizing their roles in initiating communication, would misunderstand them, assuming that the children wanted to be alone, or that the children did not like them. Consequently, they avoided these children, making them feel even more unloved, unwanted, and worthless.

This same thing happens in countless homes. It happened in

Tom's. And it could have been corrected with regular, warm, pleasant eye contact (unconditional love) by the parents. If they had known this (and some other basic facts about loving children yet to be mentioned), they wouldn't have had these problems with Tom.

The Failure to Thrive Syndrome

Another important finding in our research studies also took place in a pediatric ward in a university hospital. We were studying the strange phenomenon of the Failure to Thrive Syndrome. In this illness, a child, usually between six and twelve months of age, ceases to develop. Often he refuses food and stops growing, becomes listless and lethargic, and may actually die for no apparent reason. All tests and physical examinations are normal.

Why does a child lose his will to live? In most cases we know that the parents have rejected the child, often unconsciously (outside of their awareness). They are unable consciously to deal with their feelings of rejection toward their child, so unconsciously they reject him through their behavior. In our study we found these parents avoided eye contact and physical contact with their child. Otherwise, they were good parents, providing such necessities as food and clothing.

The Failure to Thrive Syndrome is a startling phenomenon, but other findings are even more so. During the World War II Nazi blitzes of London, many young children were removed for their protection from the city and placed with adults in the countryside. Their parents remained in London. These children were basically well cared for physically, in that they were clean, well fed, and comfortable. Emotionally, however, they were severely deprived because there were not enough caretakers to give the emotional nurturing of eye contact and physical contact.

Most of these children became emotionally disturbed and handicapped. It would have been far better to have kept them with their mothers. The danger of emotional damage was greater than the danger of physical damage.

The danger and pitfalls awaiting an emotionally weak child

are frightening. Parents! Make your children strong. Your greatest tool is *unconditional love*.

Eye Contact and the Learning Process

In my work with the Headstart Program, I enjoy teaching those wonderful teachers about eye contact and physical contact and how these affect anxiety and a child's ability to learn.

A teacher will identify a three-to-four-year-old child who is obviously anxious, fearful, and immature by the difficulty he has in making or maintaining eye contact. Mild to moderate emotional deprivation can cause a child to have difficulty with eye contact.

The extremely anxious child will, in addition, have problems approaching an adult (and often his peers). A normally emotionally nourished child will be able to approach the teacher by walking directly up to her, making full non-hesitating eye contact, and speaking what's on his mind—for instance, "May I have a piece of paper?" The more emotionally deprived a child is, the more difficulty he will have in doing this.

In the average schoolroom it is not hard to find at least one child (usually a boy) who is so anxious and fearful that he cannot make good eye contact, speaks with great hesitancy (and frequently cannot speak without coaxing), and will come to his teacher with a side or oblique approach. Occasionally such a child will be able to approach his teacher only by walking almost backward. Of course these children have difficulty learning because they are so anxious and tense.

When we have found such an unfortunate child, I ask the teacher to teach him something while sitting across the table from him. Then I ask the teacher to hold the child, make occasional eye contact with him (as much as the child can tolerate) while talking with him. After a short while, I again ask the teacher to teach the child something while continuing to hold him. The teacher is amazed, and I am always amazed, at how much easier it is for the child to learn when his emotional needs are cared for first. With eye contact and physical contact, the teacher has eased the child's fears and anxiety, and increased his sense of security and confidence. This, in turn, enables him to learn better. Simple? Of course. Then why don't we do it more? For many reasons, I believe, ranging from a fear that we'll appear unprofessional, or fearing we'll spoil a child, to fearing we'll somehow damage him in some vague way. If there is anything we don't have to worry about, it's giving a child too much love.

In a New Place

I am so thankful as a parent that I learned about the importance of eye contact. It has made a great difference with my own children. I'll never forget, for example, when we first moved to a new home. Our two boys were six and two at the time and were happy, energetic, and normally independent.

About a week after moving, we noticed a change coming over both boys. They were becoming whiny, clinging, easily upset, frequently fighting, constantly underfoot, and irritable. At that time, my wife Pat and I were furiously trying to get the house ready before I was to report to my new job. We were both becoming annoyed and irritated with the boys' behavior, but figured it was because of the move.

One night I was thinking about my boys, and began to try to imagine myself in their place. The answer to their behavioral problems suddenly hit me like a hammer. Pat and I were with the boys night and day and talked to them frequently. But we were so intent on the housework that we never really gave them their rightful attention; we never made eye contact and seldom made physical contact. Their emotional tanks had run dry, and *by their behavior* they were asking, "Do you love me?" In their childlike, normally irrational way, they were asking, "Do you love me now that we're in a new place? Are things still the same with us? Do you still love me?" This is so typical of children during a time of change.

As soon as I understood the problem, I shared my thoughts with Pat. I think she was a bit incredulous at first, but by then she was ready to try anything.

The next day we gave the boys eye contact whenever we could, when they talked to us (active listening), and when we talked to them. Whenever possible, we held them and gave them concentrated attention. The change was dramatic. As their emotional tanks were filled, they became their happy, radiant, rambunctious selves and soon were spending less time underfoot and more time playing with each other and keeping themselves happy. Pat and I agreed that this was time well spent. We more than made up for it when the boys were out from underfoot, but more important, they were happy again.

It's Never Too Early

Now one more illustration regarding the importance of eye contact. An infant's eyes begin focusing somewhere around two and four weeks of age. One of the first images which holds an infant's attention is a human face, but in particular he focuses on the eyes.

After a child is approximately six to eight weeks of age, you will notice that his eyes are always moving and seem to be searching for something. The eyes resemble two radar antennae constantly moving and searching. Do you know what he's looking for? I think you already know: he's searching for another set of eyes. As early as two months, these eyes lock on another set of eyes. Already he is feeling emotionally, and even at this very early age his emotional tank needs to be filled.

Awesome, isn't it? It's no wonder that a child's way of relating to his world, and his feelings toward it, are so well formed early in his life. Most researchers state that a child's basic personality, modes of thinking, style of speech, and other critical traits are well fixed by the age of five.

We cannot start too early in giving a child continuous, warm, consistent affection. He simply *must* have this unconditional love to cope most effectively in today's world. And we have a simple but extremely powerful method by which to give it to him. It's up to each parent to use eye contact to convey unconditional love.

Though we have alluded to a child's need for physical contact, let's now explore the subject in some depth.

CHAPTER 5

How to Show Love through Physical Contact

I t seems that the most obvious way of conveying our love to a child is by physical contact. Surprisingly, studies show that most parents touch their children only when necessity demands it, as when helping them dress, undress, or perhaps get into the car. Otherwise, few parents take advantage of this pleasant, effortless way of helping give their children that unconditional love they so desperately need. You seldom see a parent on his own volition or "out of the blue" take an opportunity to touch his child.

I don't mean just hugging, kissing, and the like. I'm also talking about any type of physical contact. It is such a simple thing to touch a child on his shoulder, gently poke him in the ribs, or tousle his hair. When you closely observe parents with their children, many actually attempt to make the least possible physical contact. It's as if these poor parents have the notion their children are like mechanical walking dolls, the object being to get them walking and behaving correctly with the least assistance. These parents don't know the fantastic opportunities they are missing. Within their hands they have a way of assuring their children's emotional security and their own success as parents.

It is heartening to see some parents who have discovered this secret of physical contact along with eye contact.

Scientists have discovered that touch plays a surprising role in our physical and mental well-being, and begins at birth, asserts an article "The Sense That Shapes Our Future" in *Reader's Digest* for January 1992. The author, Lowell Ponte, points out that researchers at the University of Miami Medical School's Touch Research Institute showed that premature babies who received three fifteen-minute periods of slow, firm massage strokes each day showed forty-seven percent greater weight gain than their wardmates who did not get this attention. Preemies who were massaged also exhibited improved sleep, alertness, and activity. Up to eight months later they displayed greater mental and physical skills.

Dr. Michael Meaney, a psychologist at the Douglas Hospital Research Center at McGill University in Montreal, demonstrated that touching baby rats during the first few weeks of life results in development of receptors that control the production of glucocorticoids, powerful stress chemicals that cause a multitude of problems, including impaired growth and damage to brain cells. During his research, the article concluded, Dr. Meaney's first child was born and in early childhood he made a point to hug her more than he otherwise would have done. "Our evidence," he was quoted as saying, "suggests that the hugging I give my daughter today will help her . . . lead a happier, healthier life. My touch may be shaping her future."

The article also pointed out that the caring touch of nurses and loved ones can do wonders for hospitalized patients, relieving anxiety and tension headaches and sometimes reduce rapid heartbeat and heart arrhythmias.

When our son David was eight, he played Peanut League Baseball. During the games I especially enjoyed watching one father who had discovered the secrets of eye and physical contact. Frequently, his son would run up to tell him something. It was obvious that there was a strong affectional bond between them. As they talked, their eye contact was direct with no hesitation. And their communication included much appropriate physical contact, especially when something funny was said. This father would frequently lay his hand on his son's arm, or put his arm around his son's shoulder and sometimes lovingly slap him on the knee. Occasionally, he would pat him on the back or pull the child toward him, especially when a humorous comment was made. You could tell that this father used physical contact whenever he possibly could, as long as he and the boy were comfortable and it was appropriate.

At times, this same father's teenage daughter would come to watch her brother play. She would sit with her father, either at his side or directly in front of him. Here again, this caring and knowledgeable father related to his daughter in an appropriate manner. He used much eye and physical contact but because of her age, did not hold her on his lap or kiss her (as he would have done if she were younger). He would frequently lightly touch her hand, arm, shoulder, or back. Now and then he would tap her on the knee or briefly put his arm around her shoulder and lightly jerk her toward him, especially when something funny happened.

Two Precious Gifts

Physical and eye contact are to be incorporated in all of our everyday dealings with our children. They should be natural, comfortable, and not showy or overdone. A child growing up in a home where parents use eye and physical contact will be comfortable with himself and other people. He will have an easy time communicating with others, and consequently be well liked and have good self-esteem. Appropriate and frequent eye and physical contact are two of the most precious gifts we can give our child. Eye and physical contact (along with focused attention, see chapter 6) are the most effective ways to fill a child's emotional tank and enable him to be his best.

Unfortunately, Tom's parents had not discovered the secret of physical and eye contact. They misused eye contact. They felt physical contact was all right for girls because "they needed affection." But Mr. and Mrs. Smith believed boys should be treated as men. They felt affection would feminize Tom into being a sissy. These grieving parents did not realize that the opposite is true, that the more Tom's emotional needs were met by physical and eye contact, especially by his father, the more he would identify with the male sex, and the more masculine he would be.

Mr. and Mrs. Smith also thought that as a boy gets older, his need for affection, especially physical affection, ceases. Actually a boy's need for physical contact never ceases, even though the type of physical contact he needs does change.

As an infant, he needs to be held, cuddled, fondled, hugged, and kissed — "ooey-gooey love stuff" as one of my sons called it when he was in grade school. This type of physical affection is crucial from birth until the boy reaches seven or eight years of age — and I mean crucial! Research shows that girl infants less than twelve months old receive five times as much physical affection as boy infants. I am convinced that this is one reason younger boys (three years to adolescence) have many more problems than girls. Five to six times as many boys as girls are seen in psychiatric clinics around the country. This ratio changes dramatically during adolescence.

It is apparent then how important it is for a boy to receive just as much or more affection as a girl may need during the early years. As a boy grows and becomes older, his need for physical affection such as hugging and kissing lessens, but his need for physical contact does not. Instead of primarily "ooey-gooey love stuff," he now wants "boy-style" physical contact such as playful wrestling, jostling, backslapping, playful hitting or boxing, bearhugs, "give-me-five" (slapping another person's palm in a moment of triumph). These ways of making physical contact with a boy are just as genuine a means of giving attention as hugging and kissing. Don't forget that a child *never* outgrows his need for *both* types.

As my boys, who are now grown, got older, they became less and less receptive to holding, hugging, and kissing. There were still times when they needed and wanted it, and I had to be alert in order to give it to them every chance I got. These times occurred usually when they had been hurt (either physically or emotionally), when they were very tired, when they were sick, and at special periods such as bedtime or when something sad had happened.

Remember the special moments discussed in chapter 4? Moments that are especially meaningful to a child, so meaningful that he will *never forget* them? These special opportunities to give our children affectionate physical contact (hugging, kissing), *especially as they get older,* are some of these very special times. These are the moments your child will recall when he or she is in the throes of deepest adolescence, when a teenager is in the conflict of rebellion on one hand versus affection for his parents on the other. The more special memories he has, the stronger he will be able to stand against adolescent turmoil.

These precious opportunities are limited in number. A child quickly passes from one stage to the next, and before we know it, opportunities to give him what he needs have come and gone. A somber thought, isn't it?

Here is one other point about giving physical affection to boys. It is easier to give affection to a boy when he is younger, especially around twelve to eighteen months of age. As he grows older, however, it becomes more difficult. Why? One reason, as mentioned before, is the false assumption that the physical display of affection is feminine. The reason is that most boys become less appealing to people as they grow older. For example, to many people a seven- or eight-year-old boy is unappealing and irritating. In order to give a boy what he must have emotionally, we as parents must recognize these unpleasant feelings in ourselves, resist them, and go ahead with what we must do as mothers and fathers.

Let's now discuss the needs of girls in relation to physical contact. Girls generally do not display as much directness as boys to emotional deprivation during their first seven or eight years. In other words, they do not make their affectional needs so evident. I've seen many, many emotionally deprived children and, generally, it is very easy to tell which boys are suffering — their distress is usually obvious. But the girls seem better able to cope and are less affected by the lack of emotional nurturing *prior* to adolescence. Don't let this fool you. Although girls don't show their misery as much when they are younger, they suffer intensely when not properly cared for emotionally. It becomes quite evident as they grow older, especially during adolescence.

One reason for this lies in this matter of physical contact. Remember that physical contact, especially the more affectionate type (holding, hugging, kissing, etc.), is vital to boys during their younger years. The younger the boy, the more vital affectional contact is to him. While, with a girl, physical contact (especially the more affectionate type) *increases* in importance as she becomes older and reaches a zenith at around the age of eleven. Nothing stirs my heart more than an eleven-year-old girl who is not receiving adequate emotional nourishment. What a critical age!

Sharon's Personality Change

"I can't believe it! Sharon must be a Dr. Jekyll and Mr. Hyde," exclaimed Mrs. Francisco in her first visit with me concerning her fifteen-year-old daughter. "She has always been a quiet, shy girl who never really acted up. In fact, she had to be prompted to do things, especially over the last few months. For a while I couldn't get her to do anything. She seemed bored with life. She lost interest in everything, especially her schoolwork. She seemed to lose all her energy. I took Sharon to her pediatrician, but he couldn't find anything wrong with her. Then I talked with the school counselor and her teachers. They were also concerned with Sharon's attitude and boredom. Some friends told me not to worry, that it was a stage she'd grow out of. I hoped they were right but had my doubts. Then one day a friend of mine who has a daughter Sharon's age called. She said that her daughter thought Sharon was on drugs. I didn't think Sharon was the type, but I searched her room anyway and found some marijuana.

"For the first time in her life she acted horribly. She yelled and screamed at me, saying I was prowling and I had no right to intrude on her privacy. I was shocked at her defiance.

"That seemed to be the beginning of her personality change.

Now she's angry all the time, just hateful. She demands to go out with the worst crowd in school, and it scares me to think of what they might be doing.

"Now all she cares about is being away from home with her gooney friends. What will become of her, Dr. Campbell? We can't control her."

"Is Sharon the same way with her father?" I asked.

"She's much better with him for some reason, but even he is finding it more and more difficult to reason with her. But he's not around much to help anyway. He's so busy. Gone most of the time. Even when he's here, he doesn't give us much time. The children adore him and want to be with him. But he immediately finds something they have done wrong and gets on to them about it. He really cares about the kids. I know he does. But that's his way."

A tragic story. But a common one. A normal, well-endowed girl who for almost thirteen years was open, docile, easy to love. Like any child, her main concern was, "Do you love me?" For almost thirteen years her parents had nearly continuous opportunity to answer her question and prove their love to her. As a typical girl, her need for demonstrable love increased over the years and hit a maximum around the age of eleven—that ultracritical age when girls have an almost desperate need for abundant eye contact, focused attention, and notably physical contact, especially from their fathers.

Preparation for Adolescence

Why is affectionate love so important to girls around that age of pre-adolescence? The answer: preparation for adolescence. Every girl enters adolescence with some degree of preparation for it. Some are well prepared and some are poorly prepared.

The two most important aspects of this preparation for girls are self-image and sexual identity. At this point, let's look at sexual identity in a growing girl. You have read that a girl's need for affection increases as she grows older. As she nears adolescence she intuitively or unconsciously knows that how she weathers those turbulent adolescent years depends on how she feels about herself. It is vital for her to feel OK about herself as a female. If she is comfortable as a "woman" when she enters adolescence (usually about thirteen to fifteen years old), her adolescence will be relatively smooth, pleasant, and comfortable with the usual ups and downs. The more stable and healthy her sexual identity, the better she will be able to withstand peer pressure. The less she thinks of herself as an "OK female," the less stable she will be. She will then be more susceptible to pressure of peers (especially male peers) and less able to hold to parental values.

Sexual identity is self-approval as a female, and a girl gets her sexual identify at that age primarily from her father, as long as he is living and especially if he is in the home. If a father is dead or otherwise removed from relating to his daughter, a girl must find other paternal figures to fill these needs. But when a father has any viable relationship with her, he is the primary person who can help his daughter be prepared in this particular way for adolescence. What a great responsibility!

A father helps his daughter approve of herself by showing her that he himself approves of her. He does this by applying the principles we have discussed thus far — unconditional love, eye contact, and physical contact, as well as focused attention. A daughter's need for her father to do this begins as early as two years of age. This need, although important at younger ages, becomes greater as the girl grows older and approaches that almost magic age of thirteen.

One problem in our society is that as a girl grows older, a father usually feels increasingly uncomfortable about giving his daughter the affection she needs, especially when she becomes pre-adolescent (about ten or eleven years old). So as a daughter arrives at the age when she needs her father's affection the most, a father feels more awkward and uncomfortable, especially with physical contact. This is extremely unfortunate. Yes, fathers, we must ignore our discomfort and give our daughters what is vital to them for their entire lives.

Our Juvenile Court Judge

Like most fathers, I had my difficulties giving my children everything they needed emotionally as they grew up — especially physical contact and focused attention for my teenage daughter Carey. Most evenings I came home from work physically and emotionally exhausted. After expending myself in my work, how could I find the energy and resources to give to my family, especially my daughter, at those times when they needed me? With my daughter, her need for me occurred when she had a bad encounter with her peer group, perhaps another girl being hostile toward her because of jealousy. Sometimes she didn't understand the cause of the jealousy and tried to find the fault in herself. On occasions such as this, I knew what I *should* do. I went to her room, talked with her about whatever was on her mind at the moment, gave her all the eye and physical contact she needed at the time, and patiently waited until she got around to sharing with me her pain and confusion. Then I could clarify her understanding of the whole situation. After a while the fact finally dawned on her that it wasn't anything she had done wrong or should blame herself for. Then she usually saw the situation clearly enough to avoid similar difficulties.

Anyway, that's the way I *liked* it to go, but I was seldom bursting with energy and enthusiasm to carry it out. Usually all I felt like doing was eating supper, sitting in my favorite chair, reading the newspaper, and relaxing.

Here is what helped me overcome this inertia. When my daughter (or one of my sons) needed me, and my whole body was drawn like a magnet to a chair or bed, I thought of a friend, a fine judge of the Juvenile Court. I deeply appreciated and respected the judge. One of the worst, most humiliating and tragic things that could possibly have happened to me or my family would have been to appear in his court with one of my children on, say, a drug charge. I said to myself, "Campbell, one out of every six kids appears before the Juvenile Court. If you want to make sure one of your kids isn't included, you'd better hop to it and give them what they need instead of looking after yourself." Just the thought of appearing before the judge with my child on some sort of charge was unbearable. It usually worked. I'd get off my caboose and do what I knew I should do as a father.

Back to physical contact. One day in my parenting years, I was thinking how essential physical contact is and yet how most parents seem to consider it so basic and simplistic; we assume we are doing it when, in fact, we seldom do. I was groping for an illustration to point out this problem when my dear wife ran across an article about religious cults, including the Unification Church (Moonies). A young man who was interviewed told of being brainwashed by the Moonies.

One of the most powerful techniques used was as follows. In an emotionally charged atmosphere and surrounded by several Moonies, the young man was required to think back into his childhood and remember painful moments. He told of an incident when he was three years old. He remembered feeling lonely and distressed, and tried to seek comfort in physical contact from his mother. His mother did not have time for him at that moment and he felt rejected. Then the Moonies embraced him (physical contact) repeatedly, stating that *they* loved him (implying of course that his mother did not).

Frightening, isn't it? The fact that there are dozens of such religious cults and other influences in our country today trying to capture the minds of our children is alarming enough. But even worse, they are able to do so because parents are failing to provide for basic emotional needs of their children by showing unconditional love.

Yet most parents do love their children. Again, the basic problem is that we are not aware that we must convey our love to our children *before anything else:* before teaching, before guidance, before example, before discipline. Unconditional love must be the primary relationship with a child, or everything else is unpredictable, especially their attitudes and behavior.

But we should not be pessimistic about this. The really encouraging thing is that we know what the problem is and we know how to combat it. There are reasonable answers. I am convinced that most parents, because they love their child, can be *taught* to convey this love. The difficult question is, how can we get this across to all (or at least most) parents? This is something which all concerned parents must consider. The answer will require the input and action of many.

And in addition to learning to use eye contact and physical touch, parents must learn how to make use of *focused attention.*

CHAPTER 6

How to Show Love through Focused Attention

E ye contact and physical contact seldom require real sacrifice by parents. However, focused attention does require time, and sometimes a lot of it. It may mean giving up something parents would rather do. Loving parents will detect when a child desperately needs focused attention and perhaps at a time when the parents feel least like giving it.

Just what is focused attention? Focused attention is giving a child full, undivided attention in such a way that he feels without doubt that he is completely loved. That he is valuable enough *in his own right* to warrant parents' undistracted watchfulness, appreciation, and uncompromising regard. In short, focused attention makes a child feel he is the most important person in the world in his parents' eyes.

Some may think this is going a bit too far, but take a look at Scripture and see how highly children are regarded. Notice the high priority Christ gave them: "And they began bringing children to Him, so that He might touch them . . . and [He] said . . . ,'Permit the children to come to Me . . . , for the kingdom of God belongs to such as these.' . . . And He took them in His arms and began blessing them, laying His hands upon them" (Mark 10:13-16, NASB).

Their value is also stressed in the Old Testament: "Behold, children are a gift of the Lord" (Ps. 127:3, NASB) and (when Jacob answered Esau's question, "Who are these with you?") "The children whom God has graciously given your servant" (Gen. 33:5, NASB).

A child ought to be made to feel he is the only one of his kind. Few children feel this but oh, the difference it makes in that small one when he knows he is special. Only focused attention can give him that realization and knowledge. It is so vital in a child's development of self-esteem. And it profoundly affects a child's ability to relate to and love others.

Focused attention, in my experience, is the most demanding need a child has, because we parents have extreme difficulty in recognizing it, much less fulfilling it. There are many reasons we do not recognize this particular need. One of the main reasons is that other things we do for a child seem to suffice. For example, special favors (ice cream or candy), gifts, and granting unusual requests seem to substitute for focused attention at the time. These kindnesses are good, but it is a serious mistake to use them as a stand-in for genuine focused attention. I found it a real temptation to use this type of substitution because favors or gifts were easier to give and took much less of my time. But I found over and over again that my children did not do their best, did not feel their best, and did not behave their best unless I gave them that precious commodity, focused attention.

The Tyranny of the Urgent

Why is it so difficult to give focused attention? Because it takes *time*. Numerous studies have been done and books written showing that time is our most precious possession. Put it this way. Even if you could give twenty-four hours a day, seven days a week, it is virtually impossible to fulfill all of your obligations. That is a true statement. It is not possible for you to take care of every obligation and every responsibility in your life as you would like it to be done. You *must* face up to that fact. If you do not, you will naively assume that everything will somehow get taken care of, and when you assume that, you will become controlled by the tyranny of the urgent. Urgent matters will then automatically take precedence in your life and control your time. Unfortunately, they usually are not. Take the sacred telephone, for example. I say sacred because it takes precedence over almost all else. The ringing telephone must be answered regardless of time, place, or situation. Your family may be having a few wonderful moments together at suppertime. In our home when our children were with us, this was of the highest importance to me. But if the telephone rang, it was given almost a sacred right to interfere with, disrupt, and even destroy our family fellowship. It shows how the tyranny of the urgent wins out over the important things of life once again.

You know, there is just not enough time in our short lives to be controlled by the urgent and be able to look after the important. We can't have our cake and eat it too. So what can we do about it? I'm afraid there is only one answer. And it isn't simple or easy. We must determine our priorities, set our goals, and plan our time to accomplish them. *We* must control our time in order to take care of the important things.

Set Priorities

What are the priorities in your life? Where does your child fit in? Does he take first priority? Second? Third? Fourth? You must determine this! Otherwise, your child will take a low precedence and suffer from some degree of neglect.

No one else can do this for you. A spouse cannot determine your child's priority in *your* life. Nor can your minister, counselor, employer, or friend. Only you can do this. So what is it, fellow parent? What and who gets priority in your life? — Job? Church? Spouse? House? Hobby? Children? Television? Social life? Career?

In almost all families that have found contentment, satisfaction, happiness, and genuine thankfulness among all family members, the parents possess a similar priority system. Usually their first priority is of an ethical nature, such as a strong religious faith or moral code. In most cases, this is manifested by placing God first in their lives and having a warm, comforting, loving, supportive relationship with Him. They use this stabilizing relationship to influence all other relationships. Their second priority is the spouse, as discussed previously. The children take priority number three. As you can see, real happiness is found in family orientation — spiritual family then physical family. God, spouse, children. These are essential. The remaining priorities are important, of course, but these three must come first.

I have talked with many people who sought contentment in such things as money, power, and prestige. But as they experienced life and discovered real values, they sadly realized they were investing in the wrong account. I've seen numerous wealthy persons who spent their better years making it. Tragically, they had to seek counseling when they realized that, despite their wealth and power, their lives were pathetically and painfully empty. Each would weep and consider his or her life a "failure" because of a wayward child or a spouse lost through divorce. He or she realized only then that the only worthwhile possession in life is someone who loves you and cares what happens to you — God, spouse, and child.

People who are terminally ill, I have noticed, come to the same conclusion. As they look back on life, they too know that the only thing that really matters is whether someone genuinely cares for and unconditionally loves them. If these individuals do have such loved ones, they are content. If they do not, they are to be pitied.

I once talked with the wife of a minister, a most beautiful woman who had incurable cancer. She was such a radiant wholesome person. As we talked, she explained how, since she had known of her illness, her outlook on life had been transformed. With the knowledge of impending death, her priority system was forced to change. For the first time she realized there was not enough time in the life of *any* parent to provide for the needs of spouse and children if less important things were not resisted. This minister's wife gave her husband and children first priority, and what a difference was evident in their lives. Of course, this does not mean we should neglect other areas of our lives, but we must control the time we spend on them and their influence on us.

Fleeting Moments

This illustration poignantly points out the importance of focused attention. I read of a father who was sitting in his living room one day. It was his fiftieth birthday, and he happened to be in an irritable mood. Suddenly his eleven-year-old-boy Rick bounced into the room, sat on his father's lap and began kissing him repeatedly on the cheeks. The boy continued his kissing until his father sharply asked, "What are you doing?" The child answered, "I'm giving you fifty kisses on your fiftieth birthday." Ordinarily the father would have been touched by this loving act of affection. Unfortunately, because he was depressed and irritable, he pushed the boy away and stated, "Let's do that some other time." The boy was crushed. He ran out of the house, jumped on his bike, and rode away. A few moments later the child was struck and killed by a car. You can imagine the grief, remorse, and guilt suffered by this poor father.

These stories tell us several things. First, because life is so unpredictable and uncertain, we cannot know or plan how many opportunities we will have for nurturing our children, especially times to give focused attention. We must take advantage of our timely opportunities because they are fewer than we may realize. Our children are growing up.

Second, these moments of opportunity do not happen every day. Remember those special moments which leave a lasting impression on a child? That moment when Rick tried to kiss his father fifty times was one such priceless moment. If the father had been able to spend those few moments with Rick in a positive way, Rick would have affectionately remembered that time the rest of his life, especially when tempted to act against parental values, as, for example, in the dissident days of adolescence. However, if Rick had not been killed, he would never have forgotten the pain, anguish, and humiliation of that moment.

Let's look at another story regarding focused attention. In the diary of the father of a great humanitarian was found a description of a day spent fishing with his son. The father laments how the day was a "total loss" because the son seemed "bored and preoccupied, saying very little." The father even wrote that he probably would not take his son fishing again.

Many years later a historian found these notes, and with curiosity compared them with the entries of the same day in the son's diary. The son exclaimed what a "perfect day" it had been, "all alone" with his father. He described how deeply meaningful and important it was to him.

The Goal of Focused Attention

What is it that defines focused attention? When a child feels, "I'm all alone with my mommy (or daddy)"; "I have her (him) all to myself"; "at this moment, I'm the most important person in the world to my mother (father)"; this is the goal of focused attention, to enable a child to feel this way.

Focused attention is not something that is nice to give our child only if time permits; it is a critical *need* each child has. How a child views himself and how he is accepted by his world is determined by the way in which this need is met. Without focused attention, a child experiences increased anxiety because he feels everything else is more important than he is. He is consequently less secure and is impaired in his emotional and psychological growth. Such a child can be identified in the nursery or classroom. He is less mature than children whose parents have taken the time to fill their need for focused attention. This unfortunate child is generally more withdrawn and has difficulty with peers. He is less able to cope and usually reacts poorly in any conflict. He is overly dependent upon the teacher or other adults with whom he comes into contact.

Some children, especially girls deprived of focused attention from their father, *seem* to be just the opposite. They are quite talkative, manipulative, dramatic, often childishly seductive, and are usually considered precocious, outgoing, and mature by their kindergarten and first-grade teachers. However, as these girls grow older, this behavior pattern does not change and becomes gradually inappropriate. By the time they are in the third or fourth grade they are usually obnoxious to their peers and teachers. However, even at this late date, focused attention, especially from the fathers, can go a long way in reducing the children's self-defeating behavior, decreasing their anxiety, and freeing them to resume their maturational growth.

How to Give Focused Attention

Now that we've seen how vital focused attention is to a child, how do we accomplish it? I have found the best way to give a child focused attention is to set aside time to spend with him *alone*. If you're already thinking how difficult it is to do this, you are right. Finding time to be alone with a child, free from other distractions, is what I consider to be the most difficult aspect of good child rearing. You might say this separates the best parents from other parents; the sacrificing parents from the nonsacrificing; the most caring from the least caring; the parents who set priorities from those who do not. Let's face it, good child rearing takes *time*. Finding time in our hyperactive society is hard, especially when children often are addicted to television and sometimes would rather spend time with it. This is all the more reason focused attention is so crucial. Children are being influenced by forces outside the family more than anytime in history. It takes tremendous effort to pry time from busy schedules, but the rewards are great. It is a wonderful thing to see your child happy, secure, well liked by peers and adults, and learning and behaving at his best. But believe me, fellow parent, this does not come automatically. We must pay a price for it! We must find time to spend alone with each child.

John Alexander, former president of InterVarsity Christian Fellowship, related at a conference some years ago how difficult it was for him to find time for each of his four children. His solution was to save at least one-half hour every Sunday afternoon for each of his children. Everyone must find his own way of doing this.

My time during our parenting years was also difficult to manage. I tried to conserve it as much as possible for my children. For example, when my daughter was taking music lessons close to my office Monday afternoons, I scheduled my appointments so that I could pick her up. Then we would stop at a restaurant for supper. At these times, without the pressure of interruption and time schedules, I was able to give her my full attention and listen to whatever she wanted to talk about. Only in this context of being alone without pressure can parents and their child develop that special indelible relationship which each child so desperately needs to face the realities of life. It's such moments as these that a child remembers when life becomes difficult, especially during those tumultuous years of adolescent conflict and the normal drives for independence.

It's also during times of focused attention that parents can take special opportunities to make eye contact and physical contact with a child. It is during times of focused attention that eye and physical contact have stronger meaning and impact upon a child's life.

Of course, it is more difficult to find time for focused attention when there are several children in the family. I remember counseling a seven-year-old girl for numerous problems she was having at school and at home—problems with school work, peer relationships, sibling relationships, and immature behavior. You've perhaps guessed that her parents had not given her focused attention. She had nine brothers and sisters and her parents couldn't give her the focused attention she needed. Actually, they weren't aware that this girl was suffering from lack of focused attention because all of their other children were quite well adjusted. The parents were farmers, and during the natural course of a day—milking, feeding the animals, and plowing—they spent sufficient time alone with each child to forestall problems. With this particular child, because of her age, individual chores, and birth order, the natural course of events prevented her from enjoying enough of her parents' attention. She felt neglected and unloved. Her parents loved her dearly, but the child did not feel it and so she did not know it.

Careful Planning Pays Off
This illustration indicates how important it is to *plan* our time in order to provide focused attention for *each* child. This is diffi-

cult. In a two-child family, each parent is often able to spend time with one of the children. With more than two children, the problem becomes progressively more difficult. And, of course, in a one-parent family the logistics are more difficult. However, careful planning pays off. For example, on a particular day (say next Friday) one child may be invited to a party, another may be at a relative's, leaving one child free. A careful parent whose children take priority would consider this time a golden opportunity to give focused atention to that child. Of course, our plans must consider the emotional needs of each and every child, or we'll have the same problem as in the ten-child farm family just mentioned. This is especially difficult when we have both a demanding and a nondemanding child in the same family. We must resist the concept that the loudest squeaking hinge gets the oil. Every child has the same needs whether he demands they be met or not. Especially vulnerable in this regard is a nondemanding, passive child who also is a middle child. And if his siblings happen to be demanding children, his parents will find it all too easy to pass him by until problems develop.

Watching for unexpected opportunities yields additional time. For example, times occur when a parent finds himself alone with a child, a time perhaps when the others are outside playing. Here is another opportunity to fill that child's emotional tank and prevent problems brought on by a dry one. This time of focused attention may be quite short: just a moment or two can do wonders. Every moment counts. It's like making deposits in a savings account. As long as the balance is healthy, a child's emotional life will be sound and he will have fewer problems. It's also an investment in the future, especially the years of adolescence.

Every deposit is assurance that a child's teenage years will be healthy, wholesome, pleasant, and rewarding for both child and parent. The stakes are high. What's worse than a wayward adolescent son or daughter? What's more wonderful than a well-balanced teenager?

Of course, long periods of focused attention are important also. As children grow older, this time of focus needs to be lengthened. Older children need time to warm up, let their developing defenses down, and feel free to share their innermost thoughts, especially anything that may be troubling them. As you can see, if these times of focused attention were begun early in a child's life, he accepts it very naturally and finds it much easier to share emotional things with his parents. On the other hand, if times for focused attention are not provided, how can a child learn to communicate meaningfully with his parents? Again, the stakes are high. What is worse than having a troubled child who can't share his feelings with you? What is more wonderful than for your child to be able to bring anything to you to talk over?

All this is difficult and takes time. But many people I've met have shared with me all sorts of ways they have done this. I remember listening to the late Joe Bayly, a Christian writer and publishing executive, talk about this. He marked off definite times on his appointment calendar to spend with his family, and when someone called and asked him to accept a speaking engagement at that time, he politely told the inquirer that he had another engagement.

Joe Bayly had another good way to give his children focused attention. He had personal flags for each family member. Each flag was designed to suit the personality of the child for whom it was designated and was given to the child on his or her birthday. Thereafter it was flown on the flagpole in front of the house on special occasions, for example, subsequent birthdays, when that child would return home after trips, or going away to college. This is an example of indirect focused attention.

When Others Are Present

We mentioned that focused attention is given when alone with a child, away from other family members. Although this is true, there are times when focused attention must be given with others present. This is especially true when a child is ill, has experienced some emotional pain, or for some other painful reason has regressed. By regressed, I mean he is in poor control of his feelings and/or behavior.

Here is an example of this. One day, deeply concerned parents sought my advice regarding their twelve-year-old son Tim.

The boy's first cousin, also a twelve-year-old boy had come to live with them. The cousin was a very demanding child who had overshadowed Tim by taking almost all his parents' attention. Tim felt displaced by his overpowering cousin, became depressed, withdrawn, and occasionally uncommunicative. Part of my advice to the parents was, of course, to give both Tim and his cousin much focused attention; that is to spend time with Tim alone and the cousin alone. However, the cousin continued to clearly dominate each situation when the two boys were present. Next, I advised the parents to give each boy focused attention whenever the cousin was being overly dominant. The parents were able to do this by turning directly toward Tim when it was his turn to speak, giving him full eye contact, and physical contact when convenient, and responding to his comments. Then when it was appropriately Tim's cousin's turn to speak, the parents repeated the process with him.

This type of focused attention usually works well only if a child is also receiving ample focused attention alone. By the way, I've taught teachers these simple principles which have revolutionized their teaching and perceptions toward each child.

Focused attention is time consuming, difficult to do consistently, and many times burdensome to already exhausted parents. But focused attention is the most powerful means of keeping a child's emotional tank full and investing in his future.

CHAPTER 7

Appropriate and Inappropriate Love

L et's consider the *too-much-love* controversy. Some contend that too much love will spoil a child, while others claim you can't love a child too much. The confusion in this area often causes advocates of both sides to take an extreme position. Many of the former group are severe disciplinarians, and many of the latter group are overindulgent.

Consider the issue in light of the concept of *appropriate love*, which will provide healthy nurturing and foster a child's emotional growth and self-reliance. The picture then quickly becomes clearer. We can then hold to the principle that a child needs a superabundance of appropriate love but no inappropriate love.

Inappropriate Love

We may define *inappropriate love* as affection which, when conveyed to a child, hinders a child's emotional growth by failing to meet a child's emotional needs, and which fosters an increasingly dependent relationship upon a parent and hampers self-reliance.

The four most common types of inappropriate love are possessiveness, seductiveness, vicariousness, and role-reversal. Let's take them one at a time.

Possessiveness

Possessiveness is a tendency of parents to encourage a child to be too dependent on his parents. Paul Tournier, noted Swiss counselor, deals with the subject quite well in his article, "The Meaning of Possessiveness." He states that when a child is small, dependency is "obvious and almost complete." But if this dependency does not diminish as a child grows older, it becomes an obstacle to a child's emotional development. Many parents try to keep their children in a state of dependence upon them. Dr. Tournier states that they do this "by suggestion or by emotional blackmail," or else by using their authority and insisting upon obedience. The child is theirs. They have rights over him because he belongs to them. Such parents are termed *possessive*. These parents tend to treat their child as an object or property to be possessed or owned, and not as a person who needs to grow in his own right and to become gradually independent and self-reliant.

A child must have respect from his parents to be himself. This does not, of course, mean no limit-setting or being permissive. (Every child needs guidance and discipline.) It means to encourage a child to think to be spontaneous, to realize he is a separate person who must assume more and more responsibility for himself.

If we parents disregard a child's right to gradually become independent, one of two things will happen. He may become overly dependent on us and overly submissive, failing to learn how to live in his world. He may become easy prey to strong-willed, authoritative personalities or cultish groups; or there will be deterioration of our relationship with a child as he gets older. He will become more resistant to our guidance.

Again, as Dr. Tournier suggests, we should "possess as if not possessing." Such is the great message of the Bible. Man can never truly possess anything. He is but the steward of the goods that God entrusts to him, for "the earth is the Lord's, and everything in it" (1 Corinthians 10:26, NIV).

Of course, there is some possessiveness in every parent. But we must take care to (1) identify it within ourselves; (2) separate it from true concern for a child's total welfare, especially concerning his need to become self-reliant; (3) be as continually aware of it as we can; and (4) resist its influence.

Seductiveness

The second inappropriate way of expressing love is through seductiveness. I have to start out by saying this is a difficult subject to write about because *seductiveness* is not easy to define. The word seems to be used to communicate everything from elicitation of sexual experience to pollution.

Regarding our subject at hand, I believe it sufficient to define seductiveness as attempting consciously or unconsciously to derive sensual/sexual feelings from an encounter with a child.

An example of this was discussed at a recent seminar on child psychiatry. A seven-year-old girl was seen at a psychiatric clinic for frequent masturbation and poor school performance. The evaluation disclosed that the child spent much time fantasizing (day-dreaming) her mother's death and living alone with her father. It was also noted that her father spent much time holding the child, caressing and fondling her in such a way that seemed to bring sensual enjoyment to both father and child. When these facts were gently shared with the father, his response was, "Oh, my word! I just realized that when I wash the soap off of her when we're showering together, she reacts like a mature woman." This was a case where the father was obviously seductive. However, he apparently did not fully realize what he was doing. As in almost all cases of this sort, the marital relationship in this family was hurting. In families where the marriage is not healthy, it is not uncommon for seductiveness to exist. In our day the problem is worsening.

What do you think of this letter to Ann Landers which appeared in her syndicated column some years ago?

Dear Ann Landers: I don't know if I have a problem or not. It's our beautiful twelve-year-old daughter. I've seen girls who are crazy about their fathers, but never anything quite like this.

Donna sits next to (or on top of) her father at every opportunity. They play with each other's hands and act kittenish like a couple of goofy kids. She hangs on her father when they walk or their arms are around one another's waists. Is this normal?

Signed, Me Worried."

Are you a parent of a preadolescent daughter? What do you think? Does this sound good or bad? Would you be worried? What would you do?

Here is Ann Landers' reply:

Dear W: Sounds to me as if there's entirely too much touching. Today a girl of twelve is more of a woman than a child. Donna needs to be talked to, but it would be better if the word did not come from you.

Perhaps an enlightened relative or an adult friend could tell Donna it is unbecoming and unhealthy for a young girl to have so much physical contact with her father. (Surely this behavior has been observed by others.)

If you know of no person you might call on to communicate the message tactfully but firmly, by all means enlist the help of the school counselor. I believe Donna should be approached rather than your husband. He is apt to be resentful and defensive.

I would like to reply to Ann's reply. I agree that it does sound like there is too much physical contact here, and it does sound seductive. However, this is the mother's viewpoint, and the chances are overwhelming that the marital relationship is poor. In short, neither we (nor Ann) know for sure if there is actually sensual seduction here or not. Perhaps this situation is similar to the one at the end of chapter 2 where the mother is jealous of a good relationship between daughter and father.

Supposing the relationship here is indeed a seductive one, would you go to a twelve-year-old girl and suggest that her own father was sexually improper with her? Genuine respect for parents is hard enough to find today without further undermining it.

But nonetheless there is one principal comment I'd like to make regarding Ann's reply and that is that it exemplifies the general mentality today regarding loving children. Her advice seems to suggest that, because the father was conveying his love to the child inappropriately, he should not show it at all. We have already seen how vital physical contact is to a preadolescent girl. This particular father was not doing it correctly. Is the answer to stop the physical contact completely?

I'm afraid this type of reaction has become generally accepted by our society. It is assumed that because some parents are seductive with their children, physical contact should be held to a minimum or actually be avoided. An analogy would be this: because I saw an obese person today, I should not eat at all, or at least minimally.

Another reason many parents unfortunately avoid physical contact with their children is that they may actually feel some sexual response to them. This can happen to any parents, especially fathers of older daughters. So this is indeed a dilemma. On the one hand, the child desperately needs to feel loved and physical contact is essential for this. On the other hand, the parents feel uncomfortable and fear this would be wrong or perhaps damaging to the child.

I think many loving parents would be greatly helped in this difficult area if they realized that: (1) every child regardless of age needs *appropriate* physical contact; (2) to have some occasional sexual feelings or fleeting sexual fantasies regarding a child is normal; (3) a parent should ignore these inappropriate feelings, go ahead, and give a child what he (or she) needs, including appropriate (nonseductive) physical contact.

With this confusion is it any wonder so few children feel genuinely, unconditionally loved?

Another fear many parents have regarding seductiveness is homosexuality. There seems to be a misconception that too much love expressed from mother to daughter or from father to son will lead to homosexuality, but just the opposite is the case.

It's not infrequent during my work in schools for a teacher to approach me with this concern. A woman teacher recently asked, "Dr. Campbell, I love my daughter so very much that I kiss her a lot and sometimes on the lips. Am I making a lesbian out of her?" After asking for other information to make sure the relationship was healthy, my answer was, "Keep it up."

Two Examples

Let me give you two other examples. The second example will show what appropriate love, including physical contact, does for a child concerning sexual identity. But the first example concerns what the *absence* of it causes.

The first example is drawn from Rusty, a dear friend of mine who is mean, tough, "all man," and a drill instructor in the U.S. Marine Corps. He and his wonderfully warm sensitive wife have four boys, "stair steps." Rusty decided his boys were going to be like him, tough and rugged men. He treated them like Marine recruits with strict and rigid discipline—no affection, unquestioned obedience, and no questions.

Your reaction to this is important. How do you think his four sons developed? Do you think they are following in their father's footsteps? Do you think they're becoming "all men"?

The last time I saw these boys each one was extremely effeminate. Their mannerisms, speech, and appearance were those of girls. Surprised? You shouldn't be. I see it every day. Boys with rejecting, harsh, nonaffectionate fathers generally become effeminate.

Here's the second example. Several years ago we had a pastor who was a huge man with rugged features. His very presence demanded attention, and he had a warm, loving heart. His boy at that time was three years old, the same age as my David but a head taller and about twenty pounds heavier, a "spittin' image of his ol' man." Our pastor loved his son deeply and warmly. He was very affectionate with the boy, lots of holding, hugging, kissing, and wrestling.

How do you think this boy developed? Did he follow in his

father's footsteps? You bet he did. That little fellow was just like his father. He had a strong, healthy sexual identification and was secure, happy, lovable, and all boy. He will do all right in this world with a dad like that.

If these two examples don't convince you that a superabundance of appropriate love is not only warranted, but needed by every child (girls *and* boys) from *each* parent, let me give you this one fact. In all my reading and experience, I have never known of one sexually disoriented person who had a warm, loving, and affectionate father.

So, due to these misconceptions we've just looked at (and others), few parents are able to properly nourish their children emotionally. Although there is abundant love in their hearts, there is little in practice. I am convinced that once these misconceptions are corrected, and once parents understand what a child needs, most are able to provide the superabundance of appropriate love each child must have.

Vicariousness

The third most common type of inappropriate love is vicariousness. *Vicariousness*, or vicarious love, is living one's life or dreams through the life of a child. One of the most harmful kinds of vicariousness is a mother's living out romantic fantasies or longing through her daughter. A mother does this by steering her daughter into relationships and situations where she herself longs to be. A clue to this phenomenon is a mother's obsessive interests in the intimate details of her child's dating experiences, becoming sensually excited as her daughter reveals them to her. The destructiveness of this process is obvious. A child can be led into situations which she does not have the maturity or experience to handle. Pregnancy is just one possible consequence. Another frequent outgrowth of this is a degrading reputation for the child. Such a reputation can injure a child's self-image and self-respect for life.

This type of vicariousness can also happen between father and son with similar consequences. A father who acts out his own sexual prowess through his son's conquests is harming not only his son but others involved in his life. In this way the boy is heavily influenced to view women primarily as sexual objects. He will find it difficult to relate to women as persons with feelings, and especially as equals.

Of course there are many varieties of vicariousness. The kind just described happens to be the most destructive.

Another example of vicariousness is a father using his son to satisfy athletic longings of his own. To see this phenomenon in action, go to your nearest Little League game. A vicariously oriented parent becomes emotionally involved in the game to such an extent it is as though he himself were the player. You can see him becoming outrageously angry at the umpire when the call is against his son. Worst of all such a parent will reprimand and demean his son when he makes a mistake.

What does this bring to mind? The old problem of conditional love. The more vicarious we are with our children, the more our love for them is conditional upon how well they have performed and have met our own vicarious needs.

But let's face it. We're all vicarious to some extent, aren't we? When our David played Little League baseball, I considered him a pretty good baseball player. As I sat there watching him, for some strange reason my mind drifted back to my professional baseball days. I would find myself recalling how desperately I wanted to make it to the major leagues. The pain and disappointment of failing to accomplish this focused before me as I watched David play so well. I wonder why. What a mistake it would have been if I vicariously attempted to fulfill my lost dream through my son.

Vicariousness becomes harmful when it modifies our love so that it is given in relation to a child's behavior and is, in fact, conditional love. We parents must not let our own hopes, longings, and dreams determine the type of love a child receives.

Vicariousness can be considered a kind of possessiveness if it causes us to view children as possessions to be used to fulfill our own dream. How can a child grow in his own right and think for himself and rely on himself in this situation?

We must keep our love for a child unconditional. We must love him so that he can fulfill God's plan for his life, not our vicarious ones.

Role-Reversal

Role-reversal was described some years ago by M.A. Morris and R.W. Gould in their Child Welfare League publications. They define this "as a reversal of the dependency role, in which parents turn to their infants and small children for nurturing and protection."

Brandt Steele and Carl Pollock present a description of role-reversal in the book, *The Battered Child*, (Chicago: University of Chicago Press, 1974, p. 95). They state: "These parents expect and demand a great deal from their infants and children. Not only is the demand for performance great, but it is premature, clearly beyond the ability of the infant to comprehend what is wanted and to respond appropriately. [These] parents deal with the child as if he were much older than he really is. Observation of this interaction leads to a clear impression that the parent feels insecure and unsure of being loved, and looks to the child as a source of reassurance, comfort, and loving response. It is hardly an exaggeration to say the parent acts like a frightened, unloved child, looking to his own child as if he were an adult capable of providing comfort and love. . . . We see two basic elements involved—a high expectation and demand by the parent for the child's performance and a corresponding parental disregard of the infant's own needs, limited abilities, and helplessness—a significant misperception of the infant by the parent."

Role-reversal is the primary relationship in the frightening phenomenon of child abuse. An abusing parent feels his child must take care of the parent's emotional needs, that the parent has a right to be comforted and nourished by his child. When the child fails in this, the parent feels a right to severely punish him.

Child abuse is the extreme form of role-reversal, but all parents use role-reversal to some extent. Sometimes when we ourselves are not feeling well, either physically or mentally, we expect our child to make us feel better. We may be depressed, physically ill, mentally or physically exhausted. At these times we have little or no emotional nurturing to provide our child. It can then be very difficult to give him eye contact, physical contact, or focused attention. When our emotional or physical resources are drained, we need nurturing ourselves. In this condition it's so easy to make the mistake of expecting our child to be comforting, reassuring, compliant, mature in his behavior, and passively obedient. These are not the characteristics of a normal child. If made to assume this unnatural role, a child will not develop normally. The list of possible disturbances which can result is endless.

We parents must not allow such a situation to develop. We must understand that parents do the nurturing, and a child receives it. During times when we are unable to carry this out, we must not look to our children to parent us. Of course, they can help us as they are able, running errands and getting things for us when we're sick, but they must not be expected to nurture us emotionally.

We should make every attempt to prevent times when we are unable to nurture our children. This may mean better care of our bodies to prevent illness and fatigue, for example — a sensible diet, plenty of rest, and plenty of exercise. It may mean looking out for our emotional health by engaging in hobbies or other refreshing activities to prevent depression or mental exhaustion. It may mean keeping our spiritual life fresh and exciting by allowing ample time for prayer and meditation. Most importantly, it means keeping our marriages strong, healthy, and secure. God should be first and one's spouse second and our children a close third. Remember, we will be able to give more to our child if we keep ourselves emotionally and spiritually replenished. This gets back to setting priorities and planning toward goals.

Don't Toss the Baby Out with the Bath Water

We have looked at the four most common types of inappropriate love and several common misconceptions. Of course, these are ways of relating which we want to avoid. They are good neither for the child nor the parent.

However, as we avoid these mistakes, let's not "toss out the baby with the baby water." Let's not make a worse mistake and withhold *appropriate* love from our child. This is the most common of all child rearing mistakes. Far more children suffer from the lack of appropriate love than from exposure to inappropriate love.

Appropriate love is for the benefit and welfare of the child. Inappropriate love serves the abnormal needs and hang-ups of the parent.

We must face it. Our children have essential needs which only parents can fill. If we find we cannot fill these needs, if we cannot keep their emotional tanks full, if we can't give them an abundance of eye contact, physical contact, and focused attention appropriately, we had better get help, and fast. The longer we wait, the worse the situation will become.

CHAPTER 8

A Child's Anger

A nger is a natural response with all of us, including young children. Yet handling anger in a child is, in my opinion, perhaps the most difficult part of parenting. And because it is difficult, most parents respond to a child's anger in wrong and destructive ways.

Consider this. When a child becomes angry, he is quite limited in ways to express his anger. He has only two choices — to express the anger in behavior or verbally. Both ways make it difficult for a parent to know how to respond properly.

If a young child expresses his anger, for instance, by banging his head, throwing toys, hitting, or kicking, such behavior should be dealt with. On the other hand, if a child expresses anger verbally, it will almost certainly come across to the parent as unpleasant, disrespectful, and inappropriate. And this way of showing anger likewise is intolerable and unacceptable. What can a parent do?

Like steam in a kettle, anger must come out some way. No one, including a young child, can suppress anger and continue to keep it all inside. This is one of the most destructive things we can force a young child to do. If we refuse to allow a child to express anger in any way, he then must push the anger deeper and deeper within, causing destructive problems later in life. If the child is punished for expressing his anger either verbally or behaviorally, he has no other choice but to suppress the anger and bottle it up inside. As a result, this child will never be able to learn to handle anger maturely.

I call this the "punishment trap." As parents, we need to understand that punishment in itself is not the way to teach our children how to handle their anger.

Another easy mistake parents make in the face of childhood anger is to explode and dump a load of anger on an angry child. Children are helpless in the face of parental anger. They have no defense against it. A common example is found in such a harsh rebuke as, "I never want to see you acting that way (or talking that way to me) again! Understand!" When a parent yells and screams at a child, he or she effectively closes off all normal ways for the child to express anger, and, as previously pointed out, the child must keep the anger inside and add the parent's anger to it.

Doubtless, the vast majority of parents today are not doing a good job in handling anger in their young children. If a child's anger comes out behaviorally or verbally, he is either punished or angrily scolded, or both. Again, since these are the only ways a child can express anger, the treatment forces suppressed anger.

Why is this so destructive? Because, as pointed out, the anger eventually must come out some way. If suppressed too much, the anger will come out as "passive-aggressive behavior." Passive-aggressive (PA) behavior is basically unconscious (out of the child's awareness) and antiauthority. It is an unconscious motivation on the part of the child to upset authority figures (parents and teachers, especially) by doing the opposite of what is expected of them. Once passive-aggressive features start influencing a child's behavior, discipline becomes a nightmare.

Passive-aggressive behavior, the opposite of an open, honest, direct, and verbal expression of anger, is an expression of anger that gets back at a person indirectly. A few simple examples of this are procrastination, dawdling, stubbornness, intentional inefficiency, and forgetfulness. The subconscious purpose of PA behavior is to upset the parent or authority figure and cause anger.

Passive aggressive ways of handling anger are indirect, cunning, self-defeating, and destructive. Unfortunately, since passive-aggressive behavior is subconsciously motivated, a child is not consciously aware that he is using this resistant, obstructive behavior to release pent-up anger to upset his parents.

One of the ways a small child can early show PA tendencies is by soiling his pants after he has been toilet-trained—a very effective but unhealthy way to express anger. In most cases, the parents have prohibited expression of any anger, especially verbally. There is little parents can do in such a situation. The parents have backed themselves into a corner. The more the parents punish the child, the more he will soil his pants, to subconsciously upset the parents. What a dilemma! God pity both parent and child in such a situation.

Many school-aged children use PA to express anger by making poorer grades than those of which they are capable. Their attitude is much like "You can lead a horse to water, but you can't make him drink." For a PA child who uses poor grades to make his parents angry, it's "You can make me go to school, but you can't make me get good grades." Again, with PA behavior the parents are helpless; the child's anger is in control and not visibly showing. The more the parents become upset—the subconscious purpose of all this—the worse the situation becomes.

It is important to again emphasize that a PA child does not do things consciously or purposefully to anger authority figures. They are part of an unconscious process of which he is not aware, and into which he has been forced by the "punishment trap."

Passive-aggressive behavior is very common. Why? Because most people do not understand anger or know what to do with it. They feel that anger is somehow wrong or sinful and should be "disciplined" out of a child. This is serious misunderstanding, because the feeling of anger is normal; every human being through the ages has felt anger, including Jesus, who became angry with those who misused the temple. If when your child becomes angry and you spank him or yell at him, "Stop that kind of talk! I will not allow it," or as some scream, "Shut up or I'll smack you!" What can the child do? Only two things—he can disobey you and continue to "talk that way," or obey you and "stop talking that way." If he chooses the latter and ceases to express his anger, the anger will simply be suppressed; and it will remain unresolved in his subconscious, waiting to be expressed later through inappropriate and/or passive-aggressive behavior.

Another mistake some parents make related to the suppression of anger is the inappropriate use of humor. Whenever a situation becomes tense, especially if someone is becoming angry, some parents will tease and try to interject humor to relieve the tension. Of course, humor is a wonderful asset in any family. But where it is consistently used to escape the appropriate handling of anger, children simply cannot learn to appropriately deal with it.

Passive-aggressive behavior easily becomes an ingrained, habitual pattern which can last a lifetime. If a child into his midteen years avoids honestly and openly dealing with anger in an appropriate manner, he may use passive-aggressive techniques in relationships throughout life. This can affect his relationships later with spouse, children, work, associates, and friends. PA behavior is also the primary force behind drugs, inappropriate sex, school failure, running away, and suicide. What a tragedy! And most of these unfortunate people are hardly aware of their self-defeating pattern of behavior or their problems with handling anger.

Passive-aggressive behavior is the worst way to handle anger for several reasons: (1) It can easily become an ingrained tenacious pattern of behavior which will last a lifetime; (2) it can distort a person's personality and make him/her a quite disagreeable person; (3) it can interfere in all the person's relationships; (4) it is one of the most difficult behavioral disorders to treat and correct.

Scripture instructs parents to train a child in the way he should go. Forcing a child to suppress the anger and not deal with it properly is training him in the way he should not go. It is crucial to train a child in the proper way to handle anger. This is done by teaching him to resolve the anger, not suppress it.

Teaching our children and teenagers to handle anger is what I truly consider to be the most difficult part of parenting. First, it is most difficult because it does not come naturally. As we have discussed, our natural response to a child's anger is becoming more angry than the child and dumping the anger back on the child. Second, teaching the proper way to handle anger is difficult because it is a long, tedious process. As a goal, we want our child to handle his anger maturely by the age of sixteen or seventeen. It is a slow process because the handling of anger is a *maturational* process. An immature adult handles anger immaturely; a mature adult handles anger maturely. Passive-aggressive behavior is the most immature way of handling anger. The most mature ways of handling anger are *verbally, pleasantly,* and resolving the anger toward the person at whom we are angry if at all possible.

No child can be expected to learn to handle this anger quickly. A wise parent realizes that the well-parented child will very gradually learn these critical lessons as he goes from one developmental stage to another. Not until the child becomes six or seven or even older can he be expected to learn specifically how to handle anger maturely. Until that time, we as parents must avoid passive-aggressive behavior taking root in our child. When the child is able, we can then specifically train our child to handle this anger more and more maturely as he gets older. This subject is far too extensive to cover adequately in this brief chapter. However, it is thoroughly covered in the book *Kids Who Follow, Kids Who Don't.*

Ephesians 6:4 says, "Father, do not provoke your children to anger, but bring them up in the fear and admonition of the Lord." Study this and also carefully read the following chapters in this book on discipline. Be careful to use punishment as a last resort and refrain from dumping your anger on your child. Parents, please do all in your power to remain pleasant with your child and yet be appropriately firm. If there are two words that sum up Christlike parenting, they are: *pleasant* and *firm*.

Pleasant includes loving kindness, optimism, and refraining from instilling fear or anxiety in the child, especially with our own anger. *Firm* includes fair expectations with consistency. Firmness does not mean rigidity and inflexibility. It considers the child's age, abilities, and maturity level.

Then when your child reaches adolescence, read *How to Really Love Your Teenager*, chapters 6 and 7, which will give you further guidance for that age. This includes how to train your child to handle anger maturely at least by the time he is sixteen or seventeen. Any PA behavior beyond that age can be permanent.

Yes, teaching a child to handle anger is difficult, but one of the most important responsibilities in parenting today. As parents, we must be serious about this and be quite careful that we truly know what we are doing. Too much is at stake!

CHAPTER 9

Discipline: What Is It?

Periodically, when I lecture on parent-child relationships for churches and civic groups, we spend three or four hours talking about how to love a child before we deal with discipline. Invariably, after two or three hours, a parent will come up to me and say, "I've enjoyed the lecture series so far, but when do we get to discipline? That's where I have problems and need answers."

This poor parent has usually misunderstood (1) the relationship between love and discipline and (2) the meaning of discipline. He has separated love from discipline in his mind as though they are two separate entities. No wonder this parent is confused and has problems controlling his child.

Parents who are confused in this way have usually assumed that discipline means punishment (chastisement according to some).

Both of these assumptions are false. I stress to those parents and I hope to stress to you, fellow parent, that love and discipline cannot be separated, and that punishment is a very small part of discipline.

The first fact parents must understand in order to have a well-disciplined child is that *making a child feel loved is the first and most important part of good discipline.* Of course, this is not all but it is most important.

What you have read thus far in this book is the most important aspect of discipline, and must be applied to expect the best results from disciplining your child. There is no point in reading further at this time if you have not applied what you have already read, and if you have not kept your child's emotional tank full. If you have not made an effort to make your child feel loved with an abundance of eye contact, physical contact, and focused attention in an appropriate way, *please do not read further but go back and reread the previous chapters.* The results will disappoint you. Application of behavioral control techniques without a foundation of unconditional love is barbaric and unscriptural. You may have a child who is well-behaved when he is young, but the results are most discouraging in the long run. Only a healthy love-bond relationship lasts through all of life's crises.

What Is Discipline?

Now just what is discipline? What is your definition? In the realm of child rearing, discipline is *training* a child in mind and character to enable him to become a self-controlled, constructive member of society. What does this involve? Discipline involves training through every type of communication. Guidance by example, modeling, verbal instruction, written requests, teaching, providing learning and fun experiences. The list is quite long.

Yes, punishment is on this list, but it is only one of many ways of discipline and is the most negative and primitive factor. Unfortunately, we must use it at times and we will discuss its use further. At present, it should be reemphasized that guidance toward right thought and action is far superior to punishment for wrong action.

With a clear definition of discipline in mind, consider it again in relation to unconditional love. *Discipline is immeasurably easier when the child feels genuinely loved.* This is because he wants to identify with his parents, and is able to do so only if he knows he is truly loved and accepted. He is then able to accept his parents' guidance without hostility and obstructiveness.

If a child does not feel genuinely loved and accepted, however, he has real difficulty identifying with his parents *and* their values. Without a strong, healthy love-bond with his parents, a child reacts to parental guidance with anger, hostility, and resentment. He views each parental request (or command) as an imposition and learns to resist it. In severe cases, a child learns to consider each parental request with such resentment that his total orientation to parental (and eventually to all) authority is one of doing exactly the opposite of what is expected of him. This type of emotional disorder is increasing at an alarming rate in our country, and children from Christian families are not excluded.

You are by now likely realizing how crucial unconditional love is for good discipline (training). The more you keep your child's emotional tank full, the more he will respond to discipline (training). The less full his emotional tank, the less he will respond to discipline (training).

One aspect of appropriate love not yet mentioned is focused (active) listening. Focused listening is listening to a child in such a way that he is sure you know what he is trying to communicate to you. When your child knows you understand how he feels and what he wants, he is much more willing to respond positively to discipline, especially when you disagree with him. Nothing frustrates a child more than to be told to do something when he feels his parents don't understand his position. This does not mean catering to your child's demand or whim; it simply means listening to your child so that he doesn't feel you have ignored his thoughts and feelings when you use your authority. Is that unreasonable? If you believe it is, you are not regarding your child as a valuable, separate person.

Think about it. When your child feels you have considered his position and feelings, you have assuaged your anger and resentment which would come back to haunt you later. Doesn't your Heavenly Father do as much for you? Christ said, "Ask, and you will be given what you ask for. Seek, and you will find. Knock, and the door will be opened. For everyone who asks, receives. Anyone who seeks, finds. If only you will knock, the door will open. If a child asks his father for a loaf of bread, will he be given a stone instead? If he asks for fish, will he be given a poisonous snake? Of course not! And if you hardhearted, sinful men know how to give good gifts to your children, won't your Father in heaven even more certainly give good gifts to those who ask Him for them?" (Matthew 7:7-11, TLB)

To give a child focused listening requires at least eye contact, with physical contact and focused attention if possible and if appropriate. Acknowledging that you understand your child (even if you disagree with him) is usually helpful. Repeating your child's thoughts and feelings back to him is a good way to ensure that he understands that you understand. Your child's thoughts and feelings may make a difference in your own understanding and actions also.

I recall an incident with our then 16-year-old Carey. Pat and I gave her permission to go to a wrestling match at her high school on a school night with three of her friends. She was told to come home right after the match. The match was to end around 10 o'clock. It usually takes thirty to forty-five minutes to make the trip. At 11 o'clock I became concerned; at 11:15 I called the parents of one of the boys. They said the group had stopped by there to get a car with snow tires (bad weather had begun) and the parents offered them a snack. The kids had left home about 11:10. Carey arrived home at 11:40.

I was angry. I sent her to bed after giving her a lecture about responsibility, and placed her on one week's restriction (she was grounded). Why did I react without listening to what Carey had to say? I was thinking more of myself than the actual situation. I wasn't feeling well that night and wanted to get to bed early. I had a busy schedule the next day. Secondly, my daughter was later than I expected, and she did not call to tell us that she would be late. I assumed she was totally negligent in the whole situation.

I have a wise daughter. She waited until the next day when I had recovered my composure and loving ways before giving me all the facts. She also knew that I listen better when I am not angry. As it turned out the kids took a longer but safer way home. Ice and snow were making the roads slippery. She was telling the truth; it all checked. Where she had been negligent was failing to call us when she saw that she would be later than we expected. After apologizing to her for overreacting, I decreased the restriction to be commensurate with what she had done.

There are two lessons we can learn from this experience. The first is the importance of really listening to a child when he or she is communicating. I could have saved myself frustration and my daughter's pain and possible anger and resentment toward me by listening to her before acting.

The other lesson is the importance of controlling our emotions at such times. I do believe that a mother or father's worst enemy in raising a child is uncontrolled feelings, especially anger. As in my experience, this can cause a a parent to say or do things he or she will regret later. Too much anger, especially uncontrolled anger, will frighten a child initially. It may even seem to help a child's behavior, but this is only temporary. As a child grows older, parental expression of too much anger (temper outbursts) will instill increased disrespect for the parents along with kindling a child's own anger and gradual resentment. When you stop to think about it, uncontrolled feelings draw disrespect from anyone. Why should we expect otherwise from our spouse or child?

You know as well as I that we all lose our cool at times. One thing to remember is that when we do, we shouldn't be afraid to apologize later after things have calmed down. It's very possible to make something beautiful out of something bad. It's amazing how pleasant communication can become when a family member is big enough to apologize when he is wrong, and losing one's calm inappropriately (overreacting) can be such an occasion. Believe it or not, the times of warmness and closeness that usually follow this are among those special memories that a child (and parents) never forgets. They are priceless.

Emotional overreactions, however, can only be tolerated in a family to a limited extent, especially if no apology takes place. They should be kept to a minimum. How is this accomplished?

Control Your Anger

It's important to remember that anger is difficult to control under certain conditions. Some of these are (1) when a person is depressed; (2) when a person is afraid; (3) when a person is physically not well; (4) when a person is fatigued mentally or physically; and (5) when a person's spiritual life is not healthy.

A book could be written on coping with each of these problems. For now it must suffice to warn each parent to look out for himself mentally, emotionally, physically, and spiritually. Unhealthiness in any of these areas can hamper the parent-child relationship, the marital relationship, in fact, all relationships, primarily by hurting our ability to control our anger. Let's get in shape. Uncontrolled anger is detrimental to good discipline.

Discipline and Punishment

I hope you are realizing that you may have much to do before you can expect your child to respond well to discipline. Anyone can beat a child with a rod as the primary way of controlling his behavior. That takes no sensitivity, no judgment, no understanding, and no talent. To depend on corporal punishment as the principal method of discipline is to make that critical error in assuming that discipline equals punishment. Discipline is *training* the child in the way he should go. Punishment is only one part of this, and the less the better. Please remember this statement: *the better disciplined a child is, the less punishment will be required.* How well a child responds to discipline depends primarily on how much the child feels loved and accepted. So our biggest task is to make him feel loved and accepted.

There are several reasons why so many parents fall into the punishment trap, why they somehow get the idea that their greatest responsibility in discipline (training a child) is to spank (punish) him.

One reason parents fall into this trap is because so many books, articles, seminars, institutes, radio programs, sermons, and papers advocate corporal punishment while glossing over or bypassing all other needs of a child, especially love. Few plead for a child and his real needs. Too many today are dogmatically calling for children to be punished, calling it discipline, and recommending the harshest, most extreme form of human treatment. Most perplexing of all, many of these advocates call this a biblical approach. They quote three verses from the Book of Proverbs (13:24; 23:13; 29:15) to totally justify beating a child. They neglect to mention the hundreds of Scripture verses dealing with love, compassion, sensitivity, understanding, forgiveness, nurturing, guidance, kindness, affection, and giving, as though a child has little or no right to these expressions of love.

Proponents of corporal punishment seem to have forgotten that the shepherd's rod referred to in Scripture was used almost exclusively for *guiding* the sheep, not beating them. The shepherds would *gently* steer the sheep, especially the lambs, by simply holding the rod to block them from going in the wrong direction and then gently nudge them toward the right direction. If the rod was (or is) an instrument used principally for beating, I would have a difficult time with Psalm 23 "Thy rod and Thy staff, they comfort me" (v. 4, KJV).

I have not noticed one of these advocates state that there might be times when punishment may be harmful. So many parents have come away from these gatherings or readings with the idea that corporal punishment is the primary, or even the only way to relate to a child.

The Results of This Approach

I have seen the results of this approach. Children who were passive, compliant, very quiet, withdrawn, and easily controlled when they were young, lacked a strong, healthy, love-attachment to their parents, and gradually became defiant, resentful, difficult to control, self-centered, nongiving, nonaffectionate, insensitive, nonforgiving, noncompassionate, resistant to authority, and unkind as adolescents.

I think Scripture is quite helpful here. The Apostle Paul instructed, "And, fathers, do not provoke your children to anger; but bring them up in the discipline and instruction of the

Lord" (Ephesians 6:4, NASB). What has happened to these dear children just described? Yes, they were provoked to anger by mechanical, harsh discipline (primarily punitive) without the foundation of unconditional love. I like *The Living Bible* paraphrase of the Ephesians passage: "And now a word to you parents. Don't keep on scolding and nagging your children, making them angry and resentful. Rather, bring them up with the loving discipline the Lord Himself approves, with suggestion and godly advice."

Have you noticed that one deceptive trait of a young child who is disciplined primarily with punishment? Yes, he is easily controlled. That is the other reason so many parents fall into the trap. When a child is young, his behavior can usually be well controlled by corporal punishment alone. That is, if you consider good behavior as submissive compliance, lack of spontaneity, lack of self-confidence, and anxious docility.

You may be surprised, but I have seen many young children who were raised with much punishment especially corporal punishment, but who were unmanageable. These unfortunate children would be spanked severely, but the spankings would have no effect, and the children often would not even cry. Of course before coming to me, many parents have tried every piece of advice given to them, from trying to give even more punishment (like pinching the trapezius muscle), to giving candy, to putting the children in certain types of rigidly structured nursery schools. In every case, one of the problems was a lack in the parent-child love bond. These children just don't feel genuinely loved and accepted. At that early age, resentment and defiance can develop to such an extent from a lack of unconditional love that not even corporal punishment can subdue these responses.

Put the Horse before the Cart
First things first, fellow parents. Practice uncontrolled love, *then* discipline. Putting the horse before the cart will create a positive relationship between parents and child and will keep *negative* interactions such as corporal punishment to a minimum. Notice that I did not say unconditional love will abolish the need for corporal punishment. How I wish it could, but it won't. The

more genuine and unconditional the love-bond from parents to child, the more positive is the relationship, minimizing the need for punishment. Unfortunately, punishment is required at times, and we'll explore that together later.

To summarize, in order for a child to respond well to discipline (training), we parents must give him what he needs. A child can learn (train) well only if he is happy, feels safe, content, confident, secure, accepted, and loved. Expecting a child to learn, namely, be disciplined, without our giving him what he needs is cruel enough. But then to beat him for not living up to our expectations? We treat our pets better than that.

Consider this: An aggressive junior high school football coach once threatened to beat my then thirteen-year-old Carey with a paddle for what he considered an infraction in the school cafeteria. I called a school official and asked him if his school system actually allowed children to be beaten (especially teenage girls by male teachers with all the sexual connotations connected with such an act). He answered yes. When I asked him if he beat his dog he said he didn't. We wonder why children are becoming more and more disrespectful and resistant to authority. Can you figure it out?

The Corporal Punishment Trap

One important reason why using corporal punishment as a principal means of behavioral control is dangerous is that it drastically alleviates guilt. Corporal punishment degrades, dehumanizes, and humiliates a child. As a result, a child may feel the beating is punishment enough in itself. If the corporal punishment is instituted with enough frequency and severity, there will not be sufficient guilt provocation to enable a child to develop an adequate conscience. Without the foundation of unconditional love, the required developmental phases, especially proper parental identification, will fail to evolve, further crippling the development of a healthy conscience.

Many forget the important positive factor of guilt and consider it to be an unwanted feeling. Too much guilt is harmful, but a proper amount is vital in the formation and maintenance of a normal conscience. A normal, healthy conscience which keeps a child's behavior within normal boundaries is far better than control by fear, and preferable to poor control or no control at all. What do you think enables a happy, well-adjusted teenager to control his behavior? Right—his conscience. If you want your child to develop a normal responsive conscience which will enable him to *control himself,* then refrain from building your relationship with him on a punitive basis—by controlling his behavior primarily by spanking and scolding, especially spanking.

Another tragic consequence of corporal punishment is called *identification with the aggressor.* It is also a guilt-escaping mechanism. A child identifies (sides with) the punishing parent, coming to the place where he feels being aggressive and punitive is right. Then, of course, this child grows up, has children, and treats them as he himself was treated. This is why abusing parents were themselves usually ill-treated by their parents. This use of corporal punishment (or the threat of it) as the main way of handling a child is passed on from generation to generation. This in itself is bad enough. With the frightening advent of violence in all modes of mass communication, especially television, is it any wonder that child abuse and all other forms of violence have become a national disgrace? Until we parents begin to proclaim the indispensable needs of a child, namely, unconditional love and loving discipline, the situation will continue to become worse. We must stand against the avalanche of demanding critics who insist that beating a child (confusing punishment with discipline) should be the primary way of relating to him. Are you aware that some of the critics do not have children themselves? Until we give a child what he desperately needs, he (and we) will suffer.

Dear parents, look at every statistic regarding children and adolescents in our nation today—academics, attitudes, respect for authority, emotional disturbance, motivation, drugs, crime, and so on. The situation is horrible. I maintain that the principle reason for our national dilemma with youth today is that our children do not feel genuinely loved, accepted, and cared for. With the deafening roar of disciplinarians (actually punishment-oriented) on one side and advocates of vague, difficult-to-follow programs on the other, parents are confused.

Using designed programs, such as those based on behavior modification techniques, as the *primary* way of relating to your child is also a mistake. Like punishment, these programs do have a place in child rearing and can be very helpful, *but not as the principal way of relating to a child.* Some of these programs are quite good, but usually their techniques are used in place of unconditional love and loving discipline (training). Here is the error. These designed techniques can be of great value in certain situations (which we will mention later), but we parents must first make sure that our child's emotional tank is as full as possible before we resort to punishment or designed techniques. In most cases, if a child receives his required amount of unconditional love and loving discipline, the parents seldom need to resort to punishment or programs. Yes, punishment and techniques are at times necessary, quite helpful, and often good, but let's face it; they are not the best — appropriate love and guidance are.

We want the most positive, pleasant, loving relationship we can possibly have with a child. At the same time, we want him to develop self-control and act appropriately to the extent that he is able (considering his age, development, etc.). In order to see these two priceless happenings come to pass, parents must give their child two things. First, give him unconditional love, and give it appropriately. Second, give him loving discipline — that is, training in the most positive way possible. Train by all available means, in such a way that enhances a child's self-esteem and does not demean him or hurt his self-concept. Positive guidance to good behavior is far superior to negative punishment for poor behavior.

But no matter how well we do our jobs as parents, a child will sometimes misbehave. This is inevitable. There are no perfect parents and there is no perfect child.

So how should we handle a child's misbehavior? We will consider this in the next chapter.

CHAPTER 10

Loving Discipline

U p to this point we have explored how to convey unconditional love to a child by proper use of eye contact, physical contact, focused attention, and discipline (training). We have found how important it is to make sure we keep a child's emotional tank full for only then can he develop to be his best. Only then can he develop full self-control and self-discipline. We found in chapter 8 that guidance toward right action is better than punishment for wrong action. Then we ended that chapter with the fact that every child will misbehave at times. Let's now consider how to deal with misbehavior.

In order to understand how to deal with a child's behavior, we must understand the irrational way in which all children think. This crucial area must be carefully considered. All children need and want love. They know they need love and they know they want it, but the way in which they seek it is immature and irrational.

First, let's look at a rational way to obtain love. Say a man named Jim loved a woman named Carla. How would Jim be likely to win Carla's love? Acting immaturely, putting his worst foot forward, whining, pouting, being argumentative and demanding? Of course not. If Jim were mature, he would be at his best. He would put his best foot forward, remain calm, pleasant, helpful, kind, and considerate. When he was not sure of Carla's love, he would not resort to immature behavior; rather he would try to earn Carla's love. He would try to deserve it in her eyes. That's a rational way to obtain love.

But that is not the way a child does it, folks. The younger a child, the less mature he is. That makes sense, doesn't it? And the less mature he is, the more irrational he is. A child knows by nature how desperately he needs love. But he does not by nature try to deserve it or win it. This logic is beyond his inherent understanding. Eventually, he may (or may not) learn this, but he is not born with this capability.

What does a child do then, especially a younger child? A child communicates primarily with his behavior. He continually asks the question, "Do you love me?" How we answer that question determines many things. It determines a child's self-esteem, attitudes, feelings, peer relationships, and on and on. If his emotional tank is full, you can see it in his behavior. If it is empty, it is manifested by his behavior. Put it this way. Most behavior in a child is determined by how much he feels loved.

This is the irrationality of a child. Instead of winning our love and affection by good behavior, a child by nature continually *tests* our love by his behavior. "Do you love me?" If we answer that all-important question, "Yes, we love you," great! The pressure to seek love is then off a child and his behavior can be more easily controlled. If a child does not feel loved, by nature he is compelled more earnestly to ask, "Do you love me?" through his behavior. We may not like this behavior because there are only a limited number of ways a child may act, and many of these ways may be inappropriate for the occasion. It stands to reason that when anyone is desperate enough, his behavior may become inappropriate. Nothing makes a child more desperate than the lack of love.

This is the primary cause of misbehavior in a child. When his emotional tank is empty, he cries out behaviorally, "Do you love me?"

Is it fair then, or wise, to demand good behavior from a child without first making sure he feels loved? Without first filling his emotional tank?

What Does This Child Need?

Here's an example. When our daughter Carey was sixteen, she went to summer camp. Our nine-year-old David was then the oldest child at home, and he liked it. He acted more maturely, and sought more responsibility. David liked being the oldest. It was great.

The problem was that eventually Carey had to come home. Well, on the day she returned, David's behavior regressed. He suddenly became whiny, discontented, pouty, somewhat angry, moody, and withdrawn.

What happened? Why the sudden, drastic change in David? What should I do as a parent? Punish David for his poor behavior? Send Carey back to camp? Tell David his five-year-old brother Dale acts better than he? What would you do?

Well, let me explain what I did and why. Of course, Carey's coming and again becoming the oldest kid was hard on David. That's difficult for a young boy to handle. His behavior was the pleading question, "Do you love me? Do you love me now that Carey is home and I'm not the oldest anymore? How does your love for me compare to your love for Carey? Is she more important? Can she take away your love from me?" Oh, the heartache of children at these times!

If I punished him at that time, how would David think I was answering his question, "Do you love me?" As soon as I could, I took David off to himself, held him close, and we talked for some time. Occasionally I told him in boy ways how much I loved him. I gave him eye and physical contact. As his emotional tank was filled, his mood changed back to his happy, outgoing self. It took about fifteen to twenty minutes before he was off to play. David was happy and his behavior was fine. That was one of those special moments we talked about before. I think he will never forget that precious time together. I won't.

Please don't get the idea I have been the perfect father. I have not. I've made many mistakes. But here was one situation I think I handled all right.

All this leads us to the realization that when our child misbehaves, we must ask ourselves, "What does this child need?"

The tendency is for parents to ask, "What can I do to correct this child's behavior?" Unfortunately, all too often this question leads initially to punishment. It is then difficult to consider the real needs of a child, and we may end up spanking him or sending him to his room. A child will not feel loved if we approach the handling of his misbehavior this way.

We should always begin by asking ourselves, "What does this child need?" Then we can proceed *logically* from there. Only then can we take care of the misbehavior, give him what he needs, *and* permit him to feel genuinely loved.

The next step is to ask ourselves, "Does the child need eye contact? Does he need physical contact? Does he need focused attention?" In short, does his emotional tank need filling? We parents must make sure that if the misbehavior is in any way caused by a need for any of these, we must first meet these needs. We as parents should not continue to correct a child's behavior until we have met his emotional needs.

This reminds me of a situation with our Dale when he was five. I had been out of town for a few days and had returned home. Dale was acting in a way which irritated me (and everyone else). He was doing all sorts of antics designed to aggravate the rest of the family, especially his nine-year-old brother, David. You see, Dale knew exactly what to do or say to make David climb the wall. And, of course, David could do the same to Dale. In fact, one son annoying the other was one of the first clues my dear wife and I had that an emotional tank needed filling.

Anyway, on this certain day, Dale was especially aggravating. He would needle his brother, pout, and make unreasonable demands. My first reaction, of course, was to really get on to him. Perhaps send him to his room; perhaps put him to bed; perhaps spank him. Then I stopped to think. "What does he need?" The answer came in an instant. I had been out of town. He had not seen me in three days, and I had not really paid him much attention (no focused attention). No wonder Dale was asking the old question, "Do you love me?" Actually he was asking, "Do you still love me after being gone so long and acting as though it didn't affect me?" Suddenly his behavior made sense. He desperately needed his daddy, and his daddy was not giving him what he needed. If I had done anything other than give him what he needed, *me*, his behavior would have become worse. (Yes, even if I had spanked him.) He would have been deeply hurt, resentful, and I would have lost the opportunity to give him one of those special moments.

I can't tell you how thankful I am that I didn't goof on that one. I took Dale to our bedroom, held him close, and said nothing. That normally active fellow was so still and quiet against me. He just sat there and absorbed that intangible nurturing. Gradually, as his emotional tank was filled, he came to life. He began talking in his confident, easygoing, spontaneously happy way. After a short conversation about my trip, he jumped down, and ran off. Where? To find his brother, of course. When I walked into the family room, they were playing contentedly together.

So we can see how vital it is always to be asking ourselves, "What does this child need?" If we do not, we will most assuredly skip prematurely into handling misbehavior inappropriately. We will miss chances to have those extremely important special moments with him. And we will punish a child at times which will hurt him in such a way that will create anger and resentment.

Fellow parents, if you miss this, you've wasted your time reading this book. Misbehavior should not be condoned, but if it is dealt with in an inappropriate way, that is, too harshly or too permissively, you're going to have problems with that child. Yes, we must check misbehavior. We *must* not tolerate misconduct. But the first step is *not* punishment. Punishment is occasionally necessary, but because of its negative effects from overuse, punishment should be used *only as a last resort*. It is far, far better to handle misbehavior positively, especially with genuine love and affection, than to punish a child, especially with corporal punishment. So the first step in any situation is to make sure a child's emotional needs are met. Once again, *a child's emotional tank must be full before caring parents can take any other action.*

Is There a Physical Problem?
The next question to ask in the face of misbehavior is, "Does a physical problem exist which is precipitating this behavior?" The younger a child, the more behavior is affected by physical needs. Is my child hungry? Is he tired, fatigued? Is he ill? Is he coming down with something, like a cold or flu? Is he in some kind of pain or other discomfort?

This does not mean misbehavior should be condoned if such a physical reason exists. (Misbehavior, in my opinion, should *never* be condoned.) It means that we parents must make sure we are taking care of what is *causing* the misbehavior as well as the misbehavior itself. It is certainly better to correct the misbehavior by giving a child what he needs—eye contact, physical contact, focused attention, water, food, a nap, relief of pain, or treatment of an illness—rather than punishment. Punishment may be appropriate, but we must make sure that a child has all his physical and emotional needs met first.

How can we tell when punishment is appropriate and when it will be destructive? An excellent question. It brings us to the next step in our logical way of handling misbehavior.

Learn to Forgive
In my experience, the most destructive time to punish a child for misbehavior is when a child feels genuinely sorry for what he has done. The key word here is *genuinely*. If a child is genuinely remorseful for a wrong act, punishment (especially corporal punishment) would be harmful. The harm could come about principally in two ways.

First, if a child is already sorrowful for his inappropriate act, his conscience is alive and well. That's what you want! He has learned from his mistake. A good, healthy conscience is the best deterrent to repeating misbehavior. Punishment, especially corporal punishment, would remove the feelings of guilt and remorse and enhance the possibility for a child to forget the discomfort of these feelings and to repeat the misconduct.

Second, punishing a child under these circumstances could produce feelings of anger. When a child already feels genuinely contrite and remorseful for his act, his conscience is dealing severely with him. He is punishing himself. He needs and is seeking comfort and reassurance that, even though his deed was bad, he is a good child. He desperately needs this assurance at such a time. So if you make the mistake of spanking him at a time when he painfully needs affection, he is deeply hurt. Under such circumstances a child will then feel that he is bad as a person and that you, the parents, believe this to be true. The result is feelings of anger, hurt, resentment, and frequently bitterness that a child will carry with him indefinitely.

What should we parents do when a child commits a wrongful act and is genuinely sorry and remorseful about it? Scripture is a real help at this point. When we do wrong and are sorry for our wrongdoing, what does our Heavenly Father do? He forgives us. Look at this writing of the psalmist: "Just as a father has compassion on his children, so the Lord has compassion on those who fear Him" (Psalm 103:13, NASB). With the tenderness, compassion and forgiveness that our Heavenly Father gives to us under these circumstances, how can we then turn right around and punish *our* children?

The Apostle Paul warned of this mistake when he wrote, "Fathers, do not exasperate your children; instead, bring them up in the training and instruction of the Lord" (Ephesians 6:4). I personally know of no surer way to provoke a child to anger, resentment, and bitterness than to punish him, especially physically, when he is genuinely sorry for his behavior. At these times we must learn to forgive.

Another reason it is essential to forgive a child under these circumstances is that he must learn how to feel forgiven during childhood or he will have problems handling guilt. Consider how many people are guilt-laden today (including Christians) because they have never learned to feel forgiven. These poor persons may actually be truly forgiven by God and others. But they still *feel* the guilt even though they know that they are forgiven. We can save a child untold problems with guilt if we will teach him how to deal with it—namely, by the feeling of forgiveness. And we can do this by forgiving him when he is genuinely sorry for a misconduct.

A Broken Window

I remember an experience I had in this regard, but again please remember, just because I am picking out an example of a time when I did something right as a father doesn't mean I'm a perfect father. It just means that there are advantages to being a writer. I can pick out an example to illustrate a point.

One time I came home after a long, difficult day. I was exhausted and certainly not feeling my best. As soon as I got out of the car, David, who was nine then, ran to me. Usually David had a great big smile on his face and would jump up to give me a big bear hug. This time he was different. His face was so long and forlorn. There was a look of sadness in his beautiful blue eyes as he said, "Dad, I have to tell you something."

Because of my state of mind, I didn't feel I could handle a big problem very well right then. So I said, "Let's talk about it later, OK, David?"

David looked at me very intently and replied, "Can't we talk about it now, Dad?"

Just then I reached to open the back door of our house and noticed that one of the windows was broken. Somehow I figured out what was on David's mind.

Because I was in an irritable state of mind, I decided I had surely better handle this matter after I had relaxed. But David had followed me to my bedroom and pleaded, "Please, let's talk about it now, Dad."

With that pleading look on his face, what could I say? I said, "OK, David, what would you like to talk about?" (As if I didn't know.)

David told me how he and his friends were playing baseball close to the house and how a foul ball had hit a window and broken it. He knew he had done wrong and was obviously sorry about it. He was, through his behavior, asking, "Do you love me after what I did?"

So I took my son on my lap and held him close for a little while, and said, "That's OK, David. That was an easy thing to do, and we can get the window fixed. Just play farther from the house, OK?"

That was a special moment. David was immediately filled with relief. He cried briefly and just rested in my arms for a few moments. I could just feel the love flow from this child's heart. It was one of the most wonderful moments of my life. Then David was his old happy, radiant self. He jumped up and was off.

I've learned so much from this type of experience. This was one of those opportunities that do not come every day. A child does not always feel genuinely sorry for his misconduct, so we must be constantly looking for this type of opportunity to actually do what we say we should do. At these times we are able to convey to a child that, although we do not like his misconduct, we do love him no matter what. We love him unconditionally.

When a child is forgiven a misconduct, this does not mean he should not assume responsibility for its consequences. Restitution may be indicated. In the case of David's breaking the window, it may have been constructive to have had him pay for the broken glass in an appropriate way, like working it off. But again, we must make sure that the restitution is in line with the child's age, level of development, and ability to handle it.

We mustn't be manipulated. I am sure you have heard a child say, "I'm sorry," when he wasn't. Quite frequently a child says, "I'm sorry" whenever he thinks he may be punished. Of course this is not being genuinely sorry or remorseful, and we must be able to distinguish the difference.

Fortunately, it is seldom difficult to tell if a child is really sorry or not. The most obvious indication is his repeating the misbehavior. If David continued to play baseball near the house after the incident, I could conclude that I had been manipulated and other measures should be taken.

If a child frequently attempts to manipulate his parents in this manner, I would be quite concerned. It could be indicative that a child's sense of right and wrong are developing in a twisted way. He could be learning to use untruthful statements to gain an advantage, saying, "I'm sorry" simply to escape punishment.

This particular behavior is a good example of what placing the cart before the horse will develop. When parents relate to a child primarily by using punishment to control behavior instead of first meeting a child's emotional needs, a child will develop all sorts of gimmicks to escape punishment. One of these is "I'm sorry" when the parents become angry or upset over a child's behavior.

This is a dangerous situation. A child is then learning to be insincere, dishonest, calculating, manipulative, and insensitive. There is one commodity which cuts straight across this mistake and reverses the trend. It is unconditional love.

In such a situation good judgment on the part of the parents is imperative. Parents are in the best position to discern whether a child is being truthful and sincere. If a child is frequently manipulative and untruthful, trouble is ahead and help should be sought.

However, any child can do this occasionally, just as any child occasionally will feel real sorrow and guilt for misbehavior. Wise, careful parents will realize there is a difference, discern the difference, and handle each situation appropriately.

In short, forgive a child when he is genuinely sorry, remorseful, and repentant for a misconduct. These infrequent opportunities are priceless ones and let him know beyond a doubt that you understand him, are genuinely concerned about him, and deeply love him regardless of anything else. This is unconditional love.

CHAPTER 11

Discipline — Requests, Commands, Rewards, and Punishment

W hat we have considered thus far are by far the most important and crucial aspects of child rearing. If these principles are applied properly, most problems of raising a child will be alleviated or averted. Meeting a child's emotional needs and applying loving discipline will permit a healthy, strong, positive love-bond between parents and their child. When any problem with a child occurs, parents must reexamine the child's needs and fill them before doing anything else.

Please remember the material in the preceding chapters because I am now going into the part of discipline which I do not like to put into print. Why? Because there are some parents who read a book such as this to glean from it only the material which they need to justify preconceived notions about child rearing. They are likely to apply only this section of the book and completely miss the fact that punishment should be used only as a last resort.

I hope you will apply the principles in the first ten chapters before trying to apply rules relating to discipline. Please love your child unconditionally and give him a superabundance of eye contact, physical contact, and focused attention. Please be careful not to love your child with possessiveness, seductiveness, vicariousness, or role-reversal. Please discipline (train) your child in *positive* ways such as guidance, example, modeling, and instruction. When your child misbehaves, ask yourself if he needs eye contact, physical contact, focused attention, rest, or water, and fill these needs first. When your child is sorry, re-morseful, and repentant for a misbehavior, please forgive him, and let him know he is forgiven.

Fellow parents, if you are diligently doing these things, and other factors such as marriage and home environment are satis-factory, things should be going fairly well with your child. Your child should be happy, responsive, well-behaved, doing what you ask him to do (according to his age and level of development) without too much difficulty. I'm not saying everything should be *perfect*, but you should be satisfied with your child, your relation-ship with him, and the way he is progressing.

I am saying all this now because it is a tragic mistake to expect punishment *in itself* to provide anything but negative results. Punishment without a firm foundation of unconditional love and loving discipline (training) cannot but create a poor relationship between parents and their child. Unfortunately, this is a common type of child rearing today. This is one reason children are generally having unprecedented problems today in every area, from academics to personality problems.

Requests

Proper behavior from a child is required first by requesting it. This is the most positive way of achieving good behavior. More importantly, requests instill a sense of personal responsibility in a child. A child feels that proper behavior is just as much his responsibility to do as it is his parent's responsibility to see that it is done. A child knows by nature that he had a choice in how to act. When parents *request* good behavior, a child knows his parents understand that he has ability to think and make decisions himself, has control over his behavior, and must learn to take responsibility for it. When requests instead of commands are used as much as possible, a child will consider his parents in alliance with him in helping him to mold his own behavior. This is so important.

If commands are primarily used in requiring proper behavior, a child may be obedient and well behaved. But his tendency will be to act properly only because Mommy or Daddy say so, not because proper behavior is best for him. He will not see his parents in alliance with him primarily for his own best interests. He will see them as requiring proper behavior for the sake of good order, quietness, and their own social acceptance, in fact, for their own interests.

It is crucial to understand that making requests is a very effective way of giving instructions. It does not make us permissive or less firm. Using requests is simply a more thoughtful, pleasant, considerate way of giving instructions to a child. This is especially true when you want your child to enjoy doing things without resenting it.

For example, once when I was taking a bath, I noticed there were no towels in the bathroom. Dale, then five, was passing by, so I asked, "Dale, would you go down and get your daddy a towel, please?" Dale was very happy to do so and was back with a towel before I could say "Jack Robinson."

Another example. The teacher of my son David's Sunday School class was having a problem with rowdiness from the boys. I had a choice of being very authoritarian and demanding that nine-year-old David "behave himself," or talking over the problem with him, clarifying the issues, and then requesting his cooperation. I chose the latter, and ended the conversation with, "I want you to pay attention to the teacher, join in the discussions, and learn all you can. Will you do that, David?" So far so good.

Direct Instruction

The fact must be faced, however, that requests will not always suffice. Occasionally, parents must be more forceful and give directions not by requests but by direct instruction (commands).

This usually happens when a request is given to a child and he fails to carry it out. Before parents do anything else they must make sure that their request was appropriate, that it was suitable to the child's age, understanding, and ability to carry it out. The most frequent mistake in this regard is asking a child to do something which seems to be within his ability and actually is not.

A classic example of this is asking a four-year-old child to pick up his things by himself. Unless there are only two or three things to pick up, this request is unreasonable. A parent must help the child with the task. Frequently, a parent mistakenly will believe a task such as this is appropriate, gets angry when his child refuses or fails, and punishes him instead of helping him to accomplish the task.

Another real value in using requests whenever possible is to help you determine when a task is reasonable or not. You know your child better than anyone else. If on countless previous occasions your child would very willingly do a task when requested, but on one occasion he suddenly refuses, it is harmful to get angry and punish him. Obviously, because he has had no problems with this request in the past, *there is something wrong now*. Don't you want to know what it is? I believe you would. You would do your best to find the problem, because it might be extremely important. You would certainly rather take care of the problem and see your child proceed to do the task willingly than force him to do it before understanding the situation. If the reason for your child's behavior was legitimate, then you would be the one who should be punished for forcing him to perform the task.

As a parent you have the responsibility and authority to see that your child behaves properly, but you are also responsible for your child's total welfare. You are responsible for seeing that your child is not hurt by misuse of your power and authority over him. His future happiness and welfare are heavily dependent on how you use parental authority over him.

At this point I would like to insert a very important piece of advice and warning. The more parents use such authoritative techniques as commands, scolding, nagging, or screaming, the less effective they become. It is like the boy who yelled, "Wolf, wolf!" so many times that it lost its effect. If parents normally use pleasant requests, the occasional use of direct commands will be quite effective. The more parents use authoritative ways of telling a child what to do, the less response they will have. This is especially true if they are also angry, hostile, or hysterical when they do it.

For example, have you been in a home where the tension level is high? In these homes the parents have used essentially all their authority and reserve force just to discipline (train) their children in routine, daily events. When real forcefulness and authority are needed for unusual and really important situations, these poor parents have nothing in reserve to handle the situations. Their children then react as they usually do to their parents' wishes. They are no more responsive to emergency situations, for example, than they are to such mundane matters as tying a shoestring.

Parents, we must save the big salvos for the important situations. We must have reserve ammunition to handle critical situations. It is important to maintain pleasantness with a child by considerate, reasonable requests as much of the time as possible.

Once I made the mistake of using a forceful order when a simple request would have sufficed. The two boys and I were home, and I wanted to have the house clean before Pat came home from a weekend conference. I started out pretty well. I asked the boys to start cleaning up their bedroom while I made the beds. When I returned in a few minutes, they were busy doing their chores. But I noticed that they had thrown some clothes on the floor of their closet instead of hanging them up. David and Dale were usually obedient, easy-to-handle boys, and a short word of explanation and simple request would have sufficed. But I was somewhat annoyed and I overreacted. I barked out some orders to hang up the clothes which they were "ruining." See the error I made? I should not have used such forcefulness when a simple explanation and request would have been sufficient.

I should have saved forcefulness for a time when I would really need a rapid response under difficult circumstances. For example, one Sunday after we parked in our church's parking lot, Dale was walking around the car when another car pulled out. It was a dangerous situation. I yelled at Dale to run to me. Thank goodness he understood the urgency in my voice and responded immediately. If it had been my habit to yell at Dale, I know he would have responded routinely.

Another example occurred when our David and I were playing basketball with several friends. We all got carried away because we were having so much fun and we had played much too long. Consequently, we were all extremely tired. Then David fell when someone ran into him. He hurt his ankle slightly, but this pain in a very fatigued young boy was more than he could handle at that particular moment. He became angry at the person who knocked him over and began telling him about it. I saw this as inappropriate behavior on David's part but also as a good learning experience for him.

First, I was convinced that David's emotional tank was full. He had had much affection, eye contact, physical contact, and focused attention that weekend. Second, I made a request. I asked David to go with me to a place where I could talk to him. He was too angry to respond. That is where I needed enough force to control him. The next level of use of force is to give direct instruction (command). I said, "David, come with me," in a firm tone. He immediately responded. When we were alone, and as he calmed down, we talked about getting so angry we lose control of our behavior, and how to prevent it. It was a very profitable time for David because he learned much about self-control over inappropriate anger.

Suppose David simply would not have responded as I wanted him to do and could not calm down or gain control over his anger even after I commanded him to do so. The next step would have been to take him to a place where he could be by himself. If I could not get him to do this by verbal instruction, then I would have had to go to the next level of forcefulness, the use of physical force. But even here I would have used the least harsh method. I would have taken him by the hand, perhaps have one arm around his shoulder, and lead him to a quiet place. I call this "gentle physical manipulation." The point is to control a child's behavior in the most gentle, most considerate, and most loving way possible.

Defiance

It is entirely possible that David could have remained unresponsive to any verbal approach. He could have refused to do as I wanted him to do in that situation. It could have developed into a battle of the wills. This could then be called *defiance*.

Defiance is openly resisting and challenging authority—parental authority. It is stubbornly refusing to obey. Of course, defiance, as well as any misbehavior, cannot be permitted. At these times, punishment is often indicated, and such times occasionally occur no matter what we do. However, parents must attempt to avoid such unpleasant encounters—not by catering to a child's unreasonable whims or wishes, but by constantly reexamining their own expectations of their child, making sure their expectations are reasonable, considerate, and are in accordance with their child's age, level of development, and ability to respond. Yes, times which require punishment will come, but if parents find themselves punishing their child frequently, they had better reexamine their relationship with that child and what they expect from him.

But a child's defiance does not automatically mean that punishment is indicated. In fact, punishment at the wrong time can worsen the situation greatly. Punishment, especially given often at the wrong time, can permanently harm the parent's relationship to the child. For example, if the misbehavior is passive-aggressive in nature, punishment may cause the child to use this particular behavior to an even greater extent as a way to upset the parent. The child's behavior will then worsen as the child is repeatedly punished for it. Please reread the chapter "A Child's Anger" if this is unclear to you. Misapplying punishment, especially corporal punishment during such times, can rapidly snare the parent into the "punishment trap," where the more the child is punished, the worse the behavior becomes.

A wise parent can avoid the punishment trap by using punishment as the last resort. A loving parent can use pleasant means of controlling a child's behavior first with requests, explanations, and "gentle physical manipulation." Next the parent can use commands in a pleasant tone of voice. If unsuccessful, a parent can use a "time out" chair where a child can sit for a reasonable length of time until he can calm down and be reasonable. These measures should be effective the vast majority of the time. However, there will be times when the child remains defiant. However, if the parent has diligently and pleasantly tried the above ways to control a child's behavior, then the parent can assume that the behavior is not passive-aggressive in nature, that the punishment trap has been avoided, and punishment must now be considered.

Imagine that the child becomes obviously defiant and his defiant behavior does not respond to filling his emotional tank, and there are no physical problems. He does not respond to requests nor to "gentle physical manipulation," nor to explanation, nor to commands (firm instructions). He remains defiant (again, let me say this situation should be quite rare: when it occurs, make sure you have tried everything before considering punishment). He must be punished, but how?

Appropriate Punishment

Determining the appropriate punishment is seldom easy. Why? The punishment must fit the offense. A child is sensitively aware of fairness and consistency. He knows when parents have overreacted or have been too harsh with him. He also knows when parents are too accepting of poor behavior. He detects inconsistency, either with him alone or in comparison with other children, especially siblings. This is the reason parents must be firm with their child, always demanding appropriate behavior and not being afraid to love and discipline (train) him simultaneously. But parents must remain flexible, especially regarding punishment.

Parents make mistakes. If you feel parents should not make changes in their disciplinary actions once a decision is made, you are going to back yourself into a corner. Of course, parents can change their minds, and lessen or increase the punishment. (Remember that this is a disadvantage to corporal punishment, for once done, it can't be changed.)

Naturally, parents don't want to change their minds so often that they are wishy-washy and confuse the child. For instance, if a punishment is set forth — say confinement to the bedroom for one hour, and later parents discover extenuating facts which show this punishment to be too harsh, it is logical and proper to explain this to the child and lessen the punishment. If the child has already been punished or for some other reason has suffered inappropriate punishment, it is perfectly all right for parents to apologize to the child and attempt to make the situation right.

Parents must be flexible in order to change their approach to their child when indicated. Parents must also be flexible to be able to apologize. The need occasionally to change decisions and the need to apologize occur in every home.

Being flexible in order to appropriately change our approach to handling discipline (training) and being firm are two different things. Both are essential. Firmness first of all includes what our expectations are regarding a child and his response to requests. If our expectations are too rigid (for example, expecting a two-year-old to consistently respond to first requests), we are being unreasonable. A normal two-year-old will naturally be negative most of the time and seem to be quite disobedient and defiant. But this is a normal stage of development — let's call it "two-year-old negativism." Punishment for this is unwarranted. Loving parents of a two-year-old will, of course, be firm, but firm in *limit setting*, not in punishment. These parents will control the child's behavior by gently maneuvering the child physically, for example, picking him up, turning him around, guiding him, or placing him in the correct place or position — "gentle physical manipulation."

This "two-year-old negativism" is crucial for normal child development. The child will eventually do what we ask but he must say "no" first. This is one of the ways each of us had to separate ourselves psychologically from our parents. It may appear to be defiance but it is distinctively different. One difference between two-year-old negativism and defiance is belligerence. Two-year-old negativism is normal and should not be punished. Belligerent defiance on the other hand cannot be tolerated and must be dealt with quickly. Incidentally, "two-year-old negativism" can occur in any age child.

As a child becomes older, his ability to respond to verbal requests increases, and by the time he reaches four and one-half (this varies from child to child), parents can expect him to respond to first requests. I fully expected my children to respond to first requests. If they did not, they knew that action would be taken. Of course they were free to make an appropriate statement regarding the request, if they had any question about it. But unless I changed the request, they knew they must carry it out.

It is so important to remember that being firm does not mean being unpleasant. We must be firm in our expectations and enforcement of these expectations, but we will be just as effective by doing it pleasantly. Loving firmness does not require us to be angry, loud, authoritative, or otherwise unpleasant.

Every child needs to experience all the ways of loving simultaneously. He needs eye contact, physical contact, focused attention, *and* discipline *simultaneously*. A child must have a parent's love and firmness together. None of these things are mutually exclusive. Being firm does not negate affection. Showing affection does not lessen firmness or foster permissiveness. *Lack of firmness and limit setting foster permissiveness, but love and affection do not.*

When parents have conscientiously provided all of the preceding means of loving and disciplining a child, and the youngster remains belligerently defiant, the parents must punish him. This type of defiance must be broken. The punishment must be severe enough to break the belligerent defiance, but it must also be as mild as possible to prevent the problems we have already discussed. If a command or explanation to a child is sufficient to break the defiance, why be more punitive? If sending a child to his room for a period is required and will suffice, fine. If taking a privilege away from a child is necessary to crush the defiance, proceed to do so. Let's face it, corporal punishment is sometimes necessary to break a pronounced belligerent defiance, but only as a last resort.

Another problem with punishment is that punishment for one child may mean little to another. For example, one of my boys was more sensitive than the other. The most severe punishment for him was to send him to his room. This rejection was far more devastating to him than corporal punishment. Yet, my other boy didn't mind going to his room at all. Each child is unique.

One other problem with punishment is that the type and severity of punishment usually depends on the parent's feelings at the time. At times when the parent is in a pleasant, upbeat, loving mood, the punishment will most likely be quite different and less harsh than when the parent is in a negative mood. This, of course, leads to inconsistent discipline which has its own unhealthy effects on the child. For these reasons, I suggest that parents confer with each other or with a friend and determine appropriate punishment for each child in each situation. This decision-making should be done, of course, when the parent is calm, rational, and is able to think the matter completely through.

Be Careful

When physical punishment is used, we must be careful in several respects. First, the child must understand exactly why he is being punished. Explain to him in terms of his behavior exactly what he has done wrong. Words such as "bad boy" or "bad girl" can hurt the child's self-esteem and should not be used.

Second, parents must be careful not to inflict any physical damage on the child. For example, it is easy to hurt a finger or another part of the body inadvertently.

Third, immediately after the punishment, as the child is crying, he should be left alone. Parents should stay nearby, however, listening for the crying to stop. When a child's crying has subsided and he is looking around, a child is again asking, "Do you love me? Do you still love me?" Parents should then give the child an abundance of eye contact, physical contact, and focused attention to reassure him that he is indeed loved.

Behavior Modification

Finally, I believe it appropriate to mention *behavior modification*. This is a system of thought which is in wide use today concerning the handling of children. Behavior modification utilizes positive reinforcement (interjecting a positive commodity into a child's environment), negative reinforcement (withdrawing a positive commodity from a child's environment), and punishment (interjecting a negative commodity into a child's environment). An example of positive reinforcement is rewarding a child for an appropriate behavior by giving him a piece of candy or fruit. An example of negative reinforcement is withdrawing television privileges from a child for inappropriate behavior. An example of punishment (sometimes called aversive technique) is pinching him on the trapezius muscle for inappropriate behavior.

It is beyond the scope of this book to speak to this subject in depth. However, a few important points should be made.

First of all, such emphasis has been made concerning behavior modification that such techniques are frequently substituted for emotional nurturing. If behavior modification is overused by parents in relation to a child, a child will not feel loved. Why? First of all, the very foundation of behavior modification is *conditional*. A child receives a reward only if he *behaves* a certain way. Second, behavior modification is not concerned with feelings or the emotional needs of a child (love). Consequently, parents, using behavior modification as the primary way of relating to your child, cannot convey unconditional love.

For instance, consider the example I used in the last chapter regarding filling Dale's emotional tank when he misbehaved following my three-day absence. A strict behaviorist would say I was rewarding Dale for his misbehaving by giving him affection at that time. See the difference? Parents cannot *primarily* use behavior modification in relating to their child and love their child unconditionally.

Another problem with relating to a child primarily by behavior modification is that a child will derive an inappropriate value system. He will learn to do things primarily for a reward. A "what's-in-it-for me?" orientation will develop. An example of this occurred at the home of a dear friend of ours. He happens to be a strict behaviorist and was raising his children as closely to the behavior modification concept as he could. One evening, when we were eating at their home, he said, "Jerry is just three and he can count to a hundred already. Watch this." He went up to his son and said, "Jerry, count to a hundred and I'll give you an M&M." Jerry instantly replied, "I don't want an M&M." If we want our child to do things for the satisfaction of doing them or for the pride of a job well done, we should not overuse behavior modification. The end result is inappropriate motivation.

One other problem with the use of behavior modification is this. If parents overuse these techniques, a child will learn to gain what he wants by using the same method on the parents. He will behave as the parents wish *in order to get something he wants*. Most persons would call this manipulation. One of the surest ways of encouraging your child to become cunning and manipulative is to use behavior modification techniques too often.

Now that I've expounded on the negative aspects of behavior modification, let me express the positive. There is a place for these techniques in child rearing, but not as the primary way of relating to a child (the primary way must be unconditional love).

Behavior modification should be used for specific, recurring behavioral problems for which a child is neither sorry nor defiant. This type of problem must also be specific enough to be easily defined and understood by a child.

Here is an example of this type of problem which we encountered in our home. When our two boys were nine and five years of age, they were at stages during which they frequently fought with each other. Of course, neither one was remorseful about this. Forgiveness was certainly inappropriate. And neither one was defiant about it. Requests did not work. Commands had effect only for a few hours. Punishments also had brief effects and were quite unpleasant for everyone. You know what worked? You've probably guessed it, a reward system.

We used a chart-with-stars technique. One star for every fifteen minutes of peace, gradually increasing the time interval until the fighting was extinguished. We gave each boy an appropriate reward for a certain number of stars. It worked beautifully and we had "peace in the valley."

However, one word of warning about this type of technique. It takes time, consistency, real effort, and persistence. Don't start something like this unless you are prepared to stick with it and be consistent. Otherwise it will fail.

There are numerous good books on behavior modification to tell you more about specific techniques.

This has been a long chapter, but one more point. As you can tell, good child rearing requires balance. A child needs everything we have discussed: eye contact, physical contact, focused attention, discipline, requests, firmness, flexibility, commands, forgiveness, punishment, behavior modification, instruction, guidance, example, and active listening. But we must give our children these things in *proper measure*. May our discussions help you to do this in a way that will enable your child to feel unconditionally loved.

CHAPTER 12

Children with Special Problems

W hy do children with special problems such as diabetes, learning disabilities, deafness, hyperactivity, or mental retardation generally have markedly greater emotional and behavioral problems? The answer to this question is extremely complex. To explain why children in each of these problem areas are more prone to emotional and behavioral disturbance is more than can be dealt with in this book.

However, a few very pertinent points would be helpful to every parent of such a child. Some of these facts are closely related to conveying love to our children.

Perceptual Problems

First, let's look at the general area of perceptual problems. To perceive is difficult to define, but let's try. It can mean to grasp or take in information through the senses to the mind, in which case a child with perceptual problems has difficulty taking in information from his environment and transmitting it to his mind. Consequently, when such information as visual images, sound, and touch is processed in a child's mind, he has difficulty understanding it clearly. His understanding of his environment is distorted in those areas where his misperceptions lie.

Using this very broad and simplified definition of perceptual problems, we can see that many special problems can be included. Visual problems, hearing problems, certain neurological diseases, and many type of learning disabilities have one thing in common: each child suffering from one of these disorders has a distorted conception of his surroundings. In one or more ways his incoming stimuli or information are distorted to him.

Do you see the great significance of this beyond the perceptual disability per se? Every way you have to convey your love to your child requires the use of one or more of the perceptual senses? Eye contact requires the perceiving of visual imagery. Physical contact requires the use of the sense of touch, which in itself is overwhelmingly complex. Focused attention requires the use of all of your senses. So if there is enough perceptual distortion in any of these areas, your child's understanding of how you feel about him can be distorted. This makes it more difficult to convey your love to this particular child.

This difficulty in a child's feeling loved is one big reason perceptually handicapped children generally have less than adequate self-concepts. It is one reason they usually become increasingly depressed as they grow older, frequently resulting in rather severe emotional and behavioral disorders, especially in early adolescence.

The common story of a perceptually handicapped child with resultant learning disabilities is that this unfortunate child cannot keep up academically or in other ways with his peers. He makes poor grades or is in other ways forced to endure continual degrading experiences. Even in nongraded situations he realizes his deficiencies. As he goes into the pre and early adolescent years, he becomes increasingly depressed. Depression in this age group is unlike any other. Generally these children do not look or act depressed unless the depression has reached severe depths. Typically young teenagers manifest their depression by difficulty in paying attention in the classroom (decreased attention span and ability to concentrate) with a resultant dropping of grades. Subsequently, prolonged boredom sets in with decreased interest in wholesome activities. At this stage the youngster is profoundly miserable.

If the boredom continues, eventually the teenager will act out his depression and misery. A severely depressed and bored girl in this predicament may then become promiscuous, use drugs, run away, or may try other antisocial behaviors. A boy in a comparable situation will be prone to behave similarly but is usually more inclined to such actions as stealing and fighting.

If we know that perceptually handicapped children are almost predisposed to poor self-concept feelings of being unloved and unacceptable, and of depression, how can we help them? I firmly believe that the area where they require the greatest help is the area which is largely overlooked. You guessed it, these children need most of all to feel genuinely, unconditionally loved. They will then be better able to overcome their handicaps.

How do we do this? The same way we give our love to all children, except that we must remember that, though their perceptions are distorted in some areas, they are seldom distorted in all sensual modalities. These children almost always need more affection and other means of conveying love in order to feel loved. In addition, they need our love to be given to them in more direct, simplified, straightforward, and accentuated ways. We must also give it to them in a somewhat more intense manner. All of this is necessary to make sure that these children do not misunderstand our feeling toward them. Our love-communications with such children must be clear and strong.

Other Medical Problems

Children with chronic (long standing) medical problems are also prone to emotional and behavioral problems. This is especially true of medical problems which require close supervision and continual attention such as juvenile diabetes. Taking care of young children with this disease requires tremendous time and effort by parents. So much so that it is difficult not to devote one's full attention to treating the disease and overlooking other needs of the children. This is exactly what happens concerning the emotional needs of most of these children. The caring parents become so intent, for example, on giving the right doses of insulin, regulating the diet, doing glucose determinations and the like, that these necessary procedures replace the natural giving of love. As essential as they are, these medical duties are no substitute for unconditional love given through eye contact, physical contact, and focused attention. As children grow older, especially during adolescence, they become increasingly angry, resentful, and bitter about their disease. Because of the afore-mentioned substitution of medical care for love, the children resent the disease and their parents. They become hostile and defiant not only toward parental authority but all authority. They are inclined to depression and all of its consequences. Worst of all, they frequently use the seriousness of their illness to defy parents and express anger and frustration. This may be done by taking too much insulin, eating too many carbohydrates, and so on. Some actually kill themselves as an angry defiant act.

Of course, there are other reasons in this complex illness which contribute to young patients' bitter and destructive attitudes. In my experience, however, there are two principal reasons why these unfortunate children become so intensely resentful and defiant. The first is as we just discussed, substitution of medical procedures as a manifestation of love. The other is poor limit-setting and lack of behavioral control by the parents. The parents may feel pity for the children in their illness. They may also feel guilt, fear, or depression. If the parents cannot control the children's behavior in the same manner as they would other children, namely with firmness, the children will be able to manipulate the parents. This is especially easy for chronically ill children to do. They can use their illness to control their parents by taking advantage of the parents' guilt and pity, by making the parents fearful that the children's condition may worsen, and even by using the outright threat of purposely succumbing to the illness.

These dynamics may occur to some extent with any children with a prolonged disability, illness, or other problem. Examples include asthma, chronic bronchitis, heart defects, physical deformity, mental retardation, seizure disorders, neurological diseases, muscular diseases, dental problems, and even learning disabilities. The list goes on and on.

So, dear parents, if your child has a handicap, a problem of any kind, do not become so wrapped up with the problem that you neglect the child. He needs your unconditional love far more than anything else. Far more than any medical care, no matter how necessary. Far more than braces, far more than tutoring or other academic remediation, far more than any exercise, and far more than any medicine. The most indispensable ingredients in your child's life are you and your giving unconditional love to him. With that, your child can derive the strength and will to overcome and develop.

The Resistant Child

Now, let's consider help for the resistant child, namely, one who is resistant to receiving affection. Yes, believe it or not, many children are naturally (congenitally) resistant to the natural ways of giving affection and love. They resist eye contact, they do not want to be touched, and they do not care for focused attention.

This may occur in varying degrees. Some children are only mildly resistant whereas others are quite uncomfortable with the conveying of love. Some children may be comfortable with one way of conveying love but not another. Each child is unique.

The resistant child is invariably an enigma to his parents. Caring parents instinctively know that their child needs affection and other forms of emotional nurturing; but when they try to meet this need, the child finds innumerable ways to avoid receiving love. What a dilemma. Many parents eventually resign themselves to what they conclude is "what the child wants." They assume that the child does not need their attention, love, and affection. This is a disastrous mistake.

Even the extremely resistant child needs everything we have talked about concerning unconditional love. However, since he is uncomfortable accepting it, we parents must gradually teach this child to receive love comfortably.

We can begin by understanding the five periods during which a child is able to receive love. During these periods the child's defenses are down, and he is able to relate closely enough on the emotional level to be receptive. Of course, every child is different. One child may be more receptive during one period and less receptive during another. It behooves parents to know when their child is most receptive to love and affection.

The first receptive period is when a child finds something to be quite humorous. For instance, a child may be watching television and see a funny scene. At this time parents have the opportunity to make eye contact, physical contact, and focused attention while commenting on the humorous subject. Parents must usually be quick in doing this because the defenses of a truly resistant child are down only briefly. We've got to "get in and get out" or a child may defend against similar tactics in the future.

The second period of receptivity is when a child has accomplished something for which he is justifiably proud. It cannot be just anything. The accomplishment must be something a child feels genuinely good about. At these times, parents can make eye and physical contact (and focused attention if appropriate) while praising a child. Again, we must be careful not to overdo it, especially by prolonging it; again "get in and get out."

The third receptive period is at such times when a child is not well physically. A child may be ill or hurt, and his receptivity at these times is somewhat unpredictable. Sometimes illness or pain may increase a child's ability to receive affection, but at other times a child's resistance may increase. We parents should continually monitor this in order to take advantage of opportunities to give love at these times of illness or pain. A child will never forget special moments such as these.

The fourth period of receptivity occurs when a child is hurt emotionally. This frequently happens when he has a conflict with peers and the peers have taken unfair advantage of him. At these times of emotional pain, many resistant children become able to accept our showing love to them.

The fifth receptive period largely depends upon previous experiences of a particular child. For example, one child may have had many pleasant, meaningful experiences while going on long walks with his parents. Such a child will quite likely be more receptive to parental conveying of love while on walks. Another child may have had pleasant experiences at bedtime when his parents would read, pray, and talk with him. He will naturally be inclined to be more receptive at bedtime. This is why providing routine times of pleasant, warm experiences for a child is very important and pays large dividends to child and parents. Bedtime routine, for example, is a good investment.

In a nutshell, all children need the natural ways of conveying love — eye contact, physical contact, and focused attention. If a child is not receiving an ample amount, we should find out why and correct the situation.

CHAPTER 13

Helping Your Child Spiritually

One of the chief complaints we hear from teenagers today is the failure of their parents to give them ethical or moral standards to live by in formative years. This yearning is expressed by older children in many ways. One adolescent says he needs "meaning in life." Another wants a "standard to guide her." Other seeking youngsters long for "something to hold on to" or "someone to show me how to live."

These desperate cries do not come from a few unhappy, discontented teenagers. Most adolescents are feeling and expressing these yearnings. They are confused—terribly confused—in this existential area of living. It is quite unusual to find young people who have "got it together" in regard to a meaning and purpose in this life, who are at peace with themselves and their world, and who have perspective and understanding about living in this confused, changing, fearful world today. And much goes back to their childhood.

A child first looks to his parents for direction that enables him to develop healthy values. Whether he finds what he needs from his parents depends on two things. The first is whether the parents have it themselves. The second is whether a child can identify with his parents in such a way as to incorporate and accept parental values. A child who does not feel loved will find this difficult.

The First Requirement

Let's look at the first requirement that is necessary in giving a child that longed-for meaning to life. We parents must possess a foundation upon which to base our lives and which can withstand the test of time — something that will support us through every phase of living: adolescence, young adulthood, middle age, old age, marriage crises, financial crises, children's crises, energy crises, and especially, a rapidly changing society in which spiritual values are swiftly eroding. We parents must have that crucial foundation upon which we base our lives in order to give it to our child. In my opinion, it is the most valuable treasure we can pass on to our offspring.

What is this indispensable possession which gives purpose and meaning to life and is transferable to our child? Many have sought after it since the beginning of civilization but few have really found it. Philosophers have been struggling with these questions and answers for centuries. International diplomats have occasionally claimed some answers. Government planners are claiming to have answers even now, and their diligently planned legislation will leave hearts just as empty and longing as before, but more dependent upon man's (government's) control. The field of mental health offers help concerning emotional problems, mental disturbances, psychophysiological disorders, adaptational problems, and marital disharmony.

But this treasurable, peace-giving possession which every heart craves is God Himself. He is intimately personal, yet can be shared with another. He is strengthening in times of conflict, yet is comforting in times of distress. He gives wisdom in times of confusion, yet gives correction in times of error. He provides help in times past and present, yet promises even more in the future. He gives direction and guidance at all times, yet does not send us out alone—He stays closer than a brother.

He gives directions to be carried out, yet gives amazingly wonderful promises to those who are willing to obey. He allows loss and pain at times, but He always heals and replaces the loss with something better. He does not force Himself upon us, but patiently waits to be accepted. He does not coerce us into doing His will, but is deeply distressed and hurt when we follow the wrong path. He wants us to love Him because He first loved us, but He gave us a free will to choose Him or reject Him. He wants to take care of us, but refuses to force Himself upon us. His greatest desire is to be our Father, but He will not intrude. If we want what He wants, a loving, caring, Father-child relationship with Him—we must accept His offer. He is too considerate to force it. He is waiting for you and me to open our lives to Him and become His children. Of course, as you have guessed, He must be a personal God.

This personal, intimate relationship with God through His Son Jesus Christ is the most important thing in life. This is the "something" which our young people are yearning for: the "meaning in life," "something to count on," "higher guidance," "something to bring comfort when everything seems to be falling apart." It is all there.

Do you have it? If you do not, seek help from a minister or Christian friend; or write me through the publisher, and I will send you helpful material.

The Second Requirement

The second requirement necessary in order to give a child what we have is that a child identify with his parents so as to accept and incorporate the parents' values.

As you recall, if a child does not feel loved and accepted, he has real difficulty identifying with his parents and their values. Without a strong, healthy love-bond with his parents, a child reacts to parental guidance with anger, resentment, and hostility. He views each parental request (or command) as an imposition and learns to resist it. In severe cases, a child learns to consider each parental request with such resentment that his total orientation to parental authority (and eventually to all authority, including God's) is doing the opposite of what is expected of him.

With this type of attitude and orientation, you can see how difficult it becomes to give your child your moral and ethical value system.

In order for a child to identify with his parents (relate closely with them) and be able to accept their standards, he must feel genuinely loved and accepted by them. To give a child the close relationship with God which they possess, parents must make sure that a child feels unconditionally loved. Why? Because this is the way God loves us — unconditionally. It is extremely difficult for persons who do not feel unconditionally loved by their parents to feel loved by God. This is the greatest and most common obstacle to many people in establishing a personal relationship with God. Parents must prevent this from happening to their own children.

How do parents ensure that their child is prepared and ready to accept God's love? By ensuring that they fill his emotional needs and keep his emotional tank full. Parents cannot expect a child to find a close, warm, *rewarding* relationship with God unless they have cared for him emotionally and he has such a relationship with them.

Yes, I have seen children who were raised by corporal punishment become Christians. But because they were raised primarily by inflicting physical pain instead of unconditional love, these unfortunate people seldom have a healthy, loving, warm relationship with God. They tend to use their religion punitively against others under the guise of "helping" them. They use biblical commandments and other scriptural statements to justify their own harsh, unloving behavior. They also tend to set themselves up as spiritual magistrates dictating the propriety of others. It is possible, of course, for any child eventually to find his way into God's loving arms and to accept His love. With God anything is possible. Unfortunately, a child's chances are markedly diminished if his parents have not given him a loving foundation.

So there are two requirements essential to helping a child

spiritually: A parent's personal relationship with God, and a child's assurance that he is unconditionally loved.

A Child's Memory
The next important thing to know about a child is how his memory operates. Remember that a child is much more emotional than cognitive. He therefore remembers feelings much more readily than facts. A child can remember how he felt in a particular situation much easier than he can remember the details of what went on.

Let me give you a very pertinent example. A child in a Sunday School class will remember exactly how he felt long after he forgets what was said or taught.

So, in some ways, whether a child's experience was pleasant or unpleasant is much more important than the details of what a teacher taught. By pleasant, I do not mean that a teacher need cater to a child's desire for fun and frolic. I mean treating a child with respect, kindness, and concern. Make him feel good about himself. Do not criticize, humiliate, or otherwise put him down. Naturally, what a child is taught is extremely important, but if it is a degrading or boring experience for a child, he is very likely to reject even the very best teaching, especially if morality and ethics are involved. It is from this type of situation that a child develops a bias against religious matters, and tends to consider church people as hypocrites. This attitude is difficult to rectify and can continue with him for a lifetime. On the other hand, if the learning experience is a pleasant one, a child's memories of spiritual teaching will be pleasant and can then be incorporated into a child's own personality.

As an illustration, friends of ours had an eight-year-old son, Michael, who used to enjoy Sunday School and being taught about spiritual things. There was no problem getting him to go to the Lord's house. Sadly, one Sunday morning, Michael and another energetic boy were talking and laughing during a presentation by the teacher. In anger, the teacher put Michael and his friend in a small room by themselves and made them write "Thou shalt honor thy mother and thy father" over and over until Michael's parents came to get him. The unreasonableness and insensitiveness of that unjust and humiliating punishment had dramatic effects. It induced such anger, hurt, and resentment that Michael began holding animosity toward anything spiritual. He didn't want to return to his church, and, of course, his conception of God was severely damaged. Only after several months were his loving parents able to help Michael again trust spiritual truths. This type of thing, in greater or lesser extremes, happens when the importance of a teacher's teaching is placed before the emotional welfare of a child. Emotionality and spirituality are not entirely separate entities. One is quite related to and dependent upon the other. For this reason, if parents want to help a child spiritually, they must care for him first emotionally. Because a child remembers feelings much more easily than facts, there must be a series of pleasant memories upon which to accumulate the facts, especially spiritual facts.

A Popular Misconception

At this point, let's examine a popular misconception. It goes something like this: "I want my child to learn to make his own decisions after he is exposed to everything. He shouldn't feel he has to believe what I believe. I want him to learn about different religions and philosophies; then when he has grown up he can make his own decision."

This parent is copping out or else is grossly ignorant of the world we live in. A child brought up in this manner is indeed one to be pitied. Without continual guidance and clarification in ethical, moral, and spiritual matters, he will become increasingly confused about his world. There are reasonable answers to many of life's conflicts and seeming contradictions. One of the finest gifts parents can give a child is a clear, basic understanding of the world and its confusing problems. Without this stable base of knowledge and understanding, is it any wonder many children cry to their parents, "Why didn't you give me a meaning for all this? What's it all about?"

Another reason this approach to spirituality is grossly negligent is this. More and more groups, organizations, and cults are offering destructive, enslaving, and false answers to life's questions. These people would like nothing more than to find a person who was brought up in this seemingly broad-minded way. He is easy prey for any group offering concrete answers, no matter how false or enslaving.

It is amazing to me how some parents can spend thousands of dollars and go to any length of political manipulation to make sure their child is well prepared educationally. Yet, for the most important preparation of all, for life's spiritual battles and finding real meaning in life, a child is left to fend for himself and made easy prey for cultists.

Every Child Loves a Story

How do parents prepare their children spiritually? Organized religious instruction and activities are extremely important to a developing child. However, nothing influences a child more than his home and what he is exposed to there. This holds true regarding spiritual things as well. Parents must be actively involved in a child's spiritual growth. They cannot afford to leave it to others, even superb church youth workers.

First, parents themselves must teach their children spiritual concerns. They must teach not only spiritual facts, but how to apply them in everyday life. This is not easy.

It is quite simple to give a child basic scriptural facts such as who different Bible persons were and what they did. But that is not what we are ultimately after. A child needs to understand what meaning biblical characters and principles have for him personally. We can only teach this at somewhat of a sacrifice to ourselves, as with focused attention. We must give focused attention and be willing to spend time alone with a child in order to provide for his emotional needs as well as his spiritual. In fact, whenever possible, why not do them simultaneously?

Bedtime is usually the best time to accomplish this, for most children are then eager to interact with their parents. Whether it is because their emotional tanks need filling or because they want to delay bedtime makes little difference. The point is that it is a great opportunity to meet the emotional needs of a child, give him spiritual training and guidance, and do it in an atmosphere which a child will remember fondly. By what other means can parents give so much to a child in such an economical way?

Every child loves a story. When our children were growing up, Pat and I would often read to an individual child, sometimes a secular story, at other times a story from a Christian book. I even got requests for stories that I made up — "Bing Bing and Bong Bong," "The Great Rutabaga," and other fanciful tales.

We also made it a point to read short devotional stories. My boys especially loved to answer questions about the stories, and books with questions after each story were good for our purpose. Most of the books we used when our children were young are likely out of print, but a visit to a Christian bookstore will acquaint you with many good books you can use with your children.

As a child answers questions following the reading of a story, there are always similarities and applications to what is going on in his own life. The hard part is getting the message across to a child and, because many parents feel awkward and inept at this, they usually give it up, especially if a child doesn't contribute much. Don't let these things stop you! Whether a child appears to be responding or not, you can rest assured that you are strongly influencing him. Your time spent with your child in this way will have far-reaching effects. If you don't influence your child in the area of the supernatural now, someone else will do it later.

Share Your Spiritual Life

One more point about helping a child spiritually. With the factual knowledge gained from church, Sunday School, and home, a child only has the raw materials with which to grow in his spiritual life. He must learn to use this knowledge effectively and accurately to become a mature person spiritually. To do this, a child must have the experience of walking with God daily and learning to rely on Him personally.

The best way to help a child with this is to share your own spiritual life with him. Of course, this depends on the quality of what you have to share, and how much you share depends on the child, his age, level of development, and ability to comprehend and handle it.

As a child matures, we parents want to gradually increase

sharing with him how we ourselves love God, walk daily with Him, rely on Him, seek His guidance and help, thank Him for His love, care, gifts, and answered prayer.

We want to share these things with our child *as they happen,* not afterward. Only in that way can a child get on-the-job training. Sharing past experiences is simply giving additional factual information, not letting a child learn for himself through his own experience. There is a lot of truth in the old statement, "Experience is the best teacher." Let him share in yours. The sooner a child learns to trust God, the stronger he will become.

A child needs to learn how God meets all personal and family needs, including financial. He needs to know what his parents are praying for. For example, he needs to know when you are praying for the needs of others. He should (again, as appropriate) know of problems for which you are asking God's help. And don't forget to keep him informed about how God is working in your life, how He is using you to minister to someone. And, of course, a child should certainly know you are praying for him and for his individual, particular needs.

Finally, a child must be taught by example how to forgive and how to find forgiveness both from God and people. Parents do this first of all by forgiving. Next, when they make a mistake, they apologize and ask for God's forgiveness. I cannot overstress how important this is. So many people today have problems with guilt. They cannot forgive and/or they cannot feel forgiven. What can be more miserable? But the fortunate person who has learned how to forgive those who offend him and is able to ask and receive forgiveness, demonstrates a mark of mental health and finds peace as a result.

As we end our discussion, I hope you will seriously consider the principles stressed in this book. It was written especially for you by a parent who himself has learned by experience at home and in his profession that parents must truly love their children to see them grow into strong, healthy, happy, and independent adults. Now, perhaps you will want to go back and reread this volume and underline principles that you determine to put into practice as you seek to really love your child. I challenge you to do so.

II.
HOW TO REALLY
LOVE YOUR TEENAGER

CONTENTS

Guiding a child through the teenage years is a complex venture and one with which most parents today are having great difficulty. In almost every respect, the adolescent situation is becoming worse year after year. Teenage suicide has increased so dramatically that it is now the second leading cause of death for people between the ages of fourteen and twenty. Academic achievement scores and standards have steadily gone down over the last several years. Drug abuse, juvenile crime, teenage pregnancy, sexually transmitted diseases, and feelings of despair are all statistically overwhelming.

What's wrong? The primary source of the problem usually lies with parents who do not have a balanced perspective about how to relate to their teenagers. Most parents have distorted ideas of what adolescence is and what they should expect of their young people.

Although most parents truly love their teenagers, they don't know how to convey that love in ways that make the teenagers feel loved and accepted. However, parents who really desire to give their teenagers what they need can learn to do so.

I have found that parents who put into practice the principles discussed in this book have a high degree of success in helping their teenagers develop properly and become responsible, mature, and conscientious adults.

Some of the basic material for this book is from my first book, *How to Really Love Your Child*. Since the needs of teenagers are more complex than those of younger children, it is necessary to apply the information differently.

As you integrate the ideas in this book into a solid and balanced approach for relating to your teenager, you will be pleasantly surprised to discover how exciting and fulfilling it can be to really love your teenager.

Many case studies from my files and memory are used in these pages for illustrative purposes. In all cases real names are not used, and circumstances have been changed enough to protect the identity of my clients.

Chapter 1

Teenagers: Children in Transition

I can't believe she did it," explained Mrs. Batten, as she and Mr. Batten began unfolding their painful story in my counseling room. "She was such a good girl, always content, never gave us much trouble. I thought we were giving Debbie everything she needed—clothes, church, a good home.

"Why would she ever want to try to kill herself? How could she have taken all those pills? Does she really want to die, or is she just trying to get attention? I'm so confused. And she's gotten so hateful and sullen. I can't talk to her, and she won't talk to me. She just wants to spend time by herself in her room. And her grades have become terrible."

Mrs. Batten sat in her chair, her shoulders slumped, the sparkle missing from her usually bright eyes. As she told me more of her daughter's problems, I knew that she was as confused and lonely as Debbie. This was a typical example of the gap in understanding how to love a teenager.

"When did you notice these changes in Debbie?" I asked.

"About two or three years ago," replied Mrs. Batten. "But it was so gradual we didn't think anything was seriously wrong until fairly recently. Let's see. She's fifteen now. During the last few months of sixth grade we noticed she became bored—first with school. Her grades began falling. A teacher complained of her daydreaming and nonparticipation in class. She was very concerned about Debbie then. I wish we had listened to Mrs. Collins. She was such a fine teacher.

"Then Debbie gradually became bored with life. She gave up her favorite activities one by one and seemed to lose interest in everything, including church. She began to avoid her good friends and spend more and more time by herself. She talked less and less.

"But everything became even worse when she began seventh grade. She completely withdrew from her old standby friends and began running around with kids who were in trouble most of the time. Debbie's attitude worsened as she became more like her new friends. And they often led her into trouble—deep trouble.

"Yet we've tried almost everything," Mrs. Batten continued. "First, we spanked her. Then we began taking away her privileges and freedoms. We've grounded her. We've tried rewarding her for good behavior. We've talked to everyone we thought might be able to help us. I really believe we have tried everything. Can Debbie really be helped?"

"We're desperate," Mr. Batten interjected. "Did we do a poor job as parents? We've certainly *tried* hard enough. Is it inherited? Maybe physical? Should we get a sugar test or an EEG? Will vitamins or minerals help? We love Debbie, Dr. Campbell. What can be done? Is it hopeless?"

I saw Debbie after her parents left. She was a pretty girl with likable ways. Although unquestionably intelligent, she had difficulty speaking in a clear, audible way. She communicated mostly in grunts with many "uh-huhs." Debbie did not have the natural spontaneity and enthusiasm we like to see in a fifteen-year-old girl. She was obviously unhappy, and it was difficult to communicate with her.

However, when Debbie felt more comfortable, she spoke more freely, and her eye contact improved. She stated by her behavior and in her words that she had lost interest in all she once cared for. She finally said, "Nothing really matters. No one cares about me and I don't care about anything. It doesn't matter anyway."

As the conversation continued, it became clear that Debbie was suffering from an increasingly frequent and serious adolescent problem—depression. She seldom had times when she felt content with herself or her life. For years Debbie had longed for a close, warm relationship with her parents, but during the past few months, she had gradually given up hope in this dream. More and more she turned to her peers, who she thought would accept her more lovingly; but her unhappiness deepened even more.

Sad to say, Debbie is typical of many adolescent girls. Debbie *seemed* to be happy and content during her earlier years. During those years, she was a complacent child who made few demands on her parents, teachers, or others. So no one suspected that she did not feel genuinely loved and accepted by her parents. Though she had parents who deeply loved her and cared for her, Debbie did not *feel* genuinely loved. Yes, Debbie intellectually knew of her parents' love and care for her, and never would have told you that they did not love her. But Debbie did not have the precious and crucial feeling of being completely and unconditionally loved and accepted.

This situation is difficult to understand because Debbie's parents loved their daughter and looked after her needs to the best of their ability and knowledge. Mr. and Mrs. Batten had attempted to carry out all that they had learned, and had also followed good advice from experts. In addition, their marriage was indeed a good one. They had a stable relationship and loved each other. Each treated the other with respect.

Yet, the Battens, like many parents today, were experiencing real difficulty in raising a teenager, and in understanding how to effectively guide her through the stages of her life to young adulthood. With pressures increasing every day upon the American family, it is easy to become disheartened, confused, and pessimistic. Rising rates of divorce, economic and financial crises, decreasing quality of education, and declining trust in leadership—all place emotional hardships on everyone. As we parents suffer increasing physical, emotional, and spiritual strain, it becomes more and more difficult to care for our teenagers. I believe that a child, especially a teenager, pays the greatest price during these difficult times. A teenager is the most vulnerable person in our society, and his deepest need is love.

Debbie's parents had carried out their parental responsibility in raising their daughter to the best of their ability—but something was not right. As pointed out, Debbie did not *feel* genuinely loved. Was it her parents' fault? Were they to be blamed? I do not believe they should have been. Mr. and Mrs. Batten had always loved Debbie but had never known how to convey their love. As with most parents, they had a vague notion of the needs of a child—protection, shelter, food, clothes, education, guidance, love, etc. They had met essentially all these needs except unconditional love.

Teenagers Are Still Children

Teenagers are children in transition. They are not young adults. Their needs, including their emotional needs, are those of children. One of the most common mistakes parents, teachers, and others make regarding adolescents is to consider them junior adults. Many people in authority over teenagers overlook their childlike needs for feeling love and acceptance, for being taken care of, and for knowing that someone really cares for them.

Far too many teenagers today feel that no one really cares about them. As a result, many of them have feelings of worthlessness, hopelessness, helplessness, poor self-esteem, and self-depreciation.

Today's teenagers are sometimes described as the "apathetic generation." This apathy is on the surface. Beneath this surface are anger and confusion. Why is this? Because so many teens see themselves in a negative way, as unappreciated and worthless. Such a self-concept is the natural result of a child not feeling genuinely loved and cared for.

Two of the most frightening results of this apathy are depression and revolt against authority. Apathetic teens can become easy prey for unscrupulous persons who use young people for their own ends. They are susceptible to being influenced by authoritarian persons who themselves are antiauthority against legitimate authority. As a result our society is becoming increasingly angry against authority and authority figures. This is a dangerous threat in a democratic society where security rests on trust and personal responsibility. But there are ways that we will discuss later to prevent apathy in our teenagers, and to promote healthy, energetic, productive, and creative attitudes.

Influence of the Home

Parenting teenagers in today's world is difficult. One important reason for this is that most of a teenager's time is spent under the control and influence of others—schoolteachers, peers, neighbors, and television entertainers. Many people feel that regardless of how well they do their jobs as parents, their efforts have a small effect on their teenagers. But the opposite is true, for evidence indicates that the home still maintains the greatest influence. The home is stronger than any other influence in determining how happy, secure, and stable a teenager is; how he relates to adults, peers, or children; how confident he is in himself; and how he responds to new or strange situations. Regardless of the many distractions in the life of a teenager, the home has the deepest influence on his life.

A teenager may be bigger, smarter, stronger, or in other ways superior to his parents. But emotionally he is still a child. He continues to need to feel loved and accepted by his parents. Unless the teenager feels that priceless assurance of love and acceptance by his parents, he will not be his best or do his best. He cannot reach his potential.

Relatively few teenagers are fortunate enough to feel truly loved and accepted as they should be. True, most parents have deep feelings of love toward their teenagers. They assume, however, that they naturally and effectively convey this love. This is indeed the greatest error parents make today, for most parents are simply not transmitting or conveying their own heartfelt love to their teenagers. The reason is that they do not know how.

As I work with teenagers who come to me with problems, a common, interweaving thread constantly presents itself as either the cause or the aggravator of their troubled situations—a feeling of not being loved and cared for by their parents.

That is what this book is all about. It is a how-to book, to help parents know *how* to love their teenagers so they will be their best, act their best, and grow to become their best. I pray that it will be not only a book of answers for the weary, confused parent, but also a book of hope.

I, for one, love teenagers. They are among the dearest people I know. Given what they need emotionally, they are able to respond in such wholesome and joyful ways that sometimes I think my heart will burst.

Yes, they are definitely capable of trying us to our utter limits of tolerance and patience. Yes, sometimes we lose our cool and our tempers, and feel we simply do not have what it takes to meet their needs. We may even want to run away or give up.

But, dear parent, hang in there! Our perseverance is indeed worth it. For it is a priceless wonder to see our teenagers develop into pleasant and productive adults. But we must be realistic. This doesn't just happen. We must pay a price.

I truly want this book to be a source of hope to you. The last thing I want is to cause you to feel guilty. We all make mistakes. Just as there are no perfect children, there are no perfect parents. Don't let guilt from past mistakes damage your efforts to raise your teenagers well.

Most adolescent problems can be alleviated or rectified by correcting tensions in the parent-teenager relationship. However, there are some teenage problems which are caused or aggravated by neurological ills or physiological depression. These medical problems must be alleviated before attempting to correct parent-teenager relationships.

But most teenage problems do not require professional help. Relationships can be improved when parents learn how to genuinely and effectually transmit their love to their teenagers. And that is what this book is all about.

Chapter 2

The Home

The first responsibility of parents is to provide a loving and happy home. And the most important relationship in the home is the marriage bond, which takes primacy over the parent-child relationship. The security of a teenager and the quality of the parent-child bonding are largely dependent on the quality of the marital bonding. You can see how important it is to assure the best possible relationship between husband and wife, since this is the basis for seriously attempting to relate to a teenager in a more positive way.

Chuck

Chuck's parents brought him to me because he had problems of truancy, stealing, and disobedience. The Hargraves talked about their teenage son with frustration and anger. The intensity of their negative feelings toward the boy concerned me.

Chuck said nothing but sat solemnly with his eyes downcast

while he listened to his parents' accusations. When he finally spoke, he did so in a soft, meek voice and with short phrases rather than sentences.

I spent some time with Chuck alone after his parents left the office. He was angry, but he couldn't tell me exactly why. It soon became evident that Chuck was a confused boy. He was confused about himself and about the relationship between his parents. He was also puzzled regarding his misconduct, for he was a bright boy who had not experienced academic problems. He was well liked by his peers, and had no unusual problems with his teachers. He was also confused about his stealing, since he did not need the items that he took. And it was obvious that he had set himself up to be caught.

Chuck's case is not unusual. Although his parents meant well, they had made several mistakes in raising Chuck. Their marriage was in trouble, largely because they had not learned to share their feelings and opinions with each other. Mrs. Hargrave had never been able to express her normal anger in an open, healthy, direct way to her husband; therefore she manifested her anger by getting back at him in subtle and indirect ways—such as overspending. Mr. Hargrave, who was unable to be openly honest with his wife expressed his anger by being silent, avoiding eye contact, and evading family and home responsibilities.

Chuck had learned his lesson well. Because open, honest discussion and expression of feelings did not exist in the Hargrave home, Chuck demonstrated his anger by doing things which embarrassed and upset his parents.

Due to lack of normal communication, Mr. and Mrs. Hargrave had never understood each other's feelings and expectations regarding Chuck. So they had never agreed on behavioral limits or appropriate discipline for Chuck.

This had been confusing to Chuck, for he had never known his parents' expectations of him. He was a boy who naturally wanted to please. But how could he? He gave up trying to live up to his parents' standards, because he never knew what they were.

All these problems existed because the parents were never able to talk things out between them and come to mutual decisions.

Roger

Here is another illustration that shows the importance of the marital relationship in raising a teenager. Fourteen-year-old Roger was caught breaking into a home and stealing several items. His parents brought him to me because he was failing in school, had developed a defiant attitude, and was usually in a sullen mood. A history revealed that Roger's parents had been having problems with him for several years. He usually disobeyed, constantly challenged parental authority, and would get his way by manipulation. He used what one parent said against the other. These tactics caused conflict between the parents. Mom and Dad fought about how to handle Roger, while Roger did as he pleased.

Evaluation revealed that Roger had perceptual problems, was deeply depressed, and exhibited passive-aggressive traits (see chapter 7). When I gave them my recommendations, Roger's parents, in their typical way of handling problems, argued with each other about what should be done. Even with professional recommendations, these unfortunate parents were unable to come to logical and sensible decisions regarding their son.

Of course, one of my main objectives in this case was to help the parents improve their own relationship, so that they would be united in the discipline of Roger. For only then would the boy respect his parents, stop using one against the other, and learn to control himself in appropriate ways.

Need for Communication

These brief case histories from my files reveal how problems in marital relationships can produce difficulties among our teenagers. Every teenager needs parents whose marital relationship is one of stability, respect, love, and good communication.

The ability to communicate feelings, particularly unpleasant feelings, is critical in the marital relationship. Especially during times of stress, this honest, open talking it out is absolutely critical and can determine whether stress will enhance or break a marriage.

In my own marriage I have discovered this importance of communication over and over, and usually the hard way. Probably the most stressful period of our marriage was right after the birth of our second daughter, Cathy, who was born with several physical deformities. I had a difficult enough time handling this. But when she was about a year old, it slowly became apparent that Cathy was profoundly mentally retarded along with having cerebral palsy, and a severe seizure disorder. As a twenty-four-year-old husband and father, I experienced feelings that I did not know were possible. I felt anger, rage, extreme pain, and feelings of guilt and inadequacy as a man, father, and husband. I could hardly bear it. Many times I just wanted to run, especially as we saw no improvement in Cathy's condition. She was developing no self-help skills or physical abilities.

Cathy was a child-care nightmare. When she could finally move herself along the floor, she would head straight for trouble; she would try to eat garbage or anything else she could put in her mouth. She had little sense of pain and would often attempt to place her hands on the hot stove burners. Cathy had to be watched closely every second because her constant striving was toward doing things which were dangerous to her.

All this began in my first year of medical school. With Cathy's expenses and the pressures of medical school, our financial situation was quite bleak. I remember wondering many times how our marriage could possibly survive.

Pat has always been the more emotionally mature partner in our marriage. The pain about Cathy and our untenable situation was just as difficult for her as it was for me. But her response was so different from mine. In the midst of constant heartbreak, Pat carefully looked after Cathy's every need with patience, gentleness, and devoted love. She seldom gave in to the agonizing feelings which were driving me away. Her inner beauty of love, gentleness, and patience were beyond my comprehension. And, worst of all, I couldn't appreciate her qualities as I should have, because they contrasted with my inability to cope with the situation. I felt her maturity made me look rather bad as a husband and father. I somewhat resented her for this and tended to pull away from her and Cathy whenever I reasonably could.

Yet I truly loved Pat, and I realized that instead of helping her, I was adding to her crushing burden. So I felt guilty and utterly helpless. I went to several people seeking help on how to deal with this agony. But no one knew what I was talking about.

I believe things came to their absolute worst when the "patterning" method of treating children like Cathy came into vogue. It took five people to move her arms, legs, and head in coordinated movements to simulate the movements of crawling. This required our family's total resources for several hours each day. The utterly crushing consumption of time and effort came close to being the ton that broke the Campbells' backs.

Eventually we found, as did many others, that there is flimsy rationale for patterning. It turned out to be a total waste of time. But before this conclusion was finally drawn, our family was in a shambles.

Yet even at this point of profound gloom, Pat continued her motherly care with gentleness, love, and unbelievable patience. She had not lost her inner peace and incredible inner beauty.

Me? I was hardly coping. I hurt inside for Cathy from morning to night. I had difficulty concentrating on my studies and kept wondering how we were going to manage financially. In short, I was miserable and feared that we could not survive much longer. I wondered, "How much stress can a marital relationship be expected to bear? Will it break or simply die?"

By this time Cathy was five years old. The situation was generally the same, but her seizures were becoming worse and were less and less controlled by medication. Eventually, the slightest environmental change would set off another seizure. Cathy would not eat for three days following a seizure. When the frequency increased to several a day, forced-tube feeding became necessary. It finally became obvious that Cathy could not survive outside of a hospital. Then came the most difficult, agonizing decision and day of our lives—we had to permanently place Cathy in a hospital for the mentally retarded. Imagine—turning our precious five-year-old daughter over to people we didn't even know. I wasn't sure I could handle this one at all. But, again, I noticed my dear, dear wife, Pat. Struggling with just as much pain and agony as I, she knew what we had to do, made the decision, found the courage to accept it, and never lost her inner peace and beauty.

Unfortunately, I learn rather slowly. But this time, instead of fighting an unchangeable situation right down to my last guilt-ridden ounce of energy (including resenting my wife's beautiful way of responding to life's most unbearable agonies), I decided that I had much to learn from her. She had taught me, as only a woman can do, how to live with life's most unbearable situations.

Every type of personality has its advantages and disadvantages. In the situation with Cathy, Pat was the stronger and I needed to learn from her, and sometimes lean on her. In other situations, I happen to be better able to cope, and then I can help Pat.

The point of all this is to understand that stress will come into every marriage. Whether the stress hurts and destroys the marriage, or enhances it, depends on how both husband and wife respond individually to the stress. My initial response to a cruel situation was destructive. I tended to avoid it, leaving Pat to handle the entire burden by herself. By her consistent example, she showed me how to live out my commitments as husband and father and to take my responsibility. As I did, my appreciation and love for her mushroomed. Because I learned to cope with inner pain rather than to run from it, Pat and I over the years have been able to face together those problems which produce emotional pain.

Fellow parents, if we persevere through the problems which put stress on our marriages, we will grow as spouses. If we continue to carry out our marital responsibility as a *lifelong commitment*, we will grow together in love, appreciation, and respect. We must live and think as though there are no other alternatives than to *make this marriage work*. Yes, it *is* work. It is *hard work*. And it takes this lifelong commitment of both spouses. Many marriages today are based on a "wait-and-see" attitude—"We'll give it a try and if it doesn't pan out, we'll split." No marriage can truly succeed on that basis. Is there anything more rare today than total, lifelong commitment to marriage? Our way of life has been based on the integrity of the family. Yet unless it is rekindled and enhanced, the institution of marriage may be doomed.

A Look at Single–Parent Families

In 1989, twenty-six percent of children less than eighteen years of age lived with only one parent, and this figure is steadily increasing. Over 50 percent of children born today will spend at least some of their youth in a single-parent household.

Many people today believe that a single parent is incapable of being as effective in parenting as two parents raising their children together. David Clevenger's article "Parenting in the '90s" in the American Medical Association Auxiliary magazine *Facets* (September 1992) points out that those who believe single parents cannot be effective parents are wrong. Decades of research show, as Clevenger states, that "being a single parent does not preclude anyone from being an effective parent. To some degree and in some ways, personal and societal pressures diminish the ability of most people to be good parents. And those pressures stack the odds more heavily against single parents trying to raise their children alone."

The Clevenger article states that T. Berry Brazelton, M.D., one of America's best-known and highly respected pediatricians, says, "It matters a great deal if you are single or not. But I still think you can do it. It's just harder because you are likely to be poor. It is very, very hard to be single because you have to be both the disciplinarian and somebody who offers nurturance."

Also, the single parent usually must both earn the family's living and run the household. Alvin Poussaint, M.D., Harvard psychiatrist, states: "The homemaking mother took care of a lot of those things that are so important to the family. She was there when the kids came home. She got the kids ready for school. She went to the Parent-Teacher Association meetings. She took the kids to the doctor, to the dentist. Well, if you are a single parent and you are working, who does all those things? It's just a constant pressure."

In his article, David Clevenger also points out:

> In fact, the biggest cause of diminished parental energies and competencies is poverty, a factor that disproportionately affects single mothers. Today, about eight percent of America's dual-parent families live in poverty. But of the

159

families that are headed by a mother, as a majority of single-parent families are, nearly forty-five percent struggle below the poverty line.

Why do poverty and other pressures diminish the single person's parenting effectiveness more than they do that of the traditional parent? Mothers and fathers in traditional families have each other. And they usually give each other important emotional, psychological, physical, and financial support that is not typically available to the single parent who must raise her (or his) kids alone.

The absence of this support may appear to be a good reason to argue that the single-parent family is not a viable family structure in which to raise children. But those who make this argument miss an important point—single parents can get support too. While they can't turn to spouses, they can rely on others with whom they are involved—on members of their extended families, and on friends, professional organizations, and community groups.

And this support, wherever it's obtained, is essential for overcoming the pressures that diminish effective parenting. In fact, the most successful single parents are those who have learned how to tap into available support, and use this support to overcome the pressures that would prevent their using a positive pattern of parenting. And by overcoming them, they can become effective parents.

Role Reversal

A situation that is rather common today is the role reversal in which a parent demands that a child fulfill the parent's emotional needs. While this can happen in any home, it is more likely to occur in a one-parent family.

Some single parents feel tempted to use their teenagers as colleagues or confidants. This is more difficult for them to deal with because they do not have spouses with whom to share the adult levels of the home.

Because of loneliness, feelings of inadequacy, depression, or other causes, single parents at times find it difficult to avoid relating to their teenagers as contemporaries. These parents may share intimately personal information which the teenagers are not ready to handle. Such parents tend to be "best friends" with their teenagers, instead of maintaining healthy parent-child relationships.

I have seen extreme examples of this. Jim was a sixteen-year-old who frequently would get drunk with his father in a bar. Although this happened because of the father's loneliness and lack of friends, the father rationalized to himself that he was "making a man" of his son.

I remember Julie whose mother would have her boyfriend bring a date for Julie so they could go out together. While these are obviously extreme examples, role reversal is not unusual. Lesser forms of misusing teenagers in this way are very common. For example, parents complain to teenage children about how lonely, depressed, unhappy, or misused they are. This is *not* parenting. A parent fulfills the emotional needs of a child or a teenager. For the teenager to fill the emotional needs of a parent is "reversal of roles" and is unwholesome. A teenager treated in this way *cannot* develop normally.

Whether we are single or married, we parents must always maintain our position as mother or father in the home. We are responsible to meet the emotional needs of our teenagers. If we reverse this natural course and look to them to emotionally nourish us, we will hurt them — and destroy our relationship with them. We must obtain our emotional nourishment elsewhere — not from our children.

I have never particularly enjoyed being an authority for anyone, especially for my children. As my children passed through their teenage years, I was tempted to treat them as contemporary friends, but I dared not. Yes, I was loving and friendly with them and enjoyed laughing and having fun. And on occasion, I would share appropriate personal information with them, but only for their educational benefit — *not for my emotional benefit.* I did not forget that I was their father and they they needed my authority and direction. If I relinquished or neglected my responsibility for being the authority in the home — along with Pat, for she too had to assume her position of authority — my children would not be happy. They would feel insecure, and would be very apt to develop poor behavior patterns.

As parents, we must not use our children or teenagers as counselors, shoulders to cry on, emotional support, or colleagues. Of course, we can ask their opinion or advice on occasion, as long as we are not doing it in ways that prompt them to nourish us emotionally. We cannot ask them to make us feel better. There is no way to be consistently firm with our teenagers if we are dependent on them for our emotional support.

As parents, our first responsibility is to make our children feel genuinely loved. Our second responsibility is to be authority figures for our children and to lovingly discipline them.

Chapter 3

Unconditional Love

T he basic foundation for a solid relationship with your teenager is unconditional love. For only unconditional love can prevent problems such as resentment, guilt, fear, or the insecurity of feeling unwanted.

Only when your basic relationship with your teenager is built on unconditional love can you be confident in your parenting. Without this foundation, it is impossible to really understand your teenager, or know how to guide him, or deal with his behavior.

Without unconditional love, parenting is a confusing and frustrating burden. This love acts as a guiding light, showing you where you are with your teenager and what to do next. When you begin with unconditional love, you can then build your knowledge and expertise in guiding your teenager and filling his or her needs on a daily basis. You will also know where you are succeeding as a parent and where you are not.

You want to feel good about yourself as a parent. Many people question if this is possible. Let me assure you that it is definitely possible both to *be* a good parent and to *feel* confident that you are.

What Is Unconditional Love?
Unconditional love means loving a teenager, no matter what.
- No matter what the teenager looks like.
- No matter what his assets, liabilities, and handicaps are.
- No matter how he acts.

This does not mean that you always like his behavior. Unconditional love means you love your teenager even when you detest his behavior.

Unconditional love is an ideal. You can't feel love for a teenager—or anyone else—100 percent of the time. But the closer you come to this goal, the more satisfied and confident you will feel. And the more pleasant and satisfied your teenager will be.

As I look back when my children were teenagers, there were times indeed when I didn't feel like a loving dad toward them. But I attempted to arrive at that wonderful goal of loving them unconditionally. I helped myself by trying to keep in mind the following guidelines that you will want to consider in your relationship to your teenager:

- Teenagers are children.
- Teenagers will usually act like teenagers.
- Much of teenage behavior is unpleasant.
- If you love your teenager only when they please you (conditional love) and convey your love only during those times, he will not feel genuinely loved. This, in turn, will make a teenager feel insecure, damage his self-image, and actually prevent him from developing more mature behavior. Therefore, parents are without question partially responsible for a teenager's behavioral development.
- If you love a teenager unconditionally, he will feel good about himself and be comfortable with himself. He will be able to control his anxiety and, in turn, his behavior as he grows into adulthood.

• If you love a teenager only when he meets your requirements or expectations, he will feel incompetent. He will believe it is fruitless to do his best because it is never enough.
Insecurity, anxiety, and low self-esteem will plague him.
There will be constant hindrances in his emotional and behavioral growth. Again, a teenager's total growth depends a
lot on the responsibility of his parents.

As Pat and I tried to follow these guidelines, we prayed that
our love for our teenagers would be as unconditional as we
could make it. We realized that the future of our teenagers
depended on this biblical foundation.

"Do You Love Me?"
Do you know what is the most important question on your
teenager's mind? Without realizing it, he is continually asking,
"Do you love me?" It is absolutely the most important question
in a teenager's life. And he asks the question primarily through
his behavior, rather than with words.

"Do you love me?" The answer you give behaviorally to that
question is absolutely critical. If you answer it no, your teenager
will not be or do his best. You need to answer it yes, but few
parents do. It is not that these parents don't love their teenagers. The problem is that most parents do not know how to
answer yes; they don't know how to convey their love to their
teenagers.

If you love your teenager unconditionally, he feels the answer
is yes. If you love him conditionally, he is unsure and prone to
anxiety. Your answer to that critical question, "Do you love
me?" pretty well determines your teenager's basic attitude toward life. How crucial!

One of the main reasons most parents do not know how to
convey their love to their teenagers is because teenagers, like
younger children, are *behaviorally oriented*. Adults are primarily
verbally oriented.

For example, a man away on a trip would make his wife happy
by calling her and saying, "Honey, I love you." She would be on
cloud nine. However, if he got his fourteen-year-old son on the

phone and said, "I just want to say I love you," the teenager would likely shrug and perhaps say, "Yes, Dad, but why did you really call?"

See the difference? A teenager is behaviorally oriented, whereas an adult is primarily verbally oriented.

Having a warm feeling of love in your heart for your teenager is wonderful—but it's not enough! Saying "I love you" to a teenager is great, and should be done—but it's not enough. For your teenager to *know* and *feel* you love him, you must also love him behaviorally because he is still primarily behaviorally oriented. Only then can he feel you are answering yes to the crucial question in his heart: "Do you love me?" Your teenager sees your love for him by what you *say* and *do*. But what you *do* carries more weight. Your teenager is far more affected by your actions than by your words.

It is also important to remember that your teenager has an emotional tank. This tank is figurative, of course, but the concept is very real. Your teenager has certain emotional needs, and whether these emotional needs are met (through love, understanding, discipline, etc.) helps determine how he feels—whether he is content, angry, depressed, or joyful. Also, it strongly affects his behavior—whether he is obedient, disobedient, whiny, perky, playful, or withdrawn. Naturally, the fuller the tank, the more positive the feelings and the better the behavior.

At this point please stop and ponder one of the most important statements in this book: ONLY WHEN HIS EMOTIONAL TANK IS FULL CAN A TEENAGER BE EXPECTED TO BE HIS BEST AND DO HIS BEST. It is your responsibility as a parent to do all you can to keep your teenager's emotional tank full.

Love Reflectors

Teenagers may be conceptualized as mirrors. They generally reflect rather than initiate love. If love is given to them, they return it. If none is given, they have none to return. Unconditional love is reflected unconditionally, and conditional love is returned conditionally.

As an example of mirrored love, let's think again about Debbie, whom we met in chapter 1. The love between Debbie and her parents was an example of a conditional relationship. Unfortunately, her parents felt that they should continually prompt her to do better by withholding praise, warmth, and affection, except for truly outstanding behavior (when she made them feel proud). Otherwise, they withheld showing their love, feeling that too much approval and affection would spoil her and lessen her striving to be better. As Debbie grew older, she increasingly felt that her parents really didn't love or appreciate her in her own right, that they cared only about their own esteem as parents.

By the time Debbie was a teenager, she had learned well from her parents how to love conditionally. She behaved in a way which pleased her parents only when her parents did something special for her. Of course, with both Debbie and her parents now behaving this way, neither could convey love to the other because each was waiting for the other to do something first.

This is a typical result of conditional love. Love-giving eventually stops until another person does something very pleasing to get it going again. Everyone becomes more and more disappointed, confused, and bewildered. Eventually, depression, anger, and resentment set in. In the Battens' case, this prompted them to seek help.

Emotional Tanks

As mentioned before, teenagers are children *emotionally*. To illustrate this, consider how a teenager is like a two-year-old. Both a teenager and a two-year-old have drives for independence and both have emotional tanks. Each will strive for independence, using the energy from the emotional tank. When the emotional tank has run dry, the teenager and the two-year-old will do the same thing—return to the parent for a refill so they can again strive for independence.

For example, suppose a mother brings her two-year-old to a new place, such as a PTA meeting. At first the child may cling to his mother for emotional support. With a full emotional tank, the child will then begin exerting his independence by exploring. At first he may simply stand next to his mother and look around. As his emotional tank becomes empty, the child will seek his mother again for a refill with eye contact, physical contact, and focused attention. Now the child is again ready to try his independence. This time he may get to the end of the row of seats before running out of emotional gasoline. Or he may interact with another person sitting nearby before his emotional tank runs dry.

Do you see the pattern? The child must repeatedly return to the parent to have his emotional tank refilled in order to continue his quest for independence. This is exactly what happens with the teenager, especially the early adolescent. He may use different means of exerting his drive for independence (and sometimes in disturbing or upsetting ways). He needs the energy from his emotional tank to do this. And where does he get his emotional tank refilled? Right! From his parents. A teenager will strive for independence in typical adolescent ways—doing things by himself, going places without family, testing parental rules. But he will eventually run out of emotional gasoline and come back to the parents for emotional maintenance—for a refill. As parents of teenagers, this is what we want. We want our adolescent *to be able* to come to us for emotional maintenance when he needs it.

There are several reasons why this refilling is so important.

● Teenagers need an ample amount of emotional nurturance if they are to function at their best and grow to be their best.

● They desperately need full emotional tanks in order to feel the security and self-confidence they must have to cope with peer pressure and other demands of adolescent society. Without this confidence, teenagers tend to succumb to peer pressure and experience difficulty in upholding wholesome, ethical values.

● The emotional refilling is crucial, because while it is taking place, it is possible to keep open lines of communication between parents and teenagers. When a teenager's tank is empty and he seeks parental love, communication is so much easier.

Most parents do not realize how important it is for their teenager to be able to come to them to have his emotional tank refilled. During times when a teenager is striving for independence, he may upset his parent to such an extent that the parent overreacts emotionally, and usually with excessive anger.

This emotional overreaction, if too excessive or frequent, makes it extremely difficult, and perhaps impossible, for the teenager to return to his parents for emotional refills. Then, if parent-child communication is broken, a teenager may turn to his peers for emotional nurturance. What a dangerous, and frequently disastrous, situation this is! For the teenager will then be easily susceptible to peer pressure, to influences of religious cults, and to unscrupulous persons who use young people.

When your teenager tests you by striving through inappropriate behavior to be independent, you must be careful not to overreact emotionally. This does not mean condoning the misbehavior. You need to express your feelings honestly but appropriately; that is, without extreme anger, yelling, name-calling, attacking the child verbally, or otherwise losing control of yourself. Look at it this way. If someone you know overreacts with a temper tantrum, how are your feelings toward him affected? Your respect for that person lessens, especially if he loses self-control often.

The more a parent loses self-control in a teenager's presence, the less respect a teenager will feel for his parent. You should make every effort to maintain emotional control of yourself, regardless of how your teenager expresses his drive for independence. You must keep open the avenues over which your teenager returns to you to have his emotional tank refilled. This is crucial if he is to enter adulthood as a whole person.

Chapter 4

Focused Attention

G iving focused attention to your teenager involves much more than providing eye or physical contact. Eye contact and physical contact, which we will discuss in chapter 5, seldom require real sacrifice by parents. Focused attention does. It requires time and sometimes a lot of it. It may mean giving your teenager focused attention when you would rather do something else. For there are times when a teenager desperately needs focused attention that parents least feel like giving it.

Focused attention means giving your teenager full, undivided attention in such a way that he feels truly loved, that he knows he is so valuable in his own right that he warrants your watchfulness, appreciation, and uncompromising regard. Focused attention makes your teenager feel that he is the most important person in the world to you, his parents.

In the Scriptures, we see a very high regard for children. King

David called them the heritage of the Lord. Christ said that no one should prevent the little ones from coming to Him, and warned that those who offend His little ones would be better dead. He said that unless we become as children before Him, we will not enter the kingdom of God. (See Psalm 127:3-5; Matthew 18:1-10; Mark 10:13-16.)

Teenagers ought to be made to feel that they are special. Few teenagers feel this way, but, oh, the difference it makes in them when they know they are special. Only focused attention can tell them this. It is so vital to the development of their self-esteem. And it profoundly affects their ability to relate and love others.

I believe that focused attention is the greatest need a teenager has. Most parents have real difficulty recognizing this need, much less fulfilling it. There are many reasons for this. For example, other things they do for their teenagers—favors, gifts, and granting unusual requests—seem to substitute for focused attention at the time. These things may be good, but it is a serious mistake to use them to replace genuine focused attention. This substitution is tempting to parents, because favors and gifts are easier to give and take much less time. But teenagers do not do their best, do not feel their best, and do not behave their best unless they receive that precious commodity—focused attention from their parents.

Priorities
It is not possible for me to take care of every obligation and responsibility in my life in the way I would like to. There just isn't the time. So what can I do about this? There is only one answer, and it isn't simple—I must determine my priorities, set my goals, and plan my time to accomplish them. I must control my time in order to take care of the important things first.

What are the priorities in your life? Where do your children fit into them? Do they take first priority? Second? Third? You must determine this. Otherwise, your children will take a low precedence and suffer from some degree of neglect. No one else can decide for you what is important in your life.

Because life is so unpredictable, you cannot count on unlimited opportunities for nurturing your children. Therefore, you must take advantage of opportunities which you plan or which present themselves through your teenager's need. These will be fewer than you think you will have. Your children are teenagers for such a short time.

Necessity of Focused Attention

Focused attention is not something that is simply nice to give your teenager if time permits. It is a critical need each teenager has. How he views himself and how he is accepted by his world is determined primarily by the way in which this need is met. Without focused attention a teenager experiences increased anxiety, because he feels everything else is more important to his parents than he is. He is consequently less secure and becomes impaired in his emotional and psychological growth.

Such a teenager can be identified rather easily. He is generally less mature or sure of himself than teens whose parents have taken the time to fill their need for focused attention. This unfortunate teenager is often withdrawn and has difficulty with peers. He is less able to cope and usually reacts poorly in conflict. He is overly dependent on others, including peers, and is more subject to peer pressure.

Some young teenagers, however, especially girls deprived of focused attention from their fathers, seem to react in just the opposite way. They are quite talkative, manipulative, dramatic, and often seductive. They are sometimes considered precocious, outgoing and mature as children. But as they grow older, this behavior pattern does not mature and gradually becomes more inappropriate. By the time they are older teenagers, they are usually obnoxious to their peers as well as to adults. However, even at this late date, focused attention, especially from their fathers, can go a long way in reducing their self-defeating behavior, decreasing their anxiety, and freeing them to resume their maturational growth.

How Do You Give Focused Attention?

I have found that the best way to give a teenager focused attention is to set aside time to spend with him alone. You may already be thinking how difficult that is to do. And you are right. Finding time to be alone with a teenager, free from other distractions, is what I consider to be the most difficult aspect of parenting teenagers. But let's face it—good parenting takes time. Finding time in our hyperactive society is hard, especially when teenagers have other interests with which the parents must compete. But this points all the more to the fact that focused attention is crucial. Today teenagers are more influenced by forces outside the family than ever before in history.

It takes tremendous effort to pry time from busy schedules; but when you do, the rewards are great. For it is a wonderful thing to see your teenager happy, secure, well-liked by peers and adults, and learning and behaving at his best. But such satisfaction does not come automatically. As parents you must pay a price for it. You must find time to spend time alone with each child.

Time is difficult to manage. I tried to conserve as much time as possible for my children when they were growing up. For example, when my daughter, Carey, was taking music lessons near my office on Monday afternoons, I would schedule my appointments so that I could pick her up. Then we would stop at a restaurant and have supper together. At these times, without the pressure of interruption and time schedules, I was able to give her my full attention and listen to whatever she wanted to talk about.

Only in this context of being alone without pressure can parents and their child develop that special, indelible relationship which each child so desperately needs, to face the realities of life. A child treasures moments such as these and remembers them when life becomes difficult, especially during those tumultuous years of adolescent conflict.

During times of focused attention, parents can make special opportunities for eye contact and physical contact with a teenager. For during these times of focused attention, eye and physical contact have stronger meaning and impact upon a teenager's life.

It is important that you watch for unexpected opportunities to spend additional time with your teenager. For example, you may find yourself alone with your teenager. You can take this as another opportunity to fill his emotional tank and prevent problems brought on by a dry tank. This time of focused attention may be quite short—but just a moment or two can do wonders.

Every moment counts, for the stakes are high. What is worse than a wayward, adolescent son or daughter? What is more wonderful than a well-balanced teenager?

Yes, focused attention is time-consuming, difficult to do consistently, and many times burdensome for already exhausted parents. But focused attention is the most powerful means of keeping a teenager's emotional tank full and investing in his future.

As children grow older, these times of focus need to be lengthened. Older children need time to warm up, to let their developing defenses down, and to feel free to share their innermost thoughts, especially those that may be troubling them.

As children enter adolescence, they need *more* time with family, not less. It is so easy to assume that since teens are rapidly becoming more independent and *seem* to want more and more time away from the family, that you should spend less and less time with them. This is one of the most devastating mistakes parents make today. As their children enter and progress through adolescence, parents often use their free time in ways which meet their *own* pleasure needs. Every teenager I've ever known interprets this as rejection, feeling that their parents care less and less about them.

Adolescents need parental time and attention as never before. They are facing strong influences daily and, unfortunately, many of these influences are unhealthy, unwholesome, and sometimes evil. If you want your teenager to be able to cope with today's world, you must spend constructive time with him; especially when he is going through adolescent turmoils. If you do take the time to meet these needs, your teenager will gain the confidence and personal integrity to think for himself about the kind of values he will live by. He will develop strength to stand up against divisive influences from people who have little or no regard for him, but simply want to use him.

This may seem difficult to accomplish, especially when your child is in a difficult, noncommunicative mood so commonly seen in early to middle adolescents. One secret to remember is that the psychological defenses of a moody teenager are very high, and that *time* is required for him to slowly be lowered to where he is able to genuinely communicate and share with you what is *really* on his mind. Did you catch that magic word? TIME.

I remember when our precious Carey was fourteen years old. What a year! She was undergoing the typical transitions of early adolescence and would frequently communicate only with grunts like "uh-huh," "huh-uh," or "huh?"

During this period, I made two wonderful discoveries. First, it is useless *and* harmful to try to force a child to open up and talk at such a time. Although it was a real temptation to badger her with questions, I discovered this was a mistake and actually worsened the situation. Second, if I spent at least twenty to thirty minutes with Carey in a pleasant way which did not put any pressure on her to communicate, her defenses would slowly come down and we were then able to really share thoughts and feelings.

One of the most effective ways to accomplish that was to take her to a restaurant. I would pick the restaurant with the slowest service in town and would try to arrive during the busiest time, so we could wait in a long line. I would ask the waitress to come back a couple of times—"We're not quite ready to order." I would take time eating and then order a dessert, which I normally avoid, followed by a leisurely cup of coffee.

You see, the purpose of all this was to provide a time together when Carey was under no pressure to communicate and could still be comfortable in my presence. Standing in line in a public place meets this requirement. Other examples include fishing, hunting, hiking, taking a trip (short or long), playing a game, seeing a play, listening to an orchestra. When a teenager is with his or her father or mother but under no pressure, "just being there," the defenses will *gradually* come down, and he or she will begin to talk—superficially at first, and then at more meaningful levels.

By the time we finished eating, Carey would be talking fairly freely and sharing—but with the conversation mostly at a superficial level—sports, teachers, schoolwork. Then I would pay the bill, and we would go to the car.

Let me interject an interesting piece of information here. When you are driving a car with your teenager as a passenger, especially if other teenagers are with you, you somehow lose your own identity and are considered as part of the car—an extension of the steering wheel. My wife and I have really appreciated this adolescent ability—it is amazing how this facilitates adolescent conversation while riding along in the car. It is likewise amazing how much we have learned during these times.

Anyway, back to Carey and me. We would get in the car and usually, during the last mile or so before getting home, she would finally talk about things which were very meaningful to her. Things like peer relationships, family relationships, peer pressure to take drugs. Of course, the conversation couldn't be completed before we drove up to the house, typical of teenagers. The reason for this is that teenagers need to feel they have a means of "escape" when revealing meaningful information. They must feel that they are in a position to leave, if the parents are not responding properly to their innermost feelings. What they fear most is not disagreement but anger, ridicule, disapproval, or rejection of them on a personal level. They must feel enough in control so that if they become too uncomfortable, they can remove themselves.

This is why Carey would wait until we were near home before she would share with me what was really important to her. So the best conversations I had with Carey were at these times. Sometimes she would disguise her own conflicts by talking about or asking about another teenager who happened to have similar problems. This is a favorite way many teenagers use to talk about awkward, embarrassing, difficult-to-handle situations.

Sometimes a teenager needs to talk with a parent about a problem but sometimes has a difficult time initiating the conversation. At such times, he will frequently throw out hints. These hints can take various forms. A teenager who needs to talk, but who is in a noncommunicative mood, may say something much less threatening than what he actually wants to talk about. For example, he may start out by asking a question about homework. Perhaps a question about the day which the parent has had. Or maybe a comment about the day he has had.

Parents must be alert for such unsolicited and sometimes puzzling gestures, usually a hesitant teenager's way of asking for time and for focused attention. He is "feeling us out," testing us to see what kind of mood and frame of mind we are in — to see if it is safe to approach us on an issue about which he feels uncomfortable.

At other times, a teenager may test our receptivity, to see if we are in a good mood, by putting out what I call a "red herring," or "smoke screen." These are pieces of information designed to upset or irritate us — a perfect device to see if we can be trusted with what is *really* on his mind. If we overreact, especially with anger and criticism, our teenager assumes we will react to his important question the same way. Again, the more self-control and calmness we display, the more open and sharing our teenager will be with us.

These moments of opportunity are priceless. If we do not notice these times and somehow close the door to our teenager, he will feel rejected. If we are alert and can detect these subtle clues, we can respond appropriately and help our teenager, as well as demonstrate conclusively that we love him and are sensitive to his needs.

I remember many such occasions when Carey was in her early teens. Most often she would select a time when she knew her mother and I were alone with the least likelihood of interruption. You can guess when this was — just as Pat and I were ready to turn off the light for a good night's sleep. Carey's younger brothers were fast asleep, so she had no competition. First, we would see the door slowly open as Carey came in and asked her mother if she could borrow something from the adjoining bathroom. After Carey got the item she asked for and was in the process of leaving, she would turn around and say to us, "Oh, by the way. . . . "

I can't overemphasize the importance of recognizing and noting these all too familiar words — "Oh, by the way," or their equivalent. Do you know what they usually really mean, when said by a teenager in such a situation? A translation is sometimes like this, "The real reason I'm here, and what I really want to talk about, is coming up. But first I want to know—are you in a good frame of mind to handle it? Can I trust you with this very delicate personal part of my life? Will you take it and help me, or will you use it against me? Can I trust you?"

If we do not give that focused attention at such a time, a teen will interpret the answer to be no. But if we focus our attention directly on the child, and listen intently and quietly, letting him control the conversation, our teenager will feel it is safe to take a chance and reveal a pressing problem. Incidentally, be ready for those famous four words soon after a "red herring" or "smoke screen."

I remember that I would sometimes goof and do something like telling Carey to be sure to turn out all the lights. And I would then feel a swift kick under the covers, because my wife would recognize what Carey was telling us and would know that she needed that precious commodity—focused attention. Always when we were on course, Carey continued the conversation on her own, talking initially about superficial things and gradually about items which were more and more important to her. After awhile, she would be sitting at the foot of our bed. Pretty soon she would be lying across the foot of the bed, the talk continuing to pour out. Finally, she would get to the thing which was bothering her. I remember one such time when she said, "I don't know if Jim likes me anymore. He's been so different." How difficult that was for Carey to come out with. She had to make sure the situation was safe for her to share. She had to put out her "red herrings" and "smoke screens" before she could finally reveal her problem.

Once a sensitive issue is out, it is a real temptation for parents to make light of it with a casual, seemingly flippant reply, as though it is such a trivial or easy-to-handle issue. We must take our teenagers seriously, examine their problems carefully with them, and help them come to logical and sensible solutions. In this way, we not only will help them with their problems, but more importantly, will cement our love-relationship with them.

And as we help them to solve their own problems, we can also be teaching them to think logically, rationally, and sequentially. Only by learning to think clearly can a teenager develop the ability to discern right from wrong and to develop a strong value system.

Guilt and Envy

To understand the background of most teenage problems, it is important to be aware of adolescent society. Teenage society is similar to the society of chickens — both teenagers and chickens have a "pecking order," so to speak. The adolescent society is complex, but is based primarily on popularity and acceptance. It is important to know approximately where your child is in this network of relationships, because some of the most painful adolescent problems are peer-related and involve one or more of four feelings — envy, guilt, anger, and depression. We will discuss anger and depression in detail later, so right now let's consider envy and guilt.

In dealing with peers, teenagers frequently have problems which naturally make them feel guilt or envy. Unfortunately, most teenagers are not good at identifying guilt or envy within themselves and, as a result, experience them as pain (distress) and/or confusion.

If a teenager's problem involves a peer who is lower on the adolescent society ladder, he will probably feel guilt. If his encounter was with someone above him, the feeling will usually be envy. When a conflict of interest or position arises, the teenager on the lower end, prompted by envy, will attempt to make the upper peer feel guilty.

It is important for parents to see their teenager's position in the conflict and identify the feelings the teenager is struggling with. Explaining the situation to a teenager will help him in several ways.

● It will enable him to understand exactly what is happening and *why*.

● It will help the teenager determine whether he has done anything wrong.

● It will assist him in handling this situation and others like it.

For example, if your teenager is feeling guilty, a clear understanding of the situation will usually reveal there is no blame to be laid and that the real problem is actually the other teenager's feeling of envy.

If your teenager is feeling envious, it is so helpful for him to be able to identify this within himself and to understand why. Then you will be in a position to help him correct the problem—by understanding that there is no real basis for the jealousy, if this is true, or by learning how to overcome the envy, if there *is* a basis for it.

When Carey won the Junior-Miss Pageant, nearly all of her peers were genuinely excited for her, and truly proud of her. But one evening, shortly afterward, Carey seemed troubled. As it turned out, an envious peer had made Carey feel guilty about winning the contest. The statement that produced the guilt was something like this: "Well, look at the big star! She sure thinks she's hot stuff!"

Carey felt miserable, typical of a teenager in this circumstance, and could not resolve her misery. Carey's mother helped her understand her feelings of guilt—that she had done nothing wrong, but was simply feeling a false guilt which had no basis.

Carey's experience illustrates the frequent problem of envy and guilt in the teenage world. It is vital to the emotional development of our teenagers that we help them to identify and understand envy and guilt in themselves, and learn how to handle these emotions properly. If they are unable to, they are likely to be *manipulated by guilt.*

Manipulation by Guilt

This is a great problem among adolescents today. The more sensitive a teenager is, the more susceptible he or she is to being manipulated by guilt. On the other hand, the less sensitive a teen is, the more apt he or she is to use this type of manipulation on others.

The maneuver is rather simple. Manipulator finds ways to make the manipulatee feel guilty if the manipulatee does not do what the manipulator wants. Of course, the classic example of this—and one of the most destructive—is the boy who attempts to induce a girl to have a sexual encounter with him with such remarks as, "If you really loved me, you would."

The parent of a sensitive teenager is in an excellent position to teach the child about this unwholesome device. The teenager needs to understand three things:

- How to recognize manipulation by guilt.
- That this device is unwholesome, unhealthy, and unethical—*that it is wrong.*
- That the normal and justifiable reaction to manipulation is *anger.*

In the story about the confrontation between Jesus and the money changers in the temple, I see manipulation as one element that caused Jesus' anger. The people coming to the temple needed to sacrifice to fulfill their religious obligation. They would feel guilty if they did not offer an animal sacrifice. In the scene which Jesus described as a cave full of robbers, there was manipulation by guilt. And Jesus' anger was an appropriate reaction. (See Matthew 21; Mark 11; Luke 19; John 2.)

I remember counseling a beautiful sixteen-year-old girl named Claudia. She was an extremely sensitive girl and in deep depression. During our conversation, I discovered that her boyfriend used guilt to manipulate her in many ways. As is so typical among teenagers, Claudia was not fully aware of her sensitivity, depression, or of being manipulated by guilt. First I explained to her how sensitive she was—how easy it was to hurt her and to make her feel guilty. Then I explained how others, especially her boyfriend, were able to control her by making her feel guilty if she didn't do what they wanted.

Because Claudia didn't understand at first what I was trying to tell her, I gave her an example that "wasn't so close to home." I said, "Claudia, I'm a sensitive person too, and I didn't learn how some people were able to manipulate me by guilt until a few years ago. After I finished medical school, I wanted to sell my house. I was having difficulty selling it myself, so I contracted a realtor to sell it for me. A few days later, a fellow medical student in my class who was going to remain in that city for an internship offered me a certain price for the home, but wanted to bypass the realtor and save the fees. I told him I could not do that—that he would have to go through the realtor. Later that day, the realtor came with an offer from another client and I took it. When my classmate found out that I had sold the house, he was furious and tried to talk me into changing my mind and selling it to him. The arguments that he used consisted of reminding me that we were fellow classmates, that I would make more money where I would be interning than he would make, and that the house had five years wear on it and was not worth the price the other person was offering."

Then I said, "Do you see, Claudia, how this man was trying to manipulate me into selling my house to him by making me feel guilty?"

Claudia's eyes lit up. She understood why she had so little control over her own life. The next time I saw Claudia her depression had lifted and there was a sparkle in her eye. She was learning how to think for herself and to determine her behavior rather than being manipulated by guilt.

Parents must be careful not to manipulate their teenagers by guilt. It is so easy for parents to fall into this trap, especially if they happen to have an extremely sensitive child. A teenager who has been manipulated with guilt by his own parents will be easily manipulated by others.

What is the best way to prevent teenagers from being manipulated by guilt? Within the context of unconditional love and focused attention, parents can train their teenagers to identify manipulative behavior in others, and to stay free of its trap.

Chapter 5

Eye Contact and Physical Contact

We live at a time in history when there are unprece-dented numbers of outside influences upon teenagers, many of them unwholesome, and some evil and de-structive. A teenager who does not feel loved and cared for is highly vulnerable to these influences. Many unscrupulous users of young people have seduced love-starved teenagers by giving them time, attention, and affection.

The hour is late. As a parent, you have limited time and opportunities to make your teenager feel unconditionally loved. You must be consistent every day in keeping his emotional tank full. This will enable him to grow into a person who can think competently and clearly for himself and develop good self-con-trol. Only when he truly feels that you unconditionally love him will you have the influence on him that you should. Yes, tell him, but you also want to show him your love in behavioral ways, as mentioned earlier.

183

Eye contact and physical contact should be incorporated into all of your everyday dealings with your children. They should be natural, comfortable, and not overdone. A child or teenager growing up in a home where parents use eye and physical contact will be comfortable with himself and other people. He will have an easier time communicating with others, and consequently will be well-liked and feel high self-esteem.

Appropriate and frequent eye and physical contact are two of the most precious gifts you can give your teenager. They, along with focused attention, are the most effective ways to fill your teenager's emotional tank and enable him to be his best.

Eye Contact

One of the primary reasons loving parents fail to convey unconditional love to their teenager is lack of eye contact. Loving, consistent eye contact with your teenager is crucial not only in making good communicational contact, but also in filling his emotional needs. Without realizing it, you use eye contact to express many feelings—sadness, anger, hate, rage, and love. In some homes, there is amazingly little eye contact between parents and teenagers. What exists is usually negative, as when the teenager is being reprimanded or given specific instructions. The more you are able to make eye contact with your teenager as a means of expressing love, the more your teenager will be emotionally nourished with love.

Your teenager will vary in his ability to make eye contact. One moment he will eagerly seek it. The next moment, he may actually avoid your gaze. Within this unevenness, he is learning patterns of eye contact, primarily from what he observes in his home from other members of the family.

Some time ago, I saw seventeen-year-old Bruce. Tall, well-built, and good-looking, he was an excellent student and athlete, and had a pleasant personality. Strangely enough, with all these things going for him, he had poor self-esteem and considered himself quite inadequate. It was easy to detect his low opinion of himself simply by observing his pattern of eye contact. His gaze was almost always downward. When he did make eye contact, it was for a fraction of a second. I explained to

Bruce that the way he used eye contact strongly affected the way he related to other people. His poor pattern of eye contact actually worsened his self-concept. People felt uncomfortable with Bruce—they thought he didn't like them or was ignoring them. They were actually relieved to end a conversation and get away from him. Bruce naturally misinterpreted this as rejection and felt worse than ever. With a steady diet of this pattern over many years, it is no wonder Bruce developed a horrible misrepresentation of himself. Fortunately, it was simple to help Bruce correct his pattern of eye contact.

If your teenager has developed abnormal patterns of eye contact, you can teach him how he is misapplying it and how to correct it. Good eye contact can make the difference between success and failure in almost all of life's situations.

Giving loving eye contact to your teenager can be difficult, especially during those unpleasant times when he is noncommunicative. At times, a teenager can be very difficult to talk with, especially when he merely answers your questions with "uh-huh," "huh-uh," and similar grunts.

These unpleasant times of communication usually occur from one of three causes.

- The first is regression in psychosexual age, to be discussed in chapter 6. The teenager is resolving conflicts which have occurred in the past.
- The second is when the drive for independence is especially strong and the teenager feels a need to separate from the parents.
- The third is when the teenager has had an unpleasant experience with peers and feels hurt.

These periods of sullenness, withdrawal, and quietness are also usually accompanied by resistance to love and affection from parents.

During these times, it is a mistake to force yourself on your teenager or prod him with questions. Often a parent will become irritated, worried, and even desperate, and try to open up conversation with persistent questions such as "How did your day go?"/"What happened to you today?"/"Did you have a good time?"/"Who was there?" This is irritating to anyone who is not in the mood to talk.

The secret is to *be available*. This means that instead of forcing interaction with your adolescent, you will be available at all times, so that he can communicate with you when he is comfortable in doing so.

As your child enters adolescence, he comes under increasing pressure from his drives for independence, sexual expressions, and peer acceptance. He must develop defenses against these pressures to prevent his being overwhelmed. Unfortunately, he occasionally uses rather primitive and unpleasant defenses such as retreating into states of withdrawal, noncommunication, and sullenness.

These primitive defenses cannot be penetrated or forced without damaging your relationship with the child. The only sensitive, sensible, and constructive way to manage these situations is to wait for the defenses to come down. You must *remain available* for your teenager to come to you when he is able.

However, there are definite things we can do to facilitate the lowering of these defenses, and we will discuss those later. But right now it is important to understand that attempting to batter down this extremely strong defense system is inadvisable.

A teenager's ability to use eye contact varies according to how strong this defense system is. When a child is young, he is receptive of eye contact almost continuously. But as he enters into adolescence, there are uneasy periods when he is resistant to eye contact.

Do not let your teenager's occasional tendency to avoid eye contact irritate you. Try simply to accept it, realizing if you remain available, he will come to you when his emotional tank is dry. At this time, he will be receptive of eye contact and will be communicative. It is important for his self-concept and psychological development for him to know that you will be available when he needs you.

Physical Contact

As a child becomes an adolescent, he needs continual reassurance from his parents that he is loved and accepted. The dilemma for many loving parents is their confusion as to how to meet this need.

Some parents attempt to do this by being overindulgent, providing their teens with things to keep up with their peers, like a car, stereo, or sporting equipment. These material things may be all right in themselves, but they are no substitute for what teenagers need most—unconditional love. Some parents use overindulgence by permitting, and many times even encouraging, their teenagers to go to places and do things which are not healthy for them. For example, I have known many parents who permit, and even encourage, their teens to go to parties which are designed to arouse sexual desires and where alcoholic beverages and other drugs are served. Few adolescents can handle temptations in these situations, but this type of pressure on our youth is growing. Yet few parents are helping their teenagers. Why? Because they have failed to make their teens feel that they are loved, accepted, and cared for.

Appropriate and consistent physical contact is a vital way to give your teenager that feeling and conviction that you truly care about him. This is especially true when your teenager is noncommunicative, sullen, moody, or resistant. During these times, eye contact may be difficult or even impossible. But physical contact can almost always be used effectively. Seldom does an adolescent respond negatively to a light, brief, touch on the shoulder, back, or arm. For example, suppose your teenager is just sitting in a chair watching TV. What a simple thing to briefly touch him on the shoulder as you walk by. Usually he will not even notice it, *but it registers* in his mind. You can use this vital information to give constant, consistent love by frequent, brief doses of physical contact. You can also use it by occasionally giving longer, more intense nurturance with more prolonged doses of physical contact.

Even when your teenager is in a noncommunicative mood, physical contact can be a means of conveying love to him. As long as your teenager's *focus of attention* is directed elsewhere, you are able to give prolonged physical contact *regardless* of the teenager's mood of receptiveness. For example, suppose your teenager is in an especially difficult state of mind that concerns you. You find an opportunity to talk with him about something which enables you to direct his attention *from himself*, to an object of interest, like pictures or photographs. You can really take advantage of such situations by putting your hand on his arm, shoulder, or back. You should know your teenager well enough to know how much physical contact he can accept at a particular time.

Sometimes your teenager will accept physical contact, but other times he may not be able to consciously tolerate your touch. At these times of nonacceptance, you can give physical contact when his attention is directed elsewhere so that he is *unaware* of the touch. Even when your teenager is not *consciously* aware of your physical contact, it registers. Its effect is to help him feel, "My mother and father love me and care for me, even during these times when relating to them is hard for me."

There are other ways to provide physical contact with a teenager. Frequently our 13-year-old David would strain or pull a muscle in a sport. He didn't hesitate to ask me to massage the muscle for him. I was very grateful to do so, because this gave me a wonderful opportunity to use physical contact.

Once our daughter Carey landed the wrong way on a trampoline and her neck muscles needed rubbing. This was another good opportunity for physical contact.

Fortunately, all our children liked to have their backs scratched. It was genuinely fun to scratch their backs. This has an amazing effect on a teen's psychological defenses and also helps tremendously in keeping their emotional tanks full. One summer when David came home from summer camp, what was the first thing he asked for? To have his back scratched, and to have his mother and me talk with him and read to him.

Although some parents are unwilling to provide emotional nurturance to their teenagers, especially with physical contact, I am very thankful that *most* parents love their young people enough to provide this for them. It is so simple to do, yet so wonderfully effective.

In certain situations, it is good to hug and kiss your teenager. Although you do not want to do it so often as to make him or her uncomfortable, there are times when it is appropriate: when departing or returning from a trip, or when the teenager does something of which *he* is especially proud—like winning an award. Or when your teenager comes to you feeling deeply hurt, remorseful, or otherwise troubled and seems to need it. And, of course, there are times when, for no discernible reason, your teenager simple feels a need for affection. If you are alert to provide it, what a special moment you will have with your child. *But* you must remain alert for such opportunities, because it is sometimes difficult to know when your teenager wants or needs affection.

Many times your teenager will be very subtle in *hinting* that he wants your attention or affection. He may approach you and talk about very superficial or meaningless topics. Usually, this is the key. At that moment, he seems so intense, serious, and persistent in mood, and very much out of context, considering the topic of conversation. At such a time, it is important to be patient. Your teenager is buying time in your presence until his psychological defenses have time to come down enough so that he can talk about important and meaningful things. Be careful not to be in a hurry and cut off the communication. Your teenager would naturally interpret this as rejection and your relationship with him might be harmed. If you are patient and give your teenager the time he needs, his superficial conversation will eventually give way to what he really wants to talk about. You must be an active listener, and this requires patience.

At family conferences, one of the most common questions parents ask me is this: "If I have given my teenager too little eye contact and physical contact, how can I make up for it?" This is a very good question. Such parents should not overwhelm their teenagers by suddenly giving large amounts of eye and physical contact. First, they need to obtain a baseline—a general idea of how much eye and physical contact their teenagers can accept. Starting from there, they will *gradually* increase contact over the next weeks and months. The less noticeable the increases are, the better, and the more comfortable the teenagers will be.

Someone has said, "Thank goodness adolescence is a time-limited disease." We parents need to hang in there during this period of difficult and intense change. The more we maintain our cool and self-control, the smoother and less traumatic the time will be. Our children will emerge from the teenage years more mature, and our relationships with them will be better when they reach adulthood.

When we remain available to give our teenagers the love they need whenever they can accept it, we are demonstrating the manner in which God relates to us. He is constantly available to nurture and help us, if we are truly members of His family, even when we are rejecting of Him. "If we are unfaithful to Him, He Himself will remain faithful" (2 Timothy 2:13).

Chapter 6

Parental Self-Control

Mr. and Mrs. Oliver looked at each other and shook their heads in puzzlement. Not ten minutes before, their sixteen-year-old daughter, Amy, was explaining precisely how she managed to land a much-sought-after position by impressing the employer with how mature she was. Now she was crying uncontrollably because her brother had used her shampoo.

Parents of teenagers know that adolescence is a tumultuous time in which the teenage child can swing from toddler to adult, from sweet to sour, from logical to irrational, and back again, all within the span of a day or an hour. These changes can be intense and frequent, and too few parents know exactly why they happen.

In the teenage years, young people are attempting to resolve all conflicts they have previously experienced in their lives, especially with their parents. Although teenagers are not conscious of this desire to resolve old conflicts, the drive within them to do so is so strong that it appears to others that the teenagers have chosen a deliberate course of action.

For this reason, an early adolescent between the ages of twelve and fifteen will evidence frequent and unexpected mood shifts. One minute he will seem to be very mature, and the next minute like a small child. Before he can comfortably and normally grow away from his parents and become responsibly independent, a teenager must clear his past, so to speak, of problems and conflicts he has had with people, and especially with his parents.

When our Carey was thirteen, I noticed one day that her attitude toward me was one of irritability and some hostility. I asked her, "Please tell me, Honey, have I done anything that has upset or hurt you?" Without hesitation she recounted an incident that occurred six years previously! We were riding in a station wagon; my wife and I were in the front seat, the other children in the middle seat, and Carey with a friend in the back seat. All of the kids were throwing popcorn at each other. Because it was distracting me as I was driving, I yelled for them to stop. Carey exclaimed that I had embarrassed her by "screaming at her friends." Yes, I remembered the incident but never guessed that it had affected her so deeply.

At that moment Carey had psychologically regressed to a seven-year-old in order to deal with that particular conflict. After she revealed this encounter to me (and I noted the anger in her voice), I told her that I honestly had not realized the embarrassment and pain I had caused her. When I told her I was sorry and asked her forgiveness, she was immediately relieved and became her thirteen-year-old self again.

This regression and advance in psychological age is one reason why early teenagers are so unpredictable and sometimes difficult to understand. Parents should react to them according to the age they are exhibiting at that time. For instance, let's say your early adolescent approaches you with a highly sophisticated statement such as, "Dad, what do you think of the Middle East crisis? I wonder if the displaced Palestinian Arab families should be entitled to return to their homes and be a normal part of the

Israeli nation." After a couple of gulps, you are able to communicate with him on that exact level and discuss the issue.

But that same teenager may be back thirty minutes later with what appears to be a two-year-old temper tantrum. What do you do? Right! Relate to him as would be appropriate with a two-year-old having a temper tantrum. As you can easily see, this takes real flexibility on your part to change your level of communication rapidly. This is why a good, flexible youth counselor, who is dealing with several early adolescents, can be utterly exhausted at the end of the day.

It is extremely important that you as a parent exhibit emotional self-control. Emotional overreaction will hurt your relationship with your teenager in several ways.

- Excessive and uncontrolled anger will make it difficult for your teenager to come to you when his emotional tank needs refilling.
- Emotional overreaction tends to cause your adolescent to respect you less—a very natural response to anyone who lacks self-control.
- Losing your cool tends to push your teen into the influence of others, especially peers.

Maintaining Self-Control
But how do you keep yourself in good condition emotionally? How do you maintain self-control? The most common problems which adversely affect an adult's ability to control anger are depression, fatigue, and anxiety. Most people are ineffective in preventing depression because they do not realize how closely it is related to how much time they spend with people and how much time they spend alone. In other words, time balance. Each person has a different need in this regard. Some require more time socially relating to people than others, while some require more time alone. Unfortunately, I cannot think of one person I have come across who was actually aware of this crucial fact. Most people follow this pattern: they find themselves spending more and more time with people, to the point of social saturation. They become more prone to depression because they are

emotionally drained and fatigued from the excessive social contact. Depression causes most people to withdraw and become seclusive. This, along with being tired of being around people, causes them to spend too much time alone. But then they feel lonely, yearn to be with people, seek them out, and the cycle starts again. This is one reason few people lead balanced, well-adjusted lives.

Of course, some unfortunate people do not have enough control over their lives to achieve this balance. They may be forced to spend too much time with people because they do not have the means to privacy. Others spend too much time alone, because they are old, ill, or do not have access to friends. Either way, depression is usually miserably present.

For the sake of your own mental health and for that of your teenager, you need to determine what percentage of your time should be spent with people and how much should be spent alone. This differs for every person and your own ratio can change with times and seasons and circumstances.

The quality of each kind of time is important also, especially the time alone, which should be emotionally refreshing. This may mean reading a good book, hiking, walking, exercising alone, praying, or meditating. Television seldom fills this need. In fact, TV seems to leave most people even more emotionally drained.

Emotional stability and self-control do not just happen. You must prepare yourself to cope with emotional strain and frustration. A normal teenager will bring forth both. To maintain a healthy relationship with your teenager and keep communication open, you need to be in good control of yourself, especially of your anger. Emotional overreaction is destructive if it happens too often and is not resolved. We all overreact at times, and if we don't do it too often, it is possible to produce a positive situation out of a negative one. This may involve apologizing to a son or daughter for overreacting and asking for forgiveness: "Honey, I'm sorry I overdid it and yelled yesterday. What you did was wrong, but I overreacted and should have handled it in a calmer way. Will you forgive me?" This approach not only prevents many disasters, but can actually strengthen and sweeten a parent-teenager relationship. However, if you overreact too often or in extreme ways, simply saying you're sorry and asking forgiveness will not work; it could even lower your teenager's opinion of you.

The more pleasant you are with your teenager, the firmer you can afford to be in setting limits and in discipline. Likewise, the more unpleasant you are with your teenager, the less firm you can afford to be. Why? First of all, as we have already stated, the more unpleasant you are, the less your teenager will respect you and the more he will be inclined to go against your wishes. Second, the more unpleasant you are, the more parental authority you have dissipated in ventilating your own anger and frustration. The more pleasant you are, the more parental authority you have saved to control your teenager's behavior. And this is what you want, good behavioral control! How can you really expect good self-control from your teenager if you do not have it yourself? Energy, preparation, self-discipline, and self-control are needed if you are going to be pleasant in the midst of unpleasant but normal adolescent strivings.

Anger is difficult to control if your *spiritual* life is not sound. An unhealthy spiritual life can cause depression and anxiety. It can also affect your thought control in such a way that you arrive at wrong decisions or conclusions—including your ideas regarding other people's motives. Any of these problems can make you lose spiritual perspective and can hinder your ability to control anger.

I believe a healthy spiritual life is one in which communication is open between you and God. How is this done? First, make sure you have a clean heart, by asking God to search your heart and convict you of any wrong He finds there. Next, confess these wrongs and obtain God's forgiveness and cleansing. This clears the channel of communication between you and God. Now you are ready to draw close to Him and He to you. God is then able to fill your emotional and spiritual tank. He does this by being with you, close to you, listening, guiding, comforting, and reassuring you with His promises and love.

It takes time to fellowship with God long enough to really know Him and long enough for Him to fill you and prepare you for your responsibilities as a parent.

I find it very difficult to spend time alone with God, without distractions. My time for emotional and spiritual refreshment with my Heavenly Father often happens after all the kids are in bed, usually between 9 and 9:30 at night. To escape distractions, I often take a walk or just sit outside, weather permitting, or in a quiet room. It usually takes ten to twenty minutes of solitude to feel close to God, to quiet my inner self after a typically hectic day. God doesn't hurry or rush. He is so calm and He continues to speak in a still, small voice.

Your ability to handle anger is influenced by many things, most of which have little or nothing to do with your teenager. One of these is your physical condition. Are you eating foods that will help you feel your best? I have seen many people who believe their diets are healthy, when in actuality they are not. Most authorities consider breakfast the most important meal of the day. What you eat for breakfast pretty well determines how you feel the rest of the day. Most people eat too much carbohydrate and not enough protein and bulk for breakfast. This usually produces a lack of energy later and induces them to seek stimulants such as coffee or soft drinks (many soft drinks have caffeine in them). Caffeine has differing effects on people, but none of them aid the emotional stability and calmness you need with your teenager. Therefore, a healthy, low carbohydrate breakfast with plenty of protein and bulk, and avoidance of caffeine is a good start in gaining self-control.

Many people feel that they are doing themselves a favor by skipping breakfast or even lunch. Skipping meals does not aid in weight reduction or promote a sense of well-being. For lunch, it is important not to eat too much carbohydrate and to avoid caffeine. An excessive carbohydrate diet will sap energy. Caffeine will increase irritability. It is amazing how much better I feel from lunch to supper on a green salad rather than a sandwich or hamburger.

Supper is the meal at which most people tend to overeat. This is one reason why a healthy breakfast and lunch are important. If your carbohydrate intake has been excessive or you have skipped breakfast or lunch, you may not be able to control your dietary intake later in the day, especially in the midst of depression or fear. And, of course, if you eat improperly at these times, you will not feel your best during the evening.

Employing a regular exercise program, a good diet, and recreation, and maintaining a healthy spiritual life can go a long way toward preventing depression. Unfortunately, not all depression can be prevented. Many people are biochemically or hereditarily prone to depression. If a person has done all in his power to prevent depression, yet becomes depressed, he should seek help—not only for his own sake, but also for the sake of his family. A moderately to severely depressed parent simply cannot handle a normal teenager well. The relationship between parent and child will suffer, and so will the teenager himself.

An Angry Father

Bob was a seventeen-year-old boy whom I saw because of drug usage, poor grades, and a defiant attitude. When I saw him alone, he was a calm polite boy, and exceptionally easy to communicate with. I felt he was truthful when he stated that he did not like his behavior and wanted to change. He said that he had been trying to make a change in his behavior. But after bouts of fighting and arguing with his father—which were daily occurrences—he would become so angry that all he could think of was getting back by doing the very things his father (and Bob) did not like. Of course, I wanted to check out Bob's perceptions and see if they were accurate. So I asked Bob's parents to join us.

Bob's father was an extraordinarily angry man. He immediately made a grossly hostile remark about Bob's "terrible and unacceptable behavior." His anger and the ferocity of his remarks continued and even increased. Bob made no response, but deep, painful anger was obviously welling up inside him. Finally, Bob's mother tried to intervene by telling the father that Bob's behavior had been good recently and that she could not understand why he was so angry. Also, I noticed that the behavior about which the father was complaining did not justify such vehement condemnation. The father not only ignored the mother's pleas but used Bob's behavior as an excuse to rid himself of excessive anger. When I talked with the father alone, I learned the real cause of his frustration. He was having severe problems at work, was extremely depressed, could not sleep well, could hardly eat, tired easily, and felt life was not worth living. Bob was the only "safe" place to ventilate his misery. I don't know which one made my heart ache most—Bob, his mother, or his father.

It is a common thing for teenagers to be receptacles of parents' displaced anger. Teenagers often tend to put pressure on us, make us tense, upset, and angry. Therefore it sometimes seems justifiable to dump all accumulated anger on them. This is so dangerous! Excessive and overreactive anger is an enemy of parents seeking to relate to their teenagers. Nothing else cuts off parent-adolescent communication the way poorly controlled anger does.

Most parents seem to assume that their teenagers do not need their love and affection as they did as small children. This is simply not true. Teenagers continue to need love, affection, assurance, and care as never before, even though in their biological drive for independence, they may sometimes act as though they don't.

I made that mistake with Carey. Her eighteenth birthday and graduation from high school occurred at about the same time. In my mind I unconsciously graduated her from being my child to an independent adult. Fortunately, my wife, Pat, noticed the effect of this. I was not as loving or caring with Carey as before; this hurt her because she felt that she had done something wrong. Pat told me about this and, thank goodness, I was able to again relate to her as a daughter—as my child.

We never really grow out of the need to be loved and cared for. These needs may be gradually taken over by other people in adult life. But during the years when our children are dependent on us, we parents must always stand available and ready to love and nourish them whenever we're needed, especially during the teenage years.

Chapter 7

Teenage Anger

Many parents assume that anger in a teenager is bad or abnormal, and that expression of it should be suppressed or not allowed. This is a dangerous error. We are instructed in Scripture to "train up a child in the way he should go," to educate him "according to his life requirements" (Proverbs 22:6, KJV and MLB). One of the most important areas in which a teenager needs training is in how to handle anger.

The feeling of anger is not bad or good in itself. Anger is normal and occurs in every human being. The problem is not the anger itself but in managing it. This is where most people have problems. I believe it is *imperative* to understand the different ways to handle anger and know which ways are best.

Passive-Aggressive Behavior

Let's start with what I consider the absolutely worst way to handle anger—*passive-aggressive behavior*. This is a professional term you should add to your vocabulary. Passive-aggressive behavior is the opposite of an open, honest, direct, and verbal expression of anger. Passive-aggressive behavior is an expression of anger that gets back at a person indirectly. Mild examples of this are procrastination, dawdling, stubbornness, intentional inefficiency, and "forgetfulness." The subconscious purpose of passive-aggressive behavior on the part of a child is to *upset* the parents or parent figures and make them angry. Passive-aggressive behavior is a *refusal to take responsibility for one's own behavior.*

Passive-aggressive techniques of handling anger are indirect, cunning, self-defeating, and destructive. Unfortunately, passive-aggressive behavior is subconsciously motivated; that is, the child is not consciously aware that he is using this resistant, obstructive behavior to release his pent-up anger to upset his parents.

Passive-aggressive behavior causes most problems with today's teenagers, from poor grades to drugs on to suicide. However, since, of course, there are other causes of adolescent problems, it is important to be able to clearly identify PA behavior when it occurs. It is usually handled quite differently from other types of teenage misbehavior.

First of all, consider the fact that passive-aggressive behavior is irrational—it does not make logical sense. A good example of this is a student who is really capable of good grades, wants to make good grades, tries to make good grades but makes poor grades. It makes no logical sense.

Second, you can begin to label it passive-aggressive behavior when nothing works no matter what the authority figure does. This is because the underlying, subconscious motive is to upset the parent or other authority figure. In the example of the student who should make good grades but doesn't, no matter what the parent and teacher do to help the ailing student, nothing works; a change of curriculum or even a tutor doesn't result in better grades. Since the real motivation is to upset the parent or teacher, subconsciously the student will make sure nothing works no matter what steps are taken.

It is so important to identify passive-aggressive behavior. For example, the PA student who could make good grades but doesn't, affects his or her own future. Tragically, if a teenager does not learn to handle anger maturely and grow out of the PA stage by the age of sixteen or seventeen, this PA trait will harden and become a permanent part of his or her personality for life. He or she will use PA behavior toward future professors, employers, spouses, children, and so on. This will lead to serious problems for the individual to cope with everyday life and result in endless misery for those associated with him or her.

Because few people have been properly trained in handling anger, most of us handle anger with about the same maturity as we did in adolescence and thus we suffer from our own PA traits, of which we are mostly unaware. We could use help in this area ourselves, right? Ask your spouse or best friend.

One of the earliest ways a child can show passive-aggressive tendencies is by soiling his pants, after he has been toilet-trained. In many such cases, the parents have prohibited the child from expressing any anger, especially verbally. Then, if the parents have overreacted by becoming excessively angry or even punishing him whenever he expresses his anger openly, what can the child do with his normally occurring anger?

A child in this situation may use passive-aggressive behavior to get back at the parents in ways which will upset them, like soiling his pants—a very effective but unhealthy way to express anger. You know that there's little the parents can do in such a situation. Because they have refused to permit the child to openly and directly express anger, the child has been forced to use an indirect, harmful way to do it, and the parents have backed themselves into a corner. The more the parents punish the child, the more he will soil his pants. Why? Because the subconscious purpose of passive-aggressive behavior is to *upset* the parents. What a dilemma! God pity both the parent and child in such a situation.

Many older children who use passive-aggressive means to express anger do very poor work in school. Their attitude is, "You can lead a horse to water, but you can't make him drink. You can make me go to school, but you can't make me get good grades." The children's anger is in control, and the parents are utterly helpless. The more the parents become upset—the subconscious purpose of all this—the worse the situation becomes.

It is important to know that the passive-aggressive child does not do these things consciously or purposefully. They are part of an unconscious process of which he is not aware, and into which he has been forced by his parents.

Passive-aggressive behavior in younger children is bad enough, but passive-aggressive behavior in teenagers can be utterly disastrous. I have seen this unhealthy way of handling anger cause teenagers to run the gamut—from making poor grades to using drugs, becoming pregnant, committing crimes, and attempting suicide. There are, of course, other causes for these types of behavior. The passive-aggressive tendency, however, is a most serious cause that is on the increase among teenagers.

I have seen many teenagers who do poorly in school because their parents have made themselves unapproachable—either by their own emotional overreaction or by being intolerant in not allowing their teenagers to express negative or unpleasant feelings. I have seen teenagers who break parental rules, including coming in habitually late, not because of a normal drive for independence, but as a way to upset their parents and express their anger indirectly. I have seen girls who got pregnant as an act of anger toward parents because they were never allowed to express unpleasant feelings, especially anger. I have seen teenagers who developed antisocial and antiauthority attitudes as a means to express anger.

More complexly, I have seen teenagers turn their unresolved anger onto themselves to cause psychosomatic problems such as headaches, ulcers, and skin problems. And most tragically, I have seen this passive-aggressive behavior so ingrained in teenagers that it becomes their primary way of handling any anger-provoking situation which may confront them, even to the point of committing suicide as a means to indirectly express anger.

Some time ago I saw a sixteen-year-old girl whose parents mistakenly thought they were raising their daughter correctly by refusing to allow her to express any unpleasant feelings, especially anger. They thought they would teach her to be a happy person by learning to express only pleasant feelings. She learned to avoid open expression of her anger to the source of her frustration; she would habitually express her anger in ways which would indirectly hurt the person who caused her anger. This became such a habit that most of her behavior was understandable only by knowing that she was trying to hurt someone indirectly. What finally brought her to seek help was her sixth suicide attempt. Each of the attempts was planned to make a particular person feel guilty, upset, and hurt. The first five attempts were half-hearted and no great threat to her life. However, the sixth resulted in her being in a coma and near death for several days. As I talked with her after she recovered, I saw that her conduct definitely puzzled her. She did not understand that her behavior was a long-established pattern of expressing anger in unhealthy, self-defeating, destructive, indirect, and displaced ways.

Passive-aggressive behavior is common. Why? Because most people do not understand anger or know what to do with it. They feel that anger is somehow wrong or sinful and should be "disciplined" out of a child. This is a serious misunderstanding, because the feeling of anger is normal and has been experienced by everyone since Adam and Eve. If when your teenager becomes angry and you yell at him: "Stop that kind of talk. I will not allow it!" what can he do? Only two things—he can disobey you and continue to "talk that way," or obey you and "stop talking that way." If he chooses the latter and ceases to express his anger, the anger will not go away. He will simply suppress the anger into his subconscious, where it will remain unresolved, waiting to be expressed later through inappropriate and/or passive-aggressive behavior.

Another mistake some parents make, related to expression of anger, is the inappropriate use of humor. Whenever a situation becomes tense, especially if someone is becoming angry, many parents will interject humor to relieve the tension. Of course, humor is a wonderful asset in any family. But where it is consistently used to escape the appropriate handling of anger, teenagers simply cannot learn how to appropriately deal with it.

I once visited a home where the father of the family had an

uncommonly humorous wit. Whenever his wife or one of his teenagers began expressing an unpleasant feeling, he would come up with an hilarious statement. Consequently, none of the teenagers in that family could deal with anger and resorted to passive-aggressive means of expressing it indirectly. Whenever the boy would experience frustration or anger-provoking situations, he would have severe headaches. The girl manifested her anger indirectly by voluntarily helping her mother with housework, but doing such a poor job that she often caused the mother more work than if she had not helped at all.

Passive-aggressive behavior easily becomes an ingrained, habitual pattern which can last a lifetime. If a teenager avoids honestly and openly dealing with anger in an appropriate manner, he may use passive-aggressive techniques in every relationship. This can affect his relationships later with spouse, children, work associates, and friends. What a tragedy! And most of these unfortunate people are not fully aware of their self-defeating patterns of behavior or their problems with handling anger.

Incidentally, one of the most common and dangerous types of passive-aggressiveness is seen in driving habits. Have you ever noticed how some people speed up when you try to pass them? Or the driver on the highway who passes you and then darts in front of you, forcing you to use your brakes to avoid running into him? These may be blatant examples of passive-aggressive behavior. Needless to say, it is difficult to appreciate a passive-aggressive person.

This brings to mind a thirty-nine-year old woman named Margaret. She was born and reared in a Christian home. Unfortunately, her parents believed that a child should not be permitted to express anger. So she never learned how to properly handle or resolve it. Consequently, she developed into an individual whose overall behavior pattern was designed to upset her parents. Her whole life was aimed at doing the exact opposite of what her parents would want. Her behavior patterns are unconscious, or out of her awareness. Consciously, she thinks of herself as a well-meaning Christian who earnestly desires to live a proper lifestyle. However, she has had one affair after another with married men. She has been indicted for embezzlement and fraud. Margaret is an enigma to herself. Until therapy, she could not understand why her lifestyle and behavioral patterns were entirely inconsistent with her basic beliefs. Hers was a wasted life of self-abasement and self-destruction, because her primary purpose in living is to behave in ways which are just the opposite of what her parents would want her to be. Tragic!

Passive-aggressive behavior is absolutely the worst way to express anger for several reasons:

● It can easily become an ingrained tenacious pattern of behavior which will last a lifetime.

● It can distort a person's personality and make him a quite disagreeable person.

● It can interfere in all the teenager's future relationships.

● It is one of the most difficult behavioral disorders to treat.

Scripture instructs us to train a child in the way he should go. Forcing a child to suppress the anger and not deal with it properly is training him in the way he should *not* go. It is crucial to train a child in the proper way to handle anger. This is done by teaching him to resolve the anger, not to suppress it.

The Anger Ladder

There are many more ways to express anger than in a passive-aggressive manner. The more immature a person is, the more immaturely he will express his anger. The more mature he is, the more maturely he will express his anger. Handling anger appropriately and maturely is one of the most difficult lessons in becoming a mature person, one that many adults never learn.

Children will tend to express anger immaturely, until *trained* to do otherwise. A teenager cannot be expected to *automatically* express his anger in the best, most mature way. But this is what parents are expecting, when they simply tell their teen not to get mad. Parents must train teenagers to take one step at a time in learning to deal with anger.

The Anger Ladder is designed to illustrate the different steps or levels of maturity in expressing anger, and to help parents see that a teenager must be trained to progress from one rung or level of maturity to the next, as he expresses his anger more and more appropriately.

1. As discussed, passive-aggressive behavior is the worst way to express anger. (In some cases sociopathy, including deliberate homicide, may be worse; but this is rare in early adolescence, totally abnormal, and beyond the scope of this chapter.)

2. A slightly better way to express anger is to be utterly *out of control behaviorally* in such a way that the person is in a fit of rage, actually destroys property, and/or is violent toward another person. As bad as this may sound, passive-aggressive behavior is worse. Why? Because rageous behavior is much easier to deal with, correct, and prevent than passive-aggressive behavior.

3. A somewhat better way to express anger is to be in a *fit of rage*, but maintaining enough self-control to prevent property destruction and personal violence. The outburst is confined to yelling, screaming, or cursing in such a way as to verbally hurt someone, perhaps with name-calling or accusatory remarks. The anger is expressed not only at the person with whom we are angry, but at anyone who happens to be in the vicinity. As poor and immature as these methods are in expressing anger, they are far better than passive-aggressive behavior or other ways of displaying anger behaviorally.

4. The next better way to handle anger is uncontrollably ventilating it *verbally* but without seeking to hurt anyone verbally, as with name-calling or criticizing. In this situation the anger is directed not only toward the source of the anger but toward anyone who happens to be around. As primitive and poor as this method is, it is better than any yet mentioned.

5. A somewhat better way to handle anger is to ventilate it unpleasantly, perhaps by yelling and screaming, but confining the remarks to the provoking issue, and, if possible, toward the person provoking the anger. Of course, whether expressing the anger toward the person who has angered the teenager is appropriate or not depends on the particular situation.

6. The best way to express anger is to do it as pleasantly and rationally as possible, and toward the person one is angry at. You hope that the person receiving the anger will respond in an equally mature way, attempt to understand the other's position, and that the two can resolve the issue. Resolving the issue means for both parties to rationally and logically examine the

issue, discuss it, understand it from both points of view, and to come to an agreement on what to do about it. This takes a great deal of maturity on both sides. Few people ever come to this point of maturity in their lives.

I have found that describing the different levels of maturity in expressing anger becomes very complex and difficult to understand. To simplify it as much as possible and yet give you a workable knowledge of it, I have created an Anger Ladder.

The list of fifteen ways of behaving while angry are combined in various arrangements on the Anger Ladder. Notice that most expressions of anger are primarily negative. On the ladder, only the top two rungs are totally positive.

1. Pleasant behavior
2. Seeking resolution
3. Focusing anger on source only
4. Holding to the primary complaint
5. Thinking logically and constructively
6. Unpleasant and loud behavior
7. Cursing
8. Displacing anger to sources other than the original
9. Expressing unrelated complaints
10. Throwing objects
11. Destroying property
12. Verbal abuse
13. Emotionally destructive behavior
14. Physical abuse
15. Passive-aggressive behavior

Each rung on the Anger Ladder represents a progressively better way to express anger. You want to train your teenager to take one step at a time, to go up one rung at a time. How do you do this?

As parents, you should be good examples in the proper expression of anger. Also, you can expect your teenager to become angry at times. Instead of forbidding him to become angry or overreacting to his anger, you need to meet him where he is in his handling of anger and train him from there. For example,

POSITIVE

1. PLEASANT • SEEKING RESOLUTION • FOCUSING ANGER ON SOURCE • HOLDING TO PRIMARY COMPLAINT • THINKING LOGICALLY

2. PLEASANT • FOCUSING ANGER ON SOURCE • HOLDING TO PRIMARY COMPLAINT • THINKING LOGICALLY

POSITIVE AND NEGATIVE

3. FOCUSING ANGER ON SOURCE • HOLDING TO PRIMARY COMPLAINT • THINKING LOGICALLY • unpleasant, loud

4. HOLDING TO PRIMARY COMPLAINT • THINKING LOGICALLY • unpleasant, loud • displacing anger to other sources

5. FOCUSING ANGER ON SOURCE • HOLDING TO PRIMARY COMPLAINT • THINKING LOGICALLY • unpleasant, loud • verbal abuse

6. THINKING LOGICALLY • unpleasant, loud • displacing anger to other sources • expressing unrelated complaints

PRIMARILY NEGATIVE

7. unpleasant, loud • displacing anger to other sources • expressing unrelated complaints • emotionally destructive behavior

8. unpleasant, loud • displacing anger to other sources • expressing unrelated complaints • verbal abuse • emotionally destructive behavior

9. unpleasant, loud • cursing • displacing anger to other sources • expressing unrelated complaints • verbal abuse • emotionally destructive behavior

10. FOCUSING ANGER ON SOURCE • unpleasant, loud • cursing • displacing anger to other sources • throwing objects • emotionally destructive behavior

11. unpleasant, loud • cursing • displacing anger to other sources • throwing objects • emotionally destructive behavior

NEGATIVE

12. FOCUSING ANGER ON SOURCE • unpleasant, loud • cursing • destroying property • verbal abuse • emotionally destructive behavior

13. unpleasant, loud • cursing • displacing anger to other sources • destroying property • verbal abuse • emotionally destructive behavior

14. unpleasant, loud • cursing • displacing anger to other sources • destroying property • verbal abuse • physical abuse • emotionally destructive behavior

15. passive-aggressive behavior

one teenager handles anger at the level of rung 6 on the Anger Ladder. That is, he is unpleasant about it, expresses it at inappropriate people (for example, at his little brother instead of at the person who angered him), he sticks to the primary complaint only (that is, only what is bothering him), and he is logical and constructive (he is trying to make things better, not worse).

You then determine what improvement you want for your teenager. In this example, you want him to learn to direct his anger toward the appropriate person and *not* take it out on his younger brother.

To train him, you should find a time soon after you both have calmed down and the atmosphere is pleasant. At this best of possible moments, compliment and praise your teenager in the areas of expressing his anger which he did *correctly*. *Then* ask your teenager to correct that one selected aspect which you want changed—in this case, taking his anger out on his younger brother.

We all must develop our own ways of training our teenagers in handling anger maturely. Consider ways I eventually found worked best for me. When one of my teenagers verbalized his/her anger and I saw something which needed correcting, I would, as soon as possible, find a time when we were both calm and relaxed. First, I let my teenager know that his/her bringing the anger to me verbally was fine so the teen wouldn't feel he/she had done something wrong and would be reluctant to verbalize anger again. I would say something like, "I'm glad you brought your anger to me. When you are happy, your mother and I want to know when you're happy. When you're sad, we want to know that. And when you are angry, we want to know you're angry."

Second, I sought to reinforce appropriate ways my teenagers expressed anger and praise him/her for it. Remember, when a teenager is expressing anger *verbally*, there are a lot of things he/she is doing *right*. I would then say something like this: "I'm proud of the way you handled your anger. You didn't take it out on your little brother or your dog, or throw anything, or bring up unrelated facts. You clearly told me what was on your mind regarding this problem. That's good."

Now I was ready to help my teenager take the next step up the anger ladder. Please remember, this is a five- or six-year project, and a teen can take only one step at a time. So I would determine what step I would like him or her to take next, and I would *ask* the teenager, not *tell*. For example, I would say something like, "The only thing you did wrong, Son, was to call me that name. When you're angry, please just call me 'Dad.' " Parent, this is critical. I couldn't automatically expect that the very next time my teenager verbalized anger, he or she would have made that step. It may have taken several times. Remember, maturation is slow, gradual, and difficult, and often painful. But eventually your teenager will emerge (hopefully at sixteen or seventeen) a responsible, cooperative, mature person. "No pain, no gain."

This reminds me of a saying by Mark Twain, if I may paraphrase it: "When I was fifteen years old, my father was the most ignorant person I knew. It was amazing how much he learned in the next five years." Folks, that is adolescence!

Let me clarify one point of possible confusion. It is in *verbal* expression of anger that you need to train your teenager, so that he learns to handle it better. I am not encouraging permissiveness in behavior. You must remain firm in not allowing your teenager to behave inappropriately. Limit-setting regarding behavior must be firm and consistent. This distinction between verbal and behavioral expressions of anger is critical.

David

Like most people, I have my moments when anger is a problem for me — anger within me and anger in others. However, here is one experience which I believe I handled correctly. And, best of all, I gained tremendous insight into the whole area of a child's anger. Our son David was overloaded with homework one day when he was thirteen. He arrived home at about 3:30 that afternoon, and except for ten minutes for supper, was still working on academics at 11:30 that night. He also had a book report due in a few days. At 11:30 I said, "David, I don't care how much homework you still have to do, you need your sleep and I want you in bed now."

He replied, "Please give me five more minutes, Dad; I'm almost finished."

I said, "OK, five more minutes and that's it."

I then returned to my bedroom with my wife. In a few minutes, David came into the room with a book in his hand, walked up to his mother, and said, "Mom, I think I'll use this book for my book report."

His mother looked at the book and replied, "No, David, you can't use that book because it's the same one you used last year."

David said, "I know, but I can make another book report on it and won't have to read a new book."

"I'm sorry, David," his mother replied, "that wouldn't be right. You have to read another book."

David became angry and answered his mother rudely. "OK, I'll read it. Just help me find another book and I'll read it. OK, I'll read another book!"

My first reaction was a typical one toward a child who was verbally ventilating anger in an unpleasant, loud way—I felt the anger rising within me. My first thought was, *How dare he talk to his mother that way! I'll show him that he can't get away with being nasty like that.*

But fortunately, I remembered a previous event. Three days before, I became so infuriated at a man (and at church, mind you!) that I called him a liar. Who handled his anger better? David or I? Then I realized that David had managed his anger better than I had and that he was on rung 3 on the Anger Ladder. I was near rung 5. He directed his anger at its source— his mother. He didn't take it out on his little brother, kick his dog, destroy property, attempt to hurt his mother with names or criticism, or use passive-aggressive behavior. He didn't bring up unpleasant subjects or previous grievances. He simply stated that he would read another book. Who can improve on that? The only thing David did wrong was to speak loudly to his mother. Not many people, mature adults included, can beat that.

Now what would have happened if I had lit into David and punished him? I'll tell you. Because he was on rung 3 of the

Anger Ladder, the *next* time he got angry, he would have been forced to use a more immature way of expressing his anger at a lower level on the Anger Ladder.

Then what should I do? The best thing for me to do at that time was to not respond. Not responding does *not* mean condoning. By the look on my face and on his mother's face, he knew we didn't like what he was doing. *By not responding* we were telling David, "We don't like what you are doing, but if you choose to do so, go ahead. It is not bad enough to stop, but we don't like it."

After we all calmed down, David went to bed. During our usual nighttime ritual (here's a good example where nighttime rituals pay off), and after we had prayed together, I said to David, "I was very proud of the way you handled your anger tonight. You didn't take it out on your brother or the dog. You didn't throw anything or sulk, or say anything wrong. You spoke directly to your mother without trying to hurt her with names or criticism. You simply said you would read another book. That's great. The only thing you did wrong was to yell at your mother." The effect was great. David felt relieved that I wasn't angry with him but also felt very bad about yelling at his mother. The next day he apologized to her.

Train Your Teenager

When your teenager expresses anger directly by verbal means, be glad. The more he uses verbalizations to express his anger, the better it is. Then determine where your teen is functioning on the Anger Ladder. Determine in what ways he is expressing anger appropriately and in what ways he is being inappropriate.

It is easy to confuse the verbal expression of anger with disrespect. A stumbling block for most parents. To cope with this dilemma, ask yourself, "What is my teenager's attitude toward me the majority of the time? Is it respectful or disrespectful?" In the vast majority of our teenagers, the answer is *respectful*. Most teenagers have a basic, respectful attitude toward their parents. If this is the case with your teenager, please relax on this issue and realize that when he/she verbalizes anger—especially anger about a particular item—this is what you want. Then you will be able to train your teenager to mature in this area and be able to handle anger maturely. On the other hand, if your teenager has a disrespectful attitude toward you most of the time, this is a different issue altogether. This means there is a serious problem in your relationship with your teen, and I advise you to get professional help as soon as possible.

Another way to consider this is to look at the teenager who for some reason is unable to express his/her anger verbally. This makes it difficult and sometimes impossible to train this teen in becoming mature in handling anger. In fact, one of the first problems is enabling this type of teenager to express anger verbally. This is extremely difficult. So do you see, dear parent, why we should be glad when our teenager has the ability to express anger verbally; then we can train him/her to maturity.

You want to *train* your teen in the way he should go. First, praise him for appropriate ways in which he is expressing anger. Then you can talk to him about *one of the inappropriate ways* he is using anger (like name-calling), asking him to correct it. You want to choose the best possible moment; then talk with your teenager about correcting one item at a time. You are *training* your child to gradually go up the Anger Ladder *one rung at a time.*

A certain amount of passive-aggressive behavior is normal in early adolescence—as long as this behavior does not bring harm to anyone, including the teenager or family members. Normal adolescent PA behavior usually starts gradually around the age of eleven. Remember that we want the teen to be out of this PA stage around sixteen or seventeen. Therefore, it becomes obvious that this is not a short-term project. We're talking in the range of at least five or six years. This is important to realize because we must be patient and expect slow, gradual improvement—about three steps forward, two steps back progress. This is because the handling of anger is a maturational process, and we all mature very slowly. So please, don't be impatient with your teenager's progress or you will become quite frustrated with your teen, and unwittingly destroy the whole process. Be patient!

Most parents expect their children to handle anger maturely, at the highest rung, *with no training*. This is like saying to a tennis student before his first lesson, "I believe you should be about ready for Wimbledon by now."

In some cases, it is impossible to resolve anger, as for example, when the person provoking the anger is inaccessible. At these times, the teenager must learn other appropriate ways to ventilate the anger, such as exercise, talking it over with a mature person, using diversion such as an enjoyable activity, or spending time alone in a relaxed manner.

Another way to train a teenager in handling his own anger is to teach the art of preventing certain types of anger *cognitively*. This means using active intellectual reasoning to reduce the anger. For example, I saw a wonderful change in David's ability to control anger in his early teens. Instead of strictly reacting emotionally, he learned to use his thought processes more.

In his early teens, David would occasionally lose his temper when playing baseball if another player did something which was obviously wrong, especially if it resulted in physical pain to David. But one summer evening I noticed a degree of progress. In a Little League game, David was running to home plate when the catcher caught the throw from the outfield. He was ready to tag David out when David suddenly surprised the catcher by jumping over his glove. Unfortunately in doing this, he also jumped over home plate. He was on his stomach reaching back to touch the plate when the catcher, infuriated at being tricked, hit David in the face while tagging him. I was stunned and was afraid that David, being the larger boy, would overreact with violence. Much to my relief and amazement, he just dusted himself off and calmly walked to the dugout. David had learned to intellectually nip the anger in the bud by realizing that this particular player had difficulty handling anger and would express it inappropriately. In short, David knew that the catcher did not have anything against him personally and had acted this way because of his own problems with behavior.

Most adults handle their strong anger in inappropriate ways. They may lose control of themselves and ventilate their anger toward the wrong person. They may hurt the persons at whom they are angry behind their backs, by using passive-aggressive behavior in some indirect and immature way. Why? Because no one trained them in the better ways to handle anger. Who failed to train them? Their parents.

However, at this point we must be aware that some children are more naturally prone to have difficulties handling anger than others — regardless of the type of parenting they have had. For example, young children and teenagers with certain neurological problems are especially prone to handling anger in passive-aggressive ways. This is especially true and quite frequent if there is a history of perceptual or learning problems. These children and teenagers (and later adults) tend to have problems with passive-aggressive behavior and depression.

You see immature ways of handling anger every day. You see a wife and husband yelling, screaming, and cursing at each other. You see the wife or husband having an affair to get back at the other. You see an employee doing poor work to under-mine the employer's interests. You see a principal abusing a teacher. You see a teacher subtly working against a principal. You see special interest groups attempting to materially hurt others. Immature handling of anger is on every hand. It is one of the greatest problems in business today, resulting in poor attitudes in employer and employee alike. Sixty to eighty percent of problems in any organization are personnel related, because so few people learned how to deal with anger maturely. Most are very good at hiding it superficially, when dealing face to face with others; but out it comes later, in inappropriate ways.

One of the most important things to understand about anger, whether we are dealing with employees, unions, government, or teenagers, is that it is bound to occur. It can result from any human interaction. The next important fact is that it will tend to build up and become more and more difficult to control, even explosive, if not dealt with. And the more difficult it is to control, the more destructive it may become. Therefore, we must find ways to either "nip it in the bud" if the anger is based on misunderstanding, or to see that the anger is ventilated slowly and then resolved, if it is justified. Such control does not come naturally to anyone. The maturity that comes with managing anger appropriately must be learned, through much time and practice.

Chapter 8

From Parent Control to Self-Control

A s a child moves into the teenage years, discipline and training need to gradually change from a parent-control basis to a parent-trust basis, in which privileges and freedom depend on trustworthiness. When a child is young and has little judgment to exercise in his actions, the parents take almost all the responsibility in determining his behavior. As the child becomes a preadolescent and experiences the drive of independence, he will attempt to exert more and more control and decision-making regarding his actions. Parents should work to make this transition as smooth and nontraumatic as possible.

To accomplish this, you must first accept the fact that this drive for independence is normal. Eventually, your child should become quite independent of you, whether you like it or not. What you want to be able to do is to control the rate of this gain of independence, gauging it on your teen's rate of maturity. The best indicator you have in doing this is the degree to which you can trust your youngster and his ability to control his behavior.

Your teen will likely test your limits of control as well as your love for him. So, naturally, your great concern is where to set the limits. Should you make them fair, broad, and reasonable? Or should you be very strict? It is important to remember that a normal teenager will test—and sometimes even break—limits or rules, regardless of where they are placed. If you make the rules extremely restrictive, your teenager will surely test them, and usually break them. If you make them broad, your teenager will again find some way to challenge them or break them. Common sense, then, indicates that since it is in the makeup of most teenagers to challenge and/or break rules, no matter how strict or broad they are, the sensible thing is to make rules *initially* quite strict and restrictive. Then, as the maturing child demonstrates that he can be trusted to behave appropriately, you can gradually allow him increased privileges with less and less parental control. In other words, his privileges will be contingent upon his showing you that he is trustworthy. As your teenager proves to be more trustworthy, you trust him more. As he demonstrates appropriate behavior, you increase his privileges. But in order to do this, you must begin from a restrictive position.

There are many advantages to using this approach. First, it is wise to be in the position of being able to allow more privileges and not fewer. Your relationship with your teenager is better when you are able to be positive; it is less comfortable when you must be negative. When your teen is just beginning his adolescent career, especially his social life, if you begin by being somewhat overrestrictive, then you can afford to be positive and grant privileges—you can be the "good guy." However, if you begin by being "broadminded, reasonable, understanding," allowing your budding teenager too many privileges and too few restrictions, you have only one way to go—toward increased restrictiveness or being the "bad guy." Also, if your limits are too broad and lenient, and your teenager breaks them, he will be much more likely to bring harm or disgrace on himself and the family.

I can't overemphasize how important it is to set up the rules that allow you to be as positive as possible. Begin in an overrestrictive way so that you may be able to grant more and more privileges. If you give all the privileges initially, you have nothing to work with. You have no way to reward your teen for taking increased responsibility. And, worse, you have no means to train him to be trustworthy and learn the value of being responsible.

Your goal in moving from restrictiveness to privilege is that your teenager will act as a responsible, trustworthy, independent adult by the age of eighteen.

This is not easy, for it takes courage and determination to make your teenager's privileges strictly dependent upon his ability to control his own behavior. It takes strength for you to stand against the pressure for unearned concessions, not only from your teenager, but from other teenagers, other parents, and even society.

But mark this: all teenagers at some level of consciousness realize they need guidance and control from their parents. They *want* it. I have heard numerous teenagers say that their parents do not love them because they are not strict or firm enough. And so many teenagers express their thankfulness and love to parents who showed their care and concern by their guidance and control.

Experiencing Consequences

Another factor to consider is that in order for your teenager to continue to develop a normal conscience and learn to behave responsibly as an adult, he must experience *consequences* for his behavior—positive consequences for appropriate, responsible behavior; and negative consequences for inappropriate, irresponsible behavior. These consequences must be consistent and fair, and based on behavior—not on how you are feeling at the time. Again, we're back to facing the importance of parental self-control and making decisions based on clear, logical thinking rather than on our impulsive feelings.

How do you accomplish this?

I believe that a rule or decision deserves a reason. A teenager is entitled to know why. And parents must be careful to be sure that the reason is practical and not simply moralistic. Of course, there may be moralistic reasons behind the rule, but there must also be a practical reason. Teenagers in early adolescence are in the midst of questioning their parents' rules and values. And these early teens relate much better to practical rules than to moralistic ones. One reason so many teenagers turn against spiritual values is that they are given too many moralistic reasons for rules and/or restrictions. During these rebellious, defiant, possibly hostile periods, parents are wise to give practical reasons for decisions. Once a reason is given, however, you certainly are not required to defend it like a doctoral thesis. Arguing with your teenager over the adequacy or legitimacy of the reason is seldom warranted. As long as the answer is reasonable, stating it simply is generally sufficient. Being willing to argue about it usually invites further disagreement and anger.

When our Carey wanted to date at age twelve, we told her that she could not date until she was ready—which we estimated to be in about four years. We left plenty of room for error. Remember, it is far better to be able to become less restrictive than to be forced to become more restrictive.

Carey asked, "Why not?" We explained to her that in this world it is extremely important to be able to function well in groups, and that the age when we learn to operate effectually in groups is early adolescence. There are many adults who never learned to function in groups when they were twelve to fourteen years old and who consequently are "social misfits." Then I dramatically exclaimed, "And no daughter of mine is going to be a social misfit!" We told her that when she learned to function well in groups, then we would talk about other social privileges.

This worked for about a year. Then Carey came to her mother and me and stated she had learned to operate in groups. We told her she had indeed made good progress, but that being able to function in groups was not simply getting along with everyone. It also meant offering a positive, constructive contribution to the group. It was not merely to be influenced by the group, but to have an influence on the group. We pointed out that she was making excellent progress, but that she was not yet a leader—that the other kids had more influence on her than she did on them. I'm happy to say that Carey increased her group leadership abilities and learned to have a warm, wholesome, gentle, but strong influence not only in her church group but in her school and other organizations.

Protecting Your Teenager

Parents of teenagers need to be in good communication with parents of other teenagers—on a first-name basis, if you will, and especially with the parents of the teenagers who are closest to their own teen. It is a priceless asset to be able to share information and concerns with other parents and to work together with them in providing direction and control for the young people.

I can think of many occasions when Carey would be invited to a social event which we knew nothing about. How grateful we were to be able to call different parents who were equally concerned and willing to check the appropriateness of a party.

How can parents know if a certain event is appropriate or not? Parents must not be hesitant about getting on the telephone and asking questions, no matter who is sponsoring the event. I'm sorry to say that many parents today are not only condoning immoral and destructive influences on youth, but are actively encouraging them.

You should not be afraid to call the parent or adult sponsor to find out about planned activities. How else are you going to control and protect your vulnerable teen? And when you do call, listen carefully to the attitude or tone of what that person tells you, since this usually conveys more than the actual words. For example, when the parent or adult sponsor actually sounds pleased and even thankful that you are calling regarding your teenager, that is a good sign. It's a wonderful thing to hear someone say how grateful he or she is that a parent cares enough about his child to find out what's going on. When I hear that, I thank God that there are still decent, loving, guiding parents in this world.

Unfortunately, however, you may receive a different response. I remember calling a mother who was giving a party to which Carey, then fifteen, was invited. This mother's response to my inquiry was hostile. She said, "This is a private party. Your daughter is invited and she can come or not. It's up to her, but what I do in my own home is my business!" From this response alone, I knew that her home was no place for any teenager.

But I pressed her for details. I said, "I see. But I'm concerned about my daughter, and I'd really appreciate it if you would fill me in on the details of your get-together." By now the mother was angry, but with persistence I was able to gather that the teenagers would be served wine and Bloody Marys in a sensually provocative atmosphere.

This is commonplace today. You can't sit back and assume your teenagers are experiencing wholesome influences simply because the activities may be "supervised." You need to work together with other parents to provide wholesome activities and also be able to keep each other informed of what is going on with your children. No one else will do that for you. So many influences today are not what you would want your teenager to be exposed to.

Appropriateness and Trust

Keep two things in mind as you control and train your teenager. First, allow privileges based upon the trust relationship. Second, try to make sure your teenager can handle the particular situation, before you allow him to go.

While these may seem to be conflicting statements, they are not. Too many parents become confused at this point. They may use the trust relationship in deciding on a privilege but fail to check into the circumstances and suitability of the occasion. Checking into the appropriateness of the situation does *not* mean you do not trust your teenager. Even though a teenager is trustworthy, means well, and has fine intentions, there are still situations he or she may not have the maturity to handle. In these cases, you must protect your teenager.

In regard to the party to which Carey was invited, she was quite trustworthy—it was her genuine intention to act appropriately. But she was too young and immature at that time to handle such a heavy situation.

When I told Carey she could not go to this event, her natural reaction was, "Why not?" She carefully pointed out that her previous behavior had been exemplary, that she knew how to behave appropriately, that she definitely would do so, and that I could trust her. My reply to her was that she was absolutely right. I was truly proud of her and knew that I could trust her. However, I felt she was not yet ready or able to handle such a pressurized and difficult situation as this particular event. I pointed out that, although my own behavior had also been exemplary and I was trustworthy, I was also a normal person who likewise could be tempted. I could probably handle most any social situation. One evidence of this, which I was able to point out to Carey, was during my Navy days when I was required to supervise my division of sailors during their "happy hours" in striptease and topless bars. But even there, I had certain external restraints on me—such as being in a naval officer's uniform and being completely responsible for the welfare of my men.

Even with these difficult tests of character behind me, I, as well as anyone else, can be tempted beyond my endurance if I am not careful to control my life. So, why should I take the chance of ruining my integrity, character, marriage, spiritual fellowship, welfare of my children, and my life? I pointed out to Carey that this is one reason why I don't go to bars and discos. I trust myself but I have no absolute guarantees that I can manage any temptation. I told her of a well-known minister who felt his calling was among patronizers of bars. I was not surprised to learn of his change of lifestyle which made a mockery of his ministry and his marriage.

I was able to tell Carey that I truly trusted her because of her previous good behavior, but that there were certain situations she was not yet ready to handle—and some that any right-thinking person should avoid.

Delaying

Let's say you give your teenager privileges based on your trust relationship, and also on the appropriateness of each situation. These criteria are spelled out to your teen so he or she knows why you are making your decisions and that you are trying not to be simply arbitrary. Yet this is not quite the whole picture. For frequently, these types of decisions will be difficult to make.

I remember once when Carey was fifteen that she was invited to spend the day on a large boat, to swim during the day. Then at night there would be a party aboard the boat. My wife and I were having some tough thoughts about this one. The day activities certainly seemed all right. But the thought of the party that night somehow bothered us. We knew the parents who would supervise the party were sensible people.

At this point, let me insert some good advice: if you ever get into a situation where you do not feel comfortable about an upcoming event that your teenager wants to go to—yet you can't put your finger on the reason why—your best response is *to delay*.

I usually say something like, "Wow, that's a tough one, Honey; let me think it over." In the teenager world, events and situations change so fast that this type of problem usually takes care of itself. I can think of only one or two occasions when the problem did not somehow resolve itself. Another advantage of delay is that your teenager will have time to think it over and may come to some mature decisions himself. In the example of Carey being invited to the day and night party aboard the boat, I said, "Let me think it over." And Carey said, "OK, but hurry; I have to know by Thursday."

Much to my chagrin, the situation had not resolved itself. The questionable event was still on, the weather forecast was excellent and it was Thursday evening already, with Carey saying in an irritated voice, "What's your answer, Daddy? Greg has to know tonight."

I had a terrible feeling in the pit of my stomach, because I couldn't think of any legitimate reason to say no. Carey's behavior had been exemplary. Just as I was ready to give her permission to go, she said, "Daddy, by the way." (Remember those critical words?) "Greg can't get his folks' car to go to the party; we have to go in his dune buggy—you know, the one with no seat belts—and we have to cross the bridge during the 5 o'clock traffic."

I am surely glad I was listening closely at that moment, for I immediately responded, "I'm sorry, but you may not go to the party."

Carey did not even ask why, but went directly to the phone, called Greg and said, "I'm sorry, I can't go to the party. My father won't let me."

Many times a teenager will give clues when he wants or needs a "No" to a question or privilege. You must listen closely for these clues, for they usually occur when your teenager needs a way out of a difficult peer situation. When he can use you as a defense or alibi in such a situation, this produces a wonderful sense of camaraderie between you and your teenager. You should permit your teenager to use you in this way. Of course, you must also be careful not to lie or allow your teen to be dishonest in accomplishing it.

As you can see in Carey's situation, she somehow sensed that she could not handle the boat party at that time and needed a way out. Perhaps it was her discomfort about it that made me uncomfortable. I really don't know. But at any rate I am so thankful Carey took advantage of our parental authority and removed herself from a possibly unwholesome situation.

Looking Ahead

There is another strategy I have found to be invaluable in dealing with the teenager's drive for independence and pressing for more freedom and privileges. The attitude of the parents toward their child's growth to responsible independence will strongly affect a teenager's response to control and authority.

If you approach your teenager with an attitude of keeping him dependent on you, perhaps out of fear, and attempting to actually stifle his growth to independence, he will react poorly. If your teenager yields to this type of attitude, he will be hampered in progressing to responsible adulthood and may become a passive, dependent person. If he resists this overprotective attitude, his relationship with you will, of course, deteriorate and much conflict will result.

So what should your attitude and philosophy be? The most healthy attitude is to work hand in hand with your teenager *toward his being* a responsible, *independent* person by the time he is at the legal age of adulthood. If you clearly state this to your teenager so he understands that you actually *want* him to be independent within a given time and are working toward that end, he can then feel you are for him and not against him.

A teenager needs to be reminded of this partnership from time to time, especially when he wants to go someplace which his parents feel is inappropriate. For example, let's say that your teenager wants to go to a party which you have checked out and feel is inappropriate for him. We'll assume you have done a good job in being available and in keeping your teenager's emotional tank full. Also, you have been using the trust relationship effectively in determining what privileges should be given. And you have employed the delay technique, but the problem has not resolved itself. You find that you must now say no. And you find that your teenager simply will not or cannot accept it.

This is a good time to use the strategy I mentioned. I have found it to be very effective in helping a teenager gain perspective, to understand that his parents are working on his behalf and not trying to hold him back from gaining his independence. In my experience, this difficult time seems to occur most frequently when a teenager is sixteen. He has recently gotten his driver's license which feeds his urge for new experiences. How forceful you need to be with this strategy depends, of course, on the specific situation.

I remember counseling parents of a sixteen-year-old boy named Randy who was utterly determined to go to a concert which was obviously unwholesome. Up to that time the parents had been able to control his behavior and social development fairly well by using the trust relationship and delay techniques. But this occasion was different. The parents had almost come to the point of letting Randy go. Of course, this would have been a mistake. We must remember that a teenager needs his parents to be in control at all times. It's all right for parents to change their minds for good reason, but not as capitulation to the teenager's demands.

I advised these fine parents to be pleasant but firm as they explained to Randy that they wanted him to become independent and be able to make his own decisions as soon as he was able. He was sixteen and a half, and they had only eighteen months (be sure to put it in months to make it seem sooner) to make Randy a completely independent person. In only eighteen months he would legally be an adult and after that date, he could be (notice: say *"could be,"* not *"would be"*—don't get yourself in a corner) expected to handle his own affairs, make his own living, find his own place to live, do his own laundry, cooking, etc.

If these facts still do not give your teenager perspective (they do in the majority of cases), and he remains oppositional, you may go further and state that you have no legal responsibility for him after he is eighteen—that you intend to do everything in your parental power to get him ready for adult life in the next eighteen months because your legal responsibility ends at that time. Again, be sure to say *"legal"* to avoid regretting your words later because, of course, parents have other responsibilities to their child after he is eighteen.

This strategy is a rather harsh thing to do to teenagers, and should be used only as a last resort in difficult circumstances. However, teenagers need to be aware that the parents' overall intention is to indeed prepare them for responsible independence and adulthood, not to hold them back.

You can reinforce this attitude in several ways. For example, providing your teenager with his own checking account, placing monthly deposits into it, and teaching him to be responsible for certain expenses is an excellent way to foster an attitude of cooperation between you and your teen, in working toward his independence. Initially, he should be responsible for buying only a few items. As he learns to assume more responsibility, he can be given additional items to be responsible for, on a graduated scale, with the idea of becoming able by the age of eighteen, to assume total financial responsibility.

Another way to foster this attitude of working together in gaining independence in your teenager is, during times of good communication, to talk about his future, what he wants to do after high school, what vocation he might consider, whether college is right for him, and if so, which one. Looking at colleges with your teenager is a very effective means of fostering a feeling of cooperation. Providing any new experience for your teenager, such as a new sport or hobby, also helps accomplish this.

Setting Limits

A question frequently raised by parents is how much restriction to impose on a teenager for misconduct. Teenagers, like all children, have an acute sense of fairness. They know when parents are permissive and when they are too harsh or unreasonable. I've seen parents on both ends of the spectrum. Some have extreme difficulty in consistently setting firm limits and are easily manipulated by their teenagers. Other parents take the opposite tack and impose harsh treatment. I know of one teenager who was restricted to her home for over a year for going to a bar. Parents need to remember that the punishment should fit the crime. Common sense must prevail! Lesser misbehavior, such as coming in fifteen minutes late after a date, warrants restrictions of less than a week. If it recurs, then the restriction must be lengthened. Restrictions longer than two weeks are seldom warranted, with four weeks as an extreme outside limit. If restrictions are frequent, especially in ranges greater than one week, something is wrong—possibly in the parents' expectation, the parent-child relationship, or other possibilities which we will discuss later.

Above all, remember that well-loved teenagers are so much easier to discipline and control than those who are not so loved. We must keep their emotional tanks full.

Parent Courtesy

Another point to be aware of is the great importance of parents being considerate and pleasant to their teenagers' peers. They should be cordial, regardless of their feelings toward them. Many needless problems arise as a direct result of parental hostility toward adolescent peers. Remember, parents are authority figures. Most teenagers will consequently pity and side with a peer who is being ill-treated by a parent, regardless of the situation.

One of the most tragic examples of this occurred in the Dempsey family. Jane dated a boy who upset her parents. He was several years older than Jane and was known to deal in drugs. He was also surly and disrespectful toward authority.

Due to several factors, one of the greatest being her parents' extremely hostile way of relating to the boy, Jane became more and more involved with him. Of course, this brought heartache to the parents.

Being civil to anyone, including your teenager's peers, definitely pays off. First of all, your teenager will appreciate it and can feel free to bring other teenagers home. Second, other teens often are having problems communicating with their parents. Many times they are seeking other adults to relate to. It is a wonderful privilege to befriend your teenager's friends. Not only does this help them, but it draws your own teen closer to you.

Third, when you treat "unwholesome" peers kindly, you avoid pushing your teenager toward them, as the Dempseys did in Jane's case.

In fact, what usually happens is that your teenager will later approach you with questions regarding his peers. He will want your opinion about his friends. Then your teenager will listen to your opinions of his peers. But if you are hostile toward his friends, your teenager usually will avoid discussing that issue with you, and you in turn will have lessened your influence on your child.

Abnormal Situations

What we have talked about thus far bears upon normal situations. However, there are times when parents are not facing normal problems. If a teenager, despite unconditional love and appeals to reason from parents, is continually difficult to manage, likely he has more serious problems and needs outside help.

There are several teenage behavioral problems with which parents may be unable to deal. One of these is depression, which can be complex and treacherous on the teenage level. Another problem we are encountering more and more frequently is thought disorders, or difficulty in controlling one's thinking. Still another problem that calls for professional help is neurological disorders with resultant emotional difficulties.

A physician needs to be aware of possible character disorders. One evidence of this is a teenager's inability to handle anger appropriately. Also, a teenager's behavior may be difficult to control because of problems in the family dynamics or relationships. In fact, a teenager's behavioral problems may be caused or aggravated by any combination of these factors. Since behavioral problems in teenagers are becoming more and more common and increasingly complex, a wise parent will seek help early before they become serious. Most problems can be handled effectually by competent, well-trained therapists, along with cooperation from the parents.

In recent years professionals in education, medicine, and mental health have made great strides in the understanding of the complex problem known as attention deficit disorder (ADD) or attention deficit hyperactive disorder (ADHD). We have space here to cover only a few critical points.

First of all, I regret that these unfortunate children are considered abnormal. I have seen hundreds of these children and they are *not* "abnormal." Almost all of them possess unique gifts but seldom are able to discover them because of problems with school, self-esteem, depression, and/or passive-aggressive behavior. These children are born with two basic "problems." One is "hyperactivity," which is simply a short-attention span. They have problems keeping their minds on a task in order to learn at their intellectual capacity.

Second, these young children and teenagers have "perceptual problems," which does not mean there is anything abnormal in their eyes or ears. Information is received by the brain, but as this information is processed in the brain, it becomes distorted. When the information comes to the child's awareness, it is not *exactly* what the child is seeing or hearing (and the distortion differs in each child).

We do not have the time or space here to explain the reasons in depth, but it is critical to know that these distorted perceptions cause each ADD child to feel unloved and unwanted. Young children and teenagers with perceptual problems misperceive feelings received from others just as they misperceive academic data. Unfortunately, ADD children perceive our feelings for them negatively. It is therefore difficult to make an ADD child feel genuinely loved and cared for. This, in turn, causes increasing depression and anger as the child grows older. Eventually, the depression and anger (which is primarily manifested in passive-aggressive behavior) become so strong that they become the child's (and parents') greatest problems. These can occur at any age but usually the depression becomes serious around the age of ten, and the passive-aggressive behavior becomes a worsening problem as the child enters adolescence. At this time normal adolescent passive-aggressive behavior is superimposed on the PA behavior derived from the ADD, and these children are prone to very difficult adolescence. God, help these children and their parents.

From the above, I hope that you can see how critical it is to understand that ADD kids are normal but are nonetheless prone to special problems with depression and passive-aggressive behavioral traits which eventually make hyperactivity and learning disabilities pale in comparison. Unfortunately, most ADD children receive only special education and medication in the way of help. Appropriate and carefully managed special education and medication may be beneficial, but the far more important and potentially devastating depression and passive-aggressive behavior are largely ignored.

Dear parents of ADD children, please be assured that if your teenager receives what he/she needs, the prognosis is good to excellent that your child will *eventually* do well. Remember, this is a long process because it is a *developmental* process. Keep providing what your teenager needs daily. In general, here is what you must do:

1. Study, learn, and understand all you can about ADD.

2. Realize that your ADD child is not abnormal but is prone to certain problem areas. Remember, no child is perfect.

3. Please read and reread—even memorize!—chapter nine on teenage depression. Otherwise, you are likely to miss it if and when your ADD child becomes depressed and needs help. If depression reaches the moderate range, seek professional help as soon as possible.

4. This may sound extreme, but please read chapters six and seven for a week before you fall asleep. Handling a teenager's anger is the most difficult part of child rearing in my opinion. If

you read chapters six and seven one time, you will probably do well for a few days but gradually fall back to reacting to your teenager's anger in inappropriate ways. So please read these chapters nightly with the determination to maintain the correct "mind-set" for the next twenty-four hours. You must remain consistent.

5. Remember, it is quite difficult to make an ADD teenager feel genuinely loved. We must apply the basic ways of loving a child (eye contact, physical contact, focused attention, and loving discipline) with extreme diligence to accomplish this. Also remember that corporal punishment is easily misinterpreted by an ADD child or teen as violence which he/she then uses to justify violence in him/herself.

Chapter 9

Adolescent Depression

A dolescent depression is a complex, subtle, and dangerous phenomenon. It is complex because of its many complicated causes and effects. It is subtle because it almost always goes undetected, even by teenagers who experience it, until a tragedy occurs. It is dangerous because depression can result in the worst of happenings—from school failure to suicide.

Over the years I have seen many teenagers who have attempted to harm or kill themselves. Usually their parents and friends are stunned and shocked in disbelief at the action. These distressed people believed that everything was well with their teenagers, never guessing that they were so unhappy.

Teenage depression is difficult to identify because its symptoms are different from the classical symptoms of adult depression. For example, a teenager in mild depression acts and talks normally. There are no outward signs of depression. Mild teenage depression is manifested in somber fantasies, daydreams, or dreams during sleep. Mild depression is detectable only by somehow knowing the teen's thought pattern and thought content. Few professionals are able to pick up depression in this state.

In moderate depression, also, a depressed teenager acts and talks normally. However, in moderate depression, the content of the teenager's speech is affected, dwelling primarily on depressing subjects such as death, morbid problems, and crises. Since many adults today seem to dwell on pessimistic trains of thought, a teenager's depression may go unnoticed.

Some years ago an anxious mother called me regarding her fourteen-year-old son. She was not sure if her son needed help. This loving mother said her boy was acting normally, looked normal, and talked normally—that everything seemed fine—except that after watching the news, he would say something like this: "Things are getting so bad in the world, I wonder if it would be better to be dead." This fine boy was found to be moderately depressed.

Moderate depression in adults can be quite crippling. It can cause severe sleeping and eating problems, and inability to function in various capacities, from parenting to vocation. It may lead to serious consequences, even suicide.

Moderate depression in teenagers is just as profound and serious as in adults. Biochemically and neurohormonally, the two are essentially identical. But you see how different the manifestations or symptoms are. A moderately depressed adult usually looks terrible, feels miserable, and is severely affected in his ability to function. But a teenager? In the vast majority of cases, only in severe depression does a teenager actually appear depressed. When we can say, "Boy, does that kid look depressed!" we should assume that particular teenager is profoundly depressed and probably suicidal.

There is an exception to this, however. Teenage depression is difficult to identify because teens are good at "masking" it; that is, they can cover it by appearing OK even when they are absolutely miserable. This is often called *smiling depression*. This is a front which teenagers employ unconsciously. This masking of depression is done primarily when other people are around.

When depressed teenagers are alone, they let down or relax the mask somewhat.

This is helpful to parents. If we are able to see our teenagers at times when they believe no one is looking at them, we may be able to identify depression. It is an amazing thing to see the transformation in the face. Alone they will appear terribly sad and miserable. As soon as they think someone is watching, the smiling mask of depression immediately appears as though nothing is wrong. This is one way of identifying depression, although it is not the best way.

Discovering Depression

How, then, can we discover depression in our teenagers so that we can do something about it before tragedy occurs? It is imperative that we be able to identify it early, since there are numerous ways today in which depression can bring harm to our children. A depressed teenager is quite susceptible to unhealthy peer pressure, is prone to fall victim to drugs, alcohol, criminal activity, inappropriate sexual experiences, and other antisocial behaviors, including suicide.

The best way to identify depression in a teenager is to understand the various symptoms manifested in teenage depression and how they develop. It is crucial to understand the total constellation of symptoms in detail, because one or two symptoms may or may not signify true depression. True depression is a biochemical and neurohormonal process that in teenagers usually develops slowly over a period of weeks or months.

Before we consider the specific symptoms of adolescent depression, we should understand that a depressed adolescent may also have one or more of the classic symptoms of adult depression, including feelings of helplessness, hopelessness, despondency, and despair; problems with sleep (either too much or too little); problems with eating (too much or too little with weight loss or gain); lack of energy; feelings of low self-worth; problems handling anger.

Now let's look at the more specific symptoms of adolescent depression:

1. *Shortened attention span.* In mild teenage depression, the

first symptom generally seen is a shortening of attention span. The teenager is not able to keep focused on a subject very long. His mind drifts from what he wants to focus on and he becomes increasingly distractable. He finds himself daydreaming more and more. This shortening of attention span usually becomes obvious when the teen attempts to do his homework. He finds it harder and harder to keep his mind on it. And it seems that the harder he tries, the less he accomplishes. Of course, this leads to frustration, as the teenager then blames himself for being "stupid" or "dumb." He assumes that he does not have the intellectual ability to do the work. Imagine what this does to his self-esteem.

2. *Daydreaming.* The shortened attention span affects the teenager in the classroom. At first, he may be able to pay attention to the classwork for most of the period, and then daydream the remaining minutes. As the depression deepens and the attention span becomes shorter, the teenager pays attention less, and daydreams more. At this point, his teacher is in the best position to identify depression. Unfortunately, daydreaming is usually interpreted as laziness or poor attitude. However, just one or two symptoms alone, such as daydreaming and short attention span, do not allow a person to make the diagnosis of true adolescent depression. We must see a gradual development of a constellation of symptoms.

3. *Poor grades.* As the teenager's attention span shortens, and his daydreaming increases, the natural result is lower grades. Unfortunately, this falling of grades is usually so gradual that it is difficult to notice. For this reason, it is seldom associated with depression. In fact, the teenager, the parents, and the teacher usually assume that the work is too difficult for the teenager or that he is becoming more interested in other things. It would be quite helpful if the grades took a drastic plunge, an A to a D in one grading period. This would arouse the appropriate concern. However, the grades usually go something like this: A, A-, B+, B. Therefore, depression is seldom considered.

4. *Boredom.* As the teenager daydreams more and more, he gradually falls into a state of boredom. Boredom is normal in teenagers, especially in early adolescence, but only for relatively

short periods of time. Normal boredom is frequently seen for an hour or two, sometimes for an entire evening or day, or occasionally even two days. But prolonged boredom, several days or more, is not normal, and should be a warning to us that something is not right. Few things worry me as much as prolonged boredom in an adolescent, especially in an early adolescent. Boredom usually manifests itself in the teenager by his wanting to stay alone in his room for increasingly longer periods of time. He spends this time just lying on the bed, daydreaming and listening to music. The bored teenager loses interest in things which he or she once enjoyed, for example—sports, clothes, cars, hobbies, clubs, church and social activities, and dating.

5. *Somatic depression.* As the boredom continues and deepens, the teenager gradually slips into moderate depression. At this point, he begins to suffer from what I call *somatic depression.* I use this term because, even though all depression is physiological, or has a biochemical-neurohormonal basis, at this point, the symptoms begin to affect the child in a directly physical way. For example, in moderate depression, the teenager begins to experience physical pain. This pain may occur in many places, but is most often felt in the lower midchest region or as headaches. Many teenagers suffer pain in the lower chest and/or head, secondary to depression.

6. *Withdrawal.* In this miserable state, the teenager may withdraw from peers. And to make matters worse, he doesn't simply avoid his peers, but may disengage himself from them with such hostility, belligerence, and unpleasantness that he alienates them. As a result, the teenager becomes very lonely. And since he has so thoroughly antagonized his good friends, he finds himself associated with rather unwholesome peers who may use drugs and/or are frequently in trouble. The situation becomes more frightening.

Once prolonged boredom has set in, many things can develop. The mental and physical pain at this stage may be excruciating and at times unbearable. A teenager at this stage cannot tolerate his misery indefinitely. Eventually, he becomes desperate enough to do something about his misery. Most amazingly, even at this point the teenager is hardly ever aware that he is depressed. The teenager's ability to hide behind denial is truly incredible. This is why depression is seldom suspected until tragedy occurs.

Acting Out Depression

When a teenager has been moderately to severely depressed to the extent that he can endure it no longer, he will take action in an attempt to alleviate his misery and distress. The teenager's action resulting from depression is termed "acting out his depression." There are many ways for a teenager to act out his depression.

Boys tend to be more violent than girls. Boys may attempt to relieve their depressive symptoms by stealing, lying, fighting, driving fast, or through other types of antisocial behavior. One of the most common kinds of criminal behavior seen today among boys is *breaking and entering*. Doing something which has an air of excitement and danger to it seems to somewhat relieve the pain of depression. Breaking into homes provides this air, and is therefore commonly resorted to by depressed boys.

Of course, there are also other reasons boys break into homes. Therefore, when a teenager is referred to me for behavior such as breaking and entering, one of my first concerns is to find how much depression has played into the teenager's behavior. This is critical because a depressed teenager generally does not respond well to help if the depression is not treated also. I believe that overlooking the depression in these young people is totally negligent. And unfortunately, most agencies dealing with teens focus on behavior and are unaware of the depressive component in the child's problem.

Girls tend to act out their depression in less violent ways. However, because of unhealthy, violence-oriented models in the media, this trend is changing. Girls frequently act out their depression by *sexual promiscuity*. Their depressive pain tends to be alleviated during the close physical relationship of intercourse. However, when the relationship is over, these unfortunate girls usually feel worse—more depressed—than before, because of the self-degradation involved. Depression and low self-esteem are almost always the basis of a girl's promiscuity. It is amazing how much we can help a girl with this type of problem, by taking care of her depression. It is equally true how little we can do if we neglect her depression.

A depressed teenager can also act out his or her depression by taking *drugs*. Marijuana and depression are a very dangerous combination because marijuana actually makes a depressed teenager feel better. Marijuana is not an antidepressant. Rather, it blocks the pain of depression. Unfortunately, the teenager feels better simply because he does not hurt as much. Of course, when the marijuana is out of his system, the depressive pain returns. Then in order to obtain the same degree of relief from the pain, the teenager must use a greater quantity. This is a common way for a teenager to become habituated to marijuana, to become a "pothead." Other drugs can affect a depressed teenager in the same way. So naturally, when we attempt to help a teenager on drugs, we must determine how great a role depression is playing in his or her drug usage. I am genuinely alarmed how depression is overlooked or discounted by many professionals and agencies involved in treating adolescent drug problems.

Another way a depressed teenager may act out depression is by attempting *suicide*. Sometimes the attempt is a gesture in which the teenager does not wish death, but attention. At other times, there is genuine attempt to die. Girls make many more suicide attempts than boys, but boys are more often successful in killing themselves. Girls generally use less violent means of attempting suicide, such as pills. Boys, on the other hand, use more violent means, such as guns. Of course, this makes it easier to save girls from their own attempts. However, I have seen many girls come extremely close to death or actually die. What a tragedy!

Remedy for Mild Depression

What can we do to help our depressed teenagers? First of all, we must identify depression early in order to prevent tragedy. This means we must be familiar with symptoms of adolescent depression. People who need this information most are parents and those who work with teenagers, such as teachers, school counselors, and youth workers. When the depression is mild, it is relatively easy to halt its insidious progress and alleviate it.

Although most adolescent depression is complex in its underlying causes, often there is a specific factor or event which finally overwhelms the child and triggers the constellation of symptoms. This includes, for example, a death or illness, or departure of a person important to the teenager, a disappointment such as a divorce or conflict between parents, or a move to an undesired place. In such situations, the teenager feels lonely, abandoned, and unloved. It is crucial, first of all, to show him we do care about him and love him. We show this by spending enough time with him to permit his psychological defenses to come down in order for him to be able to meaningfully communicate with us. Then our love-giving, that is, eye contact, physical contact, and focused attention, will be meaningful.

If the problem is a conflict within the family, for example a divorce, the teenager needs help in dealing with his own feelings about this. He especially needs to realize that the divorce is not his fault—that there was nothing he could do to prevent it.

Teenagers are extremely sensitive to problems between their parents. Unfortunately, most people seem to believe that once a teenager finishes high school and leaves home, he is not really affected by what happens between the parents. How utterly wrong this is.

I remember the first time we visited our Carey after she went away to college. We went with about twenty of her friends for a snack one evening. All of Carey's friends were freshmen, away from home for the first time. All of them stated how much they loved school, their new friends, and college life, but they also voiced distress that they received so little communication from their parents. Few phone calls, letters, or visits.

Most parents simply do not realize how traumatic this period is in a young person's life, and how important it is to continue to provide a solid, stable "home base." About the worst time for parents to divorce is around the time the teenager leaves home. Going away from home, especially for the first time, is one of the most unsettling, anxiety-provoking, and insecure parts of anyone's life. At that time, a teenager's primary foundation of security is in his parents and home. Divorce at that time utterly shatters these sources of teenage stability. But it is amazing how naive so many people are, and how many parents have divorced right after their child has gone off to college. This has a profound effect on the teenager's value system, undermining his faith in the sanctity of marriage. It leaves him little opportunity to resolve his feelings of frustration, anger, anxiety, rejection, and fear regarding his parents before he himself consider marriage. Some of this unresolved inner conflict may affect his own marriage and cause conflict with his spouse.

Moderate and Severe Depression

As depression deepens within a teenager, a serious complication develops. His thought process begins to be affected. In moderate and severe depression, the teenager gradually loses his ability to think clearly, logically, and rationally. His judgment deteriorates as he loses the ability to maintain healthy perspective, and he focuses more and more on morbid, depressing details. His perceptions of reality become distorted, especially concerning what he perceives other people are thinking about him. He more and more assumes that everything is bleak, nothing is worthwhile, and life is not worth living.

He now has a thought disturbance. As the teenager increasingly loses his ability to think and communicate in a clear rational way, counseling per se becomes less and less effective. This is a frightening predicament. How can you help a teenager in counseling when you cannot reason with him? When this situation occurs, medical help is mandatory. For it is usually when the teenager loses his ability to be rational, reasonable, and logical, that he begins to act out his depression in self-destructive ways.

Adolescent depression is not something you can consider a phase that will run its course. This insidious affliction tends to grow worse and worse unless the depression is identified and intervention is taken.

Depression and Drugs

As mentioned, a depressed teenager is quite susceptible to drug usage because many drugs, especially marijuana, block (or dull) the pain of depression. It is also amazing how many teenagers and adults actually believe that marijuana is harmless. Every day we see the effect of this subtly hazardous drug.

I recall admitting a fifteen-year-old boy to the hospital for drug abuse, severe depression, and behavioral problems. Included in our initial evaluation, of course, were the physician's examinations and blood tests. I found this child to be severely anemic. His body was gradually losing its ability to manufacture blood due to drug abuse. Before treating this youngster for his psychological problems, I had to transfer him to a university medical center for a blood marrow transplant. His prognosis was very poor.

All this leads back to parental control of a teenager's freedom, by allowing privileges and freedoms based on trust and trustworthiness and on the appropriateness of the activity. If your teenager genuinely feels that you love and care about him, he will likely listen to you and heed your advice regarding his safety. Therefore, you must keep his emotional tank full. Then you will be able to help your child avoid harmful consequences of yielding to peer pressure to use drugs. You must continue to remind your teenager not to carelessly drink or eat something, without being sure that no one has slipped a drug into the drink or food. At any questionable party, it is good common sense to avoid open punch bowls or accepting food and drink from someone your teenager does not know well. This may sound overly suspicious, but I have personally seen how a single ingestion of a drug can harm a teen's developing mind.

The most frightening aspect of drugs is the way they affect a teenager's thought process. I have seen numerous teenagers who could not think sequentially or logically even after one dose of drugs. This disturbance of thought process is often so subtle that no one detects it, but the results are devastating. The teenager's ability to relate positively to people deteriorates. He comes up with wrong and often bizarre ideas about people, values, authority, society, and himself. He misinterprets people and their motivations. Worst of all, because he cannot think clearly, he becomes somewhat confused and is easily led by peer groups, cults, and other people interested only in using him.

What is more frightening than people who cannot think accurately and have distorted ideas, distorted views, and distorted values? Are you willing to make sure your teenager gets through adolescence without his intellectual, social, and psychological assets being harmed or destroyed? If so, you will love your teenager, take close care to appropriately supervise him. It is a difficult job, but the reward is well worth the cost. Seeing your teenager developing into a mature, sensitive, independent, right-thinking adult, contributing to his world, is one of life's greatest rewards.

Chapter 10

Helping Your Teenager Intellectually

To prepare your adolescent for the future in this world of nonreason, you must teach him or her to think clearly. There are five basic reasons for this.

First, clear thinking is needed for a basic understanding of the world the way it is. Adolescents do not have a historical perspective and cannot understand daily events without logical reasoning.

Second, a teen must learn to think clearly to enable him or her to understand the difference between right and wrong. Without a sound, rational understanding of ethics, a teenager is easy prey to antiauthority, destructive attitudes so prevalent today. Observe the ethical and moral tone of so many influential personalities in entertainment, government, and religious life today. We must arm our teens against destructive influences. This is not easy to do as we see most adults today become increasingly confused and bewildered. Inappropriate, unethical behavior is rapidly becoming the norm in our society.

Third, we must train our teenagers to think clearly to enable them to make logical, rational decisions for themselves. We want their behavior to be based on good decision-making and sound reasoning. Too much behavior in our society today is not based on careful, rational thought but on irrational, impulsive whims. We are living in an antiauthority society due to the immature handling of anger (see chapter seven), and the tide is worsening. A well-thinking person has a vast advantage.

Fourth, clear thinking is necessary to enable teens to develop socially and become socially mature adults. The person who has the ability to be rational and to think logically in his/her dealings with different types of people and personality styles is a rare but fortunate individual. Naturally, this gift will strongly influence the teen to develop a decent, positive, strong character.

Fifth, without logical, clear thinking, a teen cannot have a strong, consistent, lasting faith or a moral value system. A faith which is solid and enduring and provides the basis for life's meaning cannot be a blind faith. It must be based on rational, logical reason. It must be consistent with the real world. And it must provide reasonable answers to life's deepest questions.

It is very important that you teach your teenager to think rationally, logically, and sequentially (keeping facts in proper order). One of the best pieces of armament you can give your teen is the ability to evaluate his own thinking so that he can have confidence in it, and be able to modify it in light of new knowledge. In addition, he should learn to see errors in faulty thinking, and understand how false conclusions are reached. How do you help your teenager do this?

Intellectual Development

It is important to understand that a child develops intellectually from one phase to another. The factor which most determines how well a child masters each stage of thought development is the degree of emotional nourishment he receives. The better job you do in unconditionally and genuinely loving your teen, the better able he will be to develop intellectually. The more your teen feels loved, the more he will be able to learn to think clearly and logically. The less a teen feels loved and cared for, the weaker his mind may be.

For his mind to grow in a strong, healthy manner, a teenager must first feel good about himself. Then he will be able to mature into a wise and understanding person who can maintain proper perspective, especially over his emotions. The young person who is not well nourished emotionally may have poor thought control and be overcome and overcontrolled by his feelings. You must meet your teenager's emotional needs first.

Some years ago I saw a muscularly built fourteen-year-old boy who had attacked his baseball coach with a bat. The boy felt totally justified in his act. He maintained he had the right to attack his coach because he and the coach's son were competing for the same position, and this put him at a disadvantage.

The poor reasoning that this boy expressed is called *loose association*. By using loose association in the thought process, a person can justify almost anything. Such confused thinking is illogical and dangerous. And it is becoming more and more common among our teenagers today. Unfortunately, this faulty thought process is subtle and difficult to identify in casual relationships. But it is one of the primary reasons many of our teens are not being prepared for mature adult life.

You should be constantly alert for opportunities to teach your teenager to make correct, accurate associations in his thinking. A typical adolescent cannot think abstractly to a significant degree until he is at least fifteen years old, and then he is just learning. This is why a teenager is often sure his parents are wrong or ignorant, during his early and middle adolescence; later, as his thought process matures and he becomes capable of abstract reasoning, he begins to understand his parents and respect their opinions.

You need to be patient and loving during these difficult times and gently train your teenager to think clearly. And one way to do this is to identify faulty association of ideas and correct it.

Intellectual Affirmation

A teenager needs intellectual affirmation to learn to think well. To be able to think creatively, a person must respect himself, not only emotionally and physically but also intellectually. He must feel approval regarding his ability to think. This does not mean giving the impression that you believe he is always right. It is rather encouraging him in a growing self-respect for his ability to reason and solve problems.

Most teenagers cannot feel this self-assurance and self-approval without first receiving assurance and approval from their parents or parent figures. Many parents make the mistake of only correcting their teenagers. But a teen will feel competent only if he receives approval, validation, and praise, as well as correction.

You can give these priceless assets to your teenager only if you engage him intellectually. This means being available to discuss with him any subject he wants to talk about. It means being willing to listen to his ideas and to fully hear him out, regardless of your own reaction. Then, instead of directly pointing out his mistakes or arguing with him, you can discuss the issues, with respect, seriously considering his viewpoint, and calmly expressing your own. Such conversation should resemble talk between good friends. In doing this, you are not giving up your parental authority. You are simply showing respect for your teenager's thinking. You are letting them know that their thoughts and opinions are worthy and valuable. If your teens feel that you love and respect them, they will gradually incorporate some of your opinions and values into their thinking.

Unfortunately, too many parents refuse to talk with their teenagers in a give-and-take manner. Instead, they persist in talking down to their teenagers as though they were small children. This makes teens feel that their opinions don't matter. They are not being intellectually affirmed. They are not feeling genuinely loved by their parents. They do not feel respected, and they become hurt and angry.

Add to this the fact that they have not learned whether their thinking is correct or incorrect, logical or irrational. They have had no feedback from parents about whether their ideas are meaningful.

Most teenagers do not know if they are right or wrong about the subjects they think about. This pushes them toward taking the opinions of others, who may not have their welfare at heart. When they become too alienated from family to accept the opinions and values of parents and other legitimate authority figures, they begin listening to people who desire to harm them mentally, emotionally, physically, or spiritually.

You want to make sure your teenager feels unconditionally loved, through use of eye contact, physical contact, and focused attention. Give him intellectual affirmation by listening to him, and carefully noticing the way he thinks and comes to conclusions. Respect him by giving your opinion, without criticizing him or denouncing his thinking.

Only when your teenager sees that you are willing to relate to him as a responsible person with a mind of his own will he feel a balanced confidence in his ability to learn to think clearly and grow to intellectual maturity.

When you criticize your teen's opinions, he will probably feel angry, resentful, and even bitter. And he may become more defiant and resistant to change. If this happens he will hold to immature, selfish, and incorrect opinions, and carry these with him into his adult life. We all know adults who believe incorrect and strange ideas. These unfortunate people have difficulty understanding social, spiritual, or emotional relationships. They tend to jump on the current bandwagon, and often hold unrealistic and antagonistic opinions.

Teach by Example

As a parent, I have made my share of mistakes. So it certainly has its advantages to be the writer of this book, because I can choose the illustrations I wish to share. Let me give you one example that involves the intellectual training of our son David as he grew up. I think I handled this situation correctly, as I attempted without criticizing him to show him where his thinking was illogical and too simplistic, and then to teach him more mature ways of thinking.

David knew which TV programs his mother and I approved of and which ones we didn't. And he was usually quite good in complying with our wishes regarding his TV viewing. One evening, however, he was watching a program we didn't like —

"Love Boat." When I reminded David that I did not want him to watch it, he asked, "Why not?" and then said he could see nothing wrong with it because "no one is hurting anyone."

Does this reasoning sound familiar? Though he said it years ago, David's statement exemplifies the current state of morality in our society: "I can do what I want as long as it doesn't hurt anyone else."

It was very tempting for me to jump on David and criticize him for this shallow and immature way of thinking. TV programs then and more so now expose young people to subtle and dangerous philosophies. But I'm glad to report that I remembered that David needed *intellectual affirmation* and *training* to learn to think maturely.

So I said, "I understand what you mean, David, but I think 'Love Boat' is hedonistic and narcissistic." (That got his attention.)

He replied, "What does that mean?"

I said, "Tell you what, David. Let's get a dictionary and look these words up." (Incidentally, using the dictionary was a tremendous help to me in teaching my children difficult concepts.)

We looked the words up *together*. Then we talked about the meaning of *hedonistic* and *narcissistic* until I was sure he understood them. But, like a typical, developing, early adolescent, after David understood the definitions, he still did not understand how they related to real life. I said, "David, do you think a hedonistic and narcissistic person could make a good husband, wife, mother, or father? How about your mother? Is she selfish? Does she care only about herself with little regard for others? Is she only concerned about her own pleasure and not in anyone else's welfare?" This certainly turned on a light in David's head. He thought about all the things his loving mother had done for him that day, even though she did not feel well.

I was overjoyed when David finally replied, "This means that a selfish person is interested only in getting pleasure for himself, instead of caring about other people."

Then David and I talked about how "Love Boat" people displayed selfish, self-gratifying attitudes, with little regard for the respect or welfare of the other person.

Teaching a teenager to think clearly is difficult, time-consuming, and tedious. But if you do not clarify issues, such as those just described, those attitudes will subtly influence your teenager.

Be Consistent

One reason teenagers are confused about moral issues is that many parents are not assuming responsibility for teaching their own convictions to their children. Other parents say they believe in spiritual values but they do not live them. Many parents—including Christians—are having difficulty with their own behavior. The rise in sexual misconduct, child abuse, and cheating is alarming.

Nothing is more confusing to a teenager than inconsistency in the life of the parent—especially about matters that the parents say they highly value and then treat as less than nothing. How can parents teach their teenagers to think clearly about moral and spiritual values, if their own lives do not demonstrate the results of clear thinking?

I believe that the undisciplined behavior which is destroying the moral fiber of our society must be dealt with. Surely God will judge us for the lack of discipline and self-control in the lives of so many who call themselves Christians.

Fellow parents, let's get our own lives in order, consistently behaving as we know God wants us to. Then we can claim God's promises to us for our children.

Chapter 11

Helping Your Teenager Spiritually

A s previously mentioned, today's generation of teenagers is often called the "apathetic generation." It is important to remember that this apathy is a covering for intense anger and rage, especially toward legitimate authority. Unfortunately, many of our teenagers are apathetic, especially regarding the future. Many of these young people who are the future hope of our country and way of life lack the vitality, vivaciousness, and eagerness which we love to see.

Why are so many of our adolescents apathetic? Why do they lack initiative and incentive? Essentially, it is because they have little hope in the future. Such hopelessness is more serious than the aggressive and violent protestings of the late 1960s. Although the young people of those years had a cause which was at times misdirected and poorly carried out, they at least had a cause which reflected a hope—a hope in their country, in their way of life, and most importantly in themselves.

We do not see this today. The prevailing mood in our young today is *hopelessness, helplessness,* and *despair.* As parents, we wonder how this heartbreaking situation can be possible. It seems as if the very heart and soul have been torn from so many of our precious teenagers. Why do they have so little hope in the future?

It is easy to point out the disheartening world and national developments, such as unemployment, disasters, AIDS, world hunger, and pollution. But these are *not* the cause of teenage hopelessness and despair.

Our forefathers faced equally difficult, dangerous, and frustrating times in the past and with even less security. They faced such hardships as the Great Depression, the holocaust, and other horrors of World War II. But the young people of those eras did not feel the hopelessness and despair seen today.

The attitudes and moods of a nation's youth reflect the attitudes and moods of its adults. Sometimes the youth rally behind their elders, especially when national security is threatened. At other times the young people march against the status quo, especially when they perceive hypocrisy. But today we see neither pro nor con, but rather a foreboding inertia. What are our youth reflecting from adults? They are reflecting depression, gloom, hopelessness, and despair. How can a teenager react positively in such an atmosphere? A teen needs to see something positive and worthwhile in life to rally behind.

Unfortunately, teenagers have little historical perspective to allow them to look back and learn from the experiences of their forebearers. They are limited to the present and future. Therefore, they form their attitudes and moods from the *current, prevailing climate of the present,* and the *current, prevailing attitudes about the future.*

One of the main reasons our teenagers are having problems in forming positive attitudes is that we adults are not passing on to them that determination, hope, and encouragement necessary for facing the future. We of the older generation seem to be offering our young people some strange and unhealthy attitudes which are largely untrue and certainly not scriptural. Almost without realizing it, we adults are rapidly developing an orientation to life which is unwholesome, noncreative, retreating, and passive. We have let other people determine our value system and outlook on life. Many of us believe:

- that we are the first generation to face crises;
- that the world was somehow a nicer, better, and safer place to live before the present problems developed;
- that the world is deteriorating so rapidly that it is hopeless and foolish to plan and prepare for the future, since there may not be a future at all.

You could rightly expect a teenager, who knows little about the history of man and less about the great promises of God, to succumb to this suffocating, hope-robbing pessimism. We have become a people whose attitudes and value systems are so easily influenced by others. We feel despair when something is not as good as it once was, ignoring the things which *are* good. We forget to count our blessings. I have seen people despair over the most inconsequential things. On the other hand, we overreact positively to equally unimportant things, like a new car or new clothes. Why should we think it strange that our young are so easily influenced by rock groups and cults when we are equally influenced by television and special interest groups?

I can understand a nonbeliever feeling this disorientation, confusion, and despair. But I find it difficult to understand the Christian person being in this trap of hopelessness. And yet I see so many Christians yielding to pessimistic influences. And I see their teenagers failing to find that critical peace-giving anchor of hope which Christ intends for His people.

I would like our teenagers to receive messages of *hope, encouragement,* and *challenge.* But our generation has generally lost contact with its *spiritual heritage.* Yes, we have problems, some of which are totally new—but so did many of our grandfathers and grandmothers. Why can't we face our crises and difficulties without foreboding, depression, without feelings of hopelessness and doom?

Doomsday?

In times of trouble some religious groups and teachers have tried to escape responsibility by withdrawing and waiting for doomsday. Instead of using biblical passages as God intended—as words of hope and promise—these self-proclaimed prophets use these Scriptures to pronounce an imminent doomsday. Their message is one of hopelessness: The end is coming soon, so there is no point in solving our problems, or providing a better life for our children. This results in a state of spiritual and emotional paralysis. It also encourages the attitude, "Eat, drink, and be merry, for tomorrow we die."

Imagine being an adolescent in such an atmosphere. At the time when a teenager should be preparing for a life of accomplishment to contribute to the world, he or she senses that the general attitude is to make the best of today, because tomorrow, even if it comes, may not be worth living.

Such preoccupations are breaking the back of responsibility in both adolescents and adults. After reading a book on the "end times" recently offered on TV, one mother admitted, "I can't help wondering why I should raise my kids or try to prepare them for a nonexistent future." A man who read another doomsday book stated, "I feel like giving up my job and just quitting. Why go on?"

In this atmosphere of escalating eschatological futility, it is difficult for people to fight cynicism, to avoid drugs, or to keep from copping out. When doomsday is proclaimed without the proper balance of hope and trust in God's promises and Christ's love, is it any wonder that Christians are finding it increasingly difficult to live responsible, courageous, and productive lives?

Periods of unhealthy overemphasis on prophecy and end-times occur every five to ten years. These periods are usually precipitated by a best-selling book on this subject which takes current conditions and compares them with biblical prophecy. We parents realize the devastating effect this can have on a teenager. If and when this occurs, be ready to equip your teenager with an understanding of the history of this phenomenon, and keep it in balance with sound understanding of biblical prophecy. Otherwise, a teenager cannot only become pessimistic and depressed about his or her existence but also may easily be drawn into astrology and fall under the growing influence of psychics, seers, and fortunetellers.

Pessimism is not the teaching of Christ. His message is one of hope and joy. Speaking of the last days, Christ said, "But of that day and that hour knoweth no man, no, not the angels which are in heaven, neither the Son, but the Father. Take ye heed, watch and pray: for ye know not when the time is" (Mark 13:32-33, KJV). We are to watch for His coming and to pray. We are not to give up, or be pessimistic about the future. We are not to withdraw from our moral responsibility to live godly lives and to pass our values on to our children. The Scriptures encourage us to be joyful, optimistic, hopeful, and to assume the best.

If we as parents can grasp the total picture of history, we will see our place in it—a place of extreme importance and excitement. We are only one chapter in God's plans and books of history. And His plans and history will never end. When our chapter is over, I for one, want to look back and know that we as His people have carried out His will, that we have stood firm in our faith in Him and in His goodness. I want to feel good about not giving in to the world's pressures to use our resources for "experiences" today at the expense of sacrificing our God-given privilege to live righteous, godly lives. I want to be able to say with Paul, "I have fought a good fight, I have finished my course, I have kept the faith" (2 Timothy 4:7, KJV).

God help us to finish our course and keep the faith. For to do this to the best of our ability will give more to our teenagers than anything else. But to give our teenagers hope, faith, and optimism, we must live it.

"Show Me How to Live"

One of the main cries of adolescents today is for their parents to provide them ethical and moral value systems to guide them. This is expressed by teenagers in various ways. One child states he wants a "standard to live by." Another teenager needs a "meaning in life." Other desperate teens yearn for "something to show me how to live" or "something to hold on to" or "a higher guidance."

These desperate yearnings are not experienced by only a few discontented, unhappy youngsters. Most teenagers are feeling these needs and are confused, so terribly confused, in this all-important area of their lives. Unfortunately, it is quite unusual to find teenagers who sense meaning and purpose in their lives, who are at peace with themselves, and who have a healthy perspective about living in a confusing, rapidly changing, and frightening world.

Initially, a child looks to his parents for guidance in life. Whether the child is successful in finding this from his parents depends on two things: whether his parents have found direction for themselves, and whether the child can accept parental values and make them his own. A child who is not able to feel genuinely loved by his parents will find this difficult.

Let's examine the first requirement in providing the meaning to life a young person so desperately needs. We parents need a foundation on which we base our own lives and which can stand the test of time. A foundation which will see us through every part of life, through marital needs, money crises, problems with our children, energy shortages, and clashes within a changing society where spiritual standards are rapidly weakening. We parents must possess that foundation to be able to pass it on to our own children.

This priceless, comfort-providing, peace-giving treasure which every heart needs is a Person. He is extremely personal, yet can be shared with another person. He gives strength in times of stress, yet offers comfort in times of sadness. He grants us wisdom when we are confused, yet corrects us when we are wrong. He provides help when we are needy, and His help will never end. For He guides us continually and stays "closer than a brother."

He gives commands to be carried out, but promises wonderful rewards for obedience. At times He allows loss, distress, and pain, but He always gives us something better. He does not impose Himself upon us, but patiently waits for us to invite Him into our lives. He does not force us to do His will, but is painfully disappointed when we do the wrong thing. He desires that we love Him because He first loved us, but He allows us a free will to choose Him or reject Him. He wants to take care of us, but refuses to force Himself upon us. His greatest desire is to be our Father, but He will not intrude. If we want what He wants — a loving, caring, Father-child relationship with Him — we must accept His offer. He is too considerate to force it. If we have not received Christ as Savior and Lord, He is waiting for us to become His child. Of course, as you have surmised, He must be a personal God.

This personal, intimate relationship with God through His Son Jesus Christ is the most important thing in life. This is the "something" which our young people are yearning for: "the meaning in life," "something to count on," "something to bring comfort when everything seems to be falling apart." It is all there.

Do you have it? If you do not, seek help from a minister or a Christian friend.

The second requirement is that a child identify with his parents so that he can accept and incorporate their values.

As you recall, if a teenager does not feel loved and accepted, he has real difficulty identifying with his parents, and tends to react to parental guidance with anger, resentment, and hostility. He views each parental request (or command) as an imposition and learns to resist it. In severe cases, a teenager learns to consider each parental request with such resentment that his total orientation to parental authority (and eventually to all authority, including God's) is to do the opposite of what is expected of him. When this degree of alienation occurs, it is nearly impossible for parents to give their moral and ethical value systems to their teenager.

In order for a teen to identify with his parents, relate closely with them, and be able to accept their standards, he must feel genuinely loved and accepted by them. To lead a teen to the close relationship with God which they possess, parents must make sure that a child feels unconditionally loved, a topic we have previously discussed. It is extremely difficult for teenagers who do not feel unconditionally loved by their parents to feel loved by God.

Religious Training

A very important thing to know about a teenager is how his memory operates. Remember that a teenager is a child emotionally and is much more emotional than cognitive. He therefore retains feelings much more readily than facts. A child can remember how he felt in a particular situation much easier than he can remember the details of what went on. For example, a child or teenager in a Sunday School class will remember exactly how he felt long after he forgets what was said or taught.

So, in some ways, whether a child's experience was pleasant or unpleasant is much more important than the details of what a teacher taught. By *pleasant* I do not mean that a teacher need cater to a child's desire for fun and frolic. I mean that the teacher should treat the child with respect, kindness, and concern, and make him feel good about himself. The child should not be criticized, humiliated, or otherwise put down.

If religious training is a degrading or boring experience for a young person, he is likely to reject even the best teaching, especially if morality and ethics are involved. It is from this type of situation that a teenager develops a bias against religious matters and tends to consider church people as hypocrites. This attitude is difficult to rectify and can continue with him for a lifetime.

On the other hand, if the learning experience is a pleasant one, a teenager's memories of religious things will be pleasant and can then be incorporated into his personality. Emotionality and spirituality are not entirely separate entities. One is quite related to and dependent upon the other. For this reason, if parents want to help a teenager spiritually, they must care for him emotionally. Because a child remembers feelings much more easily than facts, there must be a series of pleasant memories within which to accumulate the facts—especially spiritual facts.

The Wait-and-Choose Approach

Now let's examine a popular misconception that goes something like this: "I want my child to learn to make his own decisions after he is exposed to things. He shouldn't feel he has to believe what I believe. I want him to learn about different religions and philosophies; then when he has grown up he can make his own decision."

This parent is either copping out or is grossly ignorant of the world we live in. A child brought up in this manner is to be pitied. Without continual guidance and clarification in ethical, moral, and spiritual matters, he will become increasingly confused about his world. There *are* reasonable answers to many of life's conflicts and seeming contradictions. One of the finest gifts parents can give a child is a clear understanding of the world and its confusing problems. Without this stable base of knowledge and understanding, is it any wonder many children cry to their parents, "Why didn't you give me a meaning for all this? What's it all about?"

Another reason this wait-and-choose approach to spirituality is grossly negligent is that more and more organizations and cults are offering destructive, enslaving, and false answers to life's questions. These people would like nothing better than to find a person who was brought up in a seemingly broad-minded way. He is easy prey for any group offering concrete answers, no matter how false or enslaving.

It is amazing to me how some parents can spend thousands of dollars and go to any length of political manipulation to make sure their child is well prepared educationally. Yet, for the most important preparation of all, for life's spiritual battles and finding real meaning in life, a child is left to fend for himself and made easy prey to cultists.

Prepare Your Teenager Spiritually

How do parents prepare their teenagers spiritually? Organized religious instruction and activities are extremely important to a developing teenager. However, nothing influences a teenager more than his home and what he is exposed to there. Parents need to be actively involved in a teenager's spiritual growth. They cannot afford to leave it to others, even superb church youth workers.

1. Parents must teach their teenager spiritual concerns. They must teach not only spiritual facts, but how to apply them in everyday life. And this is not easy. It is quite simple to give a teenager basic scriptural facts, such as who different Bible persons were and what they did. But that is not what we are after ultimately. You need to help your teen understand what meaning biblical characters and principles have for him personally. You can do this only at somewhat of a sacrifice, as with focused attention. You must be willing to spend time alone with your teenager in order to provide for his emotional needs as well as spiritual needs.

2. Parents must share their own spiritual experiences. With the factual knowledge gained from church, Sunday School, and home, a teenager only has the raw material with which to grow spiritually. He must learn to use this knowledge effectively and accurately to become a mature person spiritually. To do this a teenager needs the experience of walking with God daily and learning to rely on Him personally.

The best way to help a teen with this is to share your own spiritual life with him. As your teenager matures, gradually increase your sharing with him about how you yourself love God, walk with Him, rely on Him, seek His guidance and help, thank Him for His love, care, gifts, and answered prayer.

Share these things with your teenager as they happen, not afterward. Only in this way can a teen get "on-the-job" training. Sharing past experiences is simply giving additional factual information, not letting a teenager learn for himself through his own experience. There is a lot of truth in the old statement, "Experience is the best teacher." Let him share in yours. The more a teenager learns to trust God, the stronger he will become.

Your teenager needs to learn how God meets all personal and family needs, including financial. He needs to know what his parents are praying for. For example, he needs to know when you are praying for the needs of others. When appropriate, he should know of problems for which you are asking God's help. Don't forget to keep him informed about how God is working in your life, and how He is using you to minister to someone. And, of course, your teenager should certainly know you are praying for him and for his particular needs.

3. Parents should be examples of forgiveness. A teenager must be taught by example how to forgive and how to find forgiveness, both from God and people. Do this first of all by forgiving others. Next, when you make a mistake which hurts your teenager, admit the mistake, apologize, and ask his forgiveness. I cannot overstress how important this is. So many people today have problems with guilt. They cannot forgive and/or they cannot feel forgiven. What can be more miserable? But the fortunate person who has learned how to forgive those who offend him, and who is able to ask and receive forgiveness, demonstrates a mark of mental health.

4. *Parents must train their teenager how to handle anger maturely.* As we discussed in chapter seven, it is normal to a certain extent for a teen to handle anger in passive-aggressive ways. This antiauthority attitude and motivation, if not checked and redirected, will cause a teenager to choose a value system (including *spiritual* values) incompatible and usually opposite of their parents. As mentioned before, normal passive-aggressive tendencies should be resolved and disappear around the ages of sixteen and seventeen. As this happens, then a teen's basic attitude toward legitimate authority (especially parents) will be positive. Then as the young person chooses his/her life's ethical/spiritual value system, usually between the ages of eighteen and twenty-five, he/she will be able to use rational, logical, clear reasoning in doing so and not be influenced by self-defeating, passive-aggressive anger. Therefore, we parents must be diligent in teaching our teenagers how to handle their anger.

Balcony People
My former pastor, Moncrief Jordan, told me a story about a friend of his. And because it has bearing on how we deal with our teenager I want to tell it to you. Pastor Jordan's friend said that when he was trying to deal with his own tendencies toward discouragement and despair, he would let his "balcony people" speak to his "cellar voices."

The cellar voices in all of us come from the basements of our lives. Sometimes they are impulses and urges we normally associate with the animal kingdom—rash temper, boiling anger, and vindictive feelings.

But the cellar voices go beyond emotional or physical reactions. They proceed from the dark side of ourselves—a dark side that most folks rarely see. The cellar is where our scenarios of hate, greed, pride, lust, and destruction are formed. And woe to that person who does not recognize the potency of this area!

The cellar voices also come from those around us who, because of low self-esteem, guilt, frustration, or pent-up hostility cut us down, telling us how bad the world is, and how bad we are. If we let them, these cellar voices can lead us to despair and hopelessness.

But fortunately, Pastor Jordan's friend also told him about balcony people. These are the people, living and dead, who have lifted us with their love, faith, hope, and courage.

We all need balcony people who show us that we can live above the petty and discordant levels of life. That we do not have to wallow in negativism and despair. That we do not have to let our inner conflicts create havoc in life. That we can live victoriously. The balcony people speak to us both with their talk and their walk.

Some of the balcony people in Scripture are beautifully summarized for us in Hebrews 11, in a roll call of people who proved that faith is workable, and that life can have meaning and purpose at *any* time of history.

Most of us can learn from our own experiences. But it takes a wise person to learn from the experience of others. It is our privilege to let our balcony people save us from unnecessary mistakes and conflicts, and to lift us up in hope.

Perhaps we should consider writing our own "eleventh chapter of Hebrews," listing our own balcony people. Do you realize we have more balcony people to draw from than any previous people in history?

From our list, there ought to be a select few balcony people who are living today and with whom we can bare our hearts and souls from time to time. These are people we utterly trust and admire, and to whom we can reveal our dark sides, knowing we will be loved and prayed for. That is part of what the church of Christ is all about.

Our teenagers need balcony people to give them hope. They are hearing more than enough cellar voices. We must be balcony people to our precious youth. But we must work at it—we do not have to be spreaders of gloom and doom. Oh, how very sensitive our teenagers are to pessimism, especially from their parents. We do not have to buy into the despair of our day. Faith in our God and in ourselves—have you read the eleventh chapter of Hebrews yet? No? Hurry up! It brings a hope that cannot be destroyed.

God gives us hope. Hope is not wishful thinking. Hope is the *knowledge* that the wonderful promises of God are true. There are numerous promises God has made to us. Read them for yourselves. Start with Romans 8:28: "And we know that all that happens to us is working for our good if we love God and are fitting into His plans" (TLB).

Or how about Jeremiah 29:11: " 'For I know the plans I have for you,' says the Lord. 'They are plans for good and not for evil, to give you a future and a hope' " (TLB).

Or consider Isaiah 41:10: "Fear not, for I am with you; be not dismayed, for I am your God! I will strengthen you, yes, I will help you; yes, I will uphold you with My vindicating right hand" (MLB).

Or look at Psalm 34:19: "Many are the afflictions of the righteous; but out of them all the Lord delivers him" (MLB).

If you wish to write to me through Victor Books, P.O. Box 1825, Wheaton, Illinois 60187, I will send you an extensive list of Scripture references which proclaim hope and assurance.

Christian Hope

There *must* be recovery of hope in our land. Our young people need hope to face an uncertain future. I know the situation does not look good right now. But, as in generations past, if we give our youth what they need to face the future, they will then be prepared and will do well. We must give them confidence, courage, moral strength, and a sense of responsibility. But we cannot give them these priceless assets without hope—the sure *knowledge* that God exists, that He loves us, and that His promises are true.

Moncrief Jordan told me of a man he visited regularly. This man had many physical ailments, and eventually both of his legs had to be amputated. Pastor Jordan thought that this would surely break his joyful and optimistic view of life. But it didn't.

The man would still swing himself with a trapeze device from his bed to a wheelchair and roll himself down to the parlor in the very depressing nursing home where he lived. There he would play the piano and sing until he had many others singing with him. During his last years, he was the channel of hope and joy to many people.

Christian hope is not dependent on what the world does to us. It is dependent on what we do in the world as we live in response to God's great love for us.

Fellow parents, let's be encouragers, dispensers of hope that our teenagers so desperately need—"balcony people," as some call those who watch over others to lovingly help them along in life. It's difficult to be a balcony person, but I guarantee you that it really pays off for it is like giving water to a drought-parched earth. And best of all, we are giving our teenagers what they need to become balcony people.

By nature, I am not as much a balcony person as my wife, Pat, is. And it has been through the years pure joy to see my daughter follow in her mother's footsteps. She is a balcony person also. How I admire that and try to become more that way!

Let's grow together, fellow parents. By working at it every day, we will gradually become more and more like Christ—the ultimate balcony Person.

Chapter 12

The Older Adolescent

A s adolescents near the time of normal separation from home, they still need their parents to help them make that precarious crossing into adulthood. Contrary to what many parents assume, this crossing does not happen instantaneously through a high school graduation or a move out of the house.

The transition into adulthood should be a gradual weaning process for which both parents and teenager prepare.

You first prepare for this change by making sure your teenager has learned to lead an independent life. There may have been "practice runs" at living away from home for periods of time, as your child was growing up, such as summer camp experiences and visits with relatives. Now you need to increase your teenager's self-sufficiency by making sure he can actually take care of himself. Can he do his own laundry? Prepare balanced meals for himself? Handle all the other necessities for independent living?

These needs are usually overlooked, especially with boys. It isn't unusual for a boy or a girl living away from home for the first time to fix the same unhealthy, starchy meal over and over, to the point of developing vitamin deficiencies and becoming susceptible to illness.

By the time your adolescent becomes independent, he should be able to handle his own finances. This means budgeting his income and balancing his checkbook. Such items may seem like common sense, trivial matters, but many adults still cannot balance a checkbook, much less discipline themselves to save money.

It takes time to train your teenager to manage his affairs; it never just happens. I am amazed, for example, at how many college students cannot even get up in the morning to arrive in class on time. Self-discipline is best learned before leaving home. Seldom is it sufficiently learned later.

Lifelong habits are usually shaped during later adolescence. Although most of a teenager's adult traits or characteristics have been partly formed, they are usually still changeable. Both parent and teenager should make use of this time to enhance favorable characteristics and hopefully modify less desirable ones.

Goal-Orientation

One of the most important aspects of a teenager's personality is his degree of goal-orientation. No one, and especially a teenager, is perfectly balanced in this area of being goal-oriented. Some people are too goal-oriented, putting almost all their personal resources into reaching what they want—good grades, a college degree, money—to the exclusion of other equally important matters such as fun, relaxation, and personal relationships. A person who is too goal-oriented tends to be perfectionistic, judgmental, rigid in his thinking, opinionated, tense, and worried. He also takes things too seriously and personally. Many people who are reading this book will fit into this category, just as I do.

It is fine to be goal-oriented and conscientious. But people who are excessively so will tend to find life a drudgery with little pleasure. They will also increasingly tend toward depression as they become older, especially during the middle years. They have made reaching for goals their meaning to life. So when they reach those goals, they wonder what meaning is left. If they do not reach their goals, they likewise see little meaning. If your older adolescent has these traits, you can be of tremendous help to him by teaching him to find significance in pleasant hobbies and other means of *relaxation*, and especially to learn the immense value of friends and personal relationships. It is still relatively easy for an older adolescent to change. However, the older a person grows, the more difficult it is to change. The more perfectionistic and goal-oriented an adult is, the more apt he is to become dull, depressed, rigid, and unpleasant in his old age.

I am reminded of two people who present stark contrasts in this area. Once I saw a sixty-seven-year-old man who had been a hard worker, devoting almost all of his energy to his job. He allowed little time for family, fostered few friendships, and was quite a perfectionist. His life was fairly satisfying until retirement. Without his goal (hard work), he lost most of his meaning in life and rapidly became profoundly depressed. When I saw him, he stared straight ahead, as though he were in a catatonic trance. He could hardly move, and just sat motionless, day after day, until his family brought him for treatment.

The exact opposite is our dear next door neighbor, a widow. She has been a woman of accomplishment, and still is involved in many projects. Yet she has always loved people and fostered close relationships. People feel wonderful just being around her.

What a difference! The man has been too perfectionistic and goal-oriented; our neighbor has achieved a wonderful balance. It is important to remember that their personal characteristics were present in late adolescence and simply intensified over the years.

The more a teenager sees the meaning and value of human relationships, the more he will develop into a pleasant, congenial person, who can roll with life's punches without crippling depression. The key is *balance*. You want your older adolescent to have the essential degree of goal-orientation to enable him to have a life of satisfying accomplishments. But you also want him to be person-oriented so that he can have truly meaningful personal relationships, as a spouse, parent, and friend.

My precious daughter Carey and I had long discussions along these lines before she went away to college. I emphasized the importance of friendships acquired in high school and college. These are truly special friendships which should be kept alive over the years, if at all possible. I recommended that she keep a notebook with the names and addresses of every meaningful friend she makes, so that she can keep in touch with them over the years.

Although we form close friendships after our school days, there is something special about high school and college friends. These are the people we can call on years later and almost always find an instant rapport. It is as though the conversation simply picks up where it left off—back in the "good old days." Appreciation for friends is especially important for the older adolescent who is so goal-oriented that he tends to devalue friendships.

However, your adolescent may be just the opposite. His orientation may be to relax, have fun, enjoy life, and to delay responsibility as long as possible. As common sense will tell you, these traits should be identified and worked on from very early adolescence.

You may have a teenager who is capable of making good grades, but who is having so much fun in activities and with friends, that he doesn't give proper time and effort to academics. It is appropriate to handle this problem directly, if your child is not strongly passive-aggressive. If you are not dealing with an anger problem, you can help your teenager become more balanced in his approach to responsibility. If you have done your job as a parent, making sure your teenager feels unconditionally loved, you have every right and responsibility to directly enforce your teenager to take the proper amount of responsibility and become properly goal-oriented.

This reminds me of an experience with our David when he was thirteen. He was capable of making good grades, and did so until the beginning of the seventh grade when he became so engrossed in football and friends that his report card showed all

Cs. Knowing this was far below his ability, and seeing his strong drift toward fun and frolic and excessive peer interaction, Pat and I knew we must make some changes. We set up a system calling for each of David's teachers to send home a weekly grade over the six-week grading period. We told David each time he brought home a grade below a B, there would be no sports for the coming week. Guidelines for good study habits were established and enforced. Not only did the next report card reveal all A's, but David's whole attitude toward academics had changed. He really felt good about his success and no longer needed coaxing from us.

Occasionally, an older adolescent will have a negative academic attitude as high school graduation approaches. This often happens to a teen who has had previous learning disabilities or perceptual problems; and it may create conflict with the parents who have high future academic expectations for him. Each situation needs to be considered separately. I have seen many instances of this kind resolved by encouraging the teen to take off a year or two to work or assume military duty. Often this course will give the adolescent the time and experience he needs to mature, settle down, and become appropriately goal-oriented, vocationally and socially.

Preparation for the Real World

One of the most difficult dilemmas that we parents face today is the preparation of our young people to handle the real world with its alcohol and other drugs, sexual license, decaying spiritual values, and general attitude of "meism" or selfishness. This is a difficult subject even to write about, because it is so controversial. I believe it is a cruel blunder to completely isolate children and teenagers from the world as it really is, but I have seen many parents do this. Eventually, of course, we must let our sons and daughters go. If our young people have not learned how to deal with these pressures while living at home, how can they cope with real life when they are on their own?

While your teenager is living at home under its haven of safety and guidance, he needs some exposure to these problem areas, in a controlled way. Of course, I don't mean encouragement or permission to "live it up" for the experience. I mean *training* your teenager how to cope with real life, and setting privileges based on trust, consequences of behavior, and appropriateness of the social occasion. These privileges should be controlled to progress in such a way that you can help your teenager handle different encounters as they arrive. He needs to be well trained on how to handle most of life's situations. Of course, this does not mean that he is to participate in unhealthy activities. Rather, he should learn how to handle himself maturely, and determine to keep himself pure and uncontaminated by the unhealthy aspects of today's society. To achieve such maturity in your teenager will take time, preparation, training, conviction, and self-control on your part.

One of the most serious mistakes you can make is to assume that school, church, or other organizations can or will handle this part of your child's development for you. The parent has the greatest effect on the teenager, especially regarding values and lifestyle. Schools and churches can help, but without the primary involvement of the parent, a teenager will not usually do well. Sending a teen off to college without preparation for life is copping out on parental responsibility. I have seen many adolescents who seem to behave well at home go wild as soon as they are away from their parents' control. They haven't learned the self-control necessary to handle independence and freedom.

To help prevent this catastrophe, work with your teenager as he *becomes* independent. You want your teenager to realize that you are working with and not against him, toward his independence and freedom. In doing so, you will want to be careful to follow the guidelines of trust vs. consequences. During the few months before he leaves home, you can gradually make your teenager's privileges similar to those he will have where he is going to live—a college dormitory or apartment. You will be training your teenager to cope by using self-control and taking responsibility, when there is little or no supervision.

Such training is hard on parents. After years of carefully training and supervising our children, we must learn to let our dear ones go, and this is a frightening experience. But it is so much easier and so much more constructive to do it at home in a carefully planned and gradual way, working as a team with our teenagers to accomplish it. This means gradually removing as many rules as possible to give our teenagers a few weeks or months of experience with the independence appropriate for an adolescent ready to leave home. We have to be careful here. If we have done our job in training our teenagers, they will handle themselves well.

However, there are a few very common conflicts which often arise, and could be disturbing to the rest of the family—such as coming in at late hours and upsetting other family members. Or being inconsiderate in not letting the household know where he or she will be, especially at mealtimes. Or failing to carry out an expected chore or errand. Or not showing up where and when expected. If such behavior persists, parents need to revert to making privileges contingent on trust and consequences of behavior, since the teen is not ready for full assumption of responsibility.

Security

Although our adolescents are nearing adulthood, their emotional needs have changed little since childhood. Even at this stage, they need to know that we genuinely love them, that we are available, and that we will help them in any way we can, for their own good. As long as they feel we truly care for them, we can continue to have constructive influence in helping them achieve independence.

One problem for many parents at this point is the old enemy—anger. Some parents who handled anger well when their adolescents were younger have a real problem handling it at this critical point. We must remember that this final separation is difficult for our teens. It is a long weaning process during which time we must remain available to offer support and help. Have you ever watched a mother bird push her youngster out of the nest when that time has come? I recently watched several nests of swallows where the mothers were performing this difficult task. Some of the young birds flew with no problems. Some had difficulty learning to fly and mother and father were available to help where needed. Then it happened. One young bird frantically tried to fly but fell through the air. The sickening thud told us the tragedy—it was not ready for departure and the parents were not available to help him in this last phase.

Even after our young person leaves home, *he still needs us.* He needs to know we are there, available, and ready to help when needed. In chapter 9, I mentioned a visit that Pat and I had with Carey's friends at college during their freshman year. All of these fine young people were happy in school and with their new friends. But they all had the same complaint—they seldom heard from their parents. Not enough calls, letters, or visits.

When we later related this to Carey, she admitted she felt the same way, which surprised me. But after thinking it over and remembering my first days away from home, I began to understand. The weaning from a good parent-child relationship is slow and often painful. After that weekend, Pat and I made it a ritual to call Carey every Sunday night to make sure she knew we were thinking about her, praying for her, and ready to help where we could.

Another characteristic about departing young ones is their need for everything to remain the same—just the way they left it. This helps the young person feel secure. It is a good idea to keep as many things as possible the same—especially rooms and personal possessions. He may feel terribly hurt if his room is turned over to a younger brother or sister. And don't be too quick to sell your house and move to smaller quarters. I've heard several teenagers say, "I sure hope my parents never sell our house. I want always to be able to go back home."

However, the most important anchor of security a teen leaves behind is the marital relationship of his or her parents. One of the most devastating things that can happen to an adolescent soon after leaving home is the separation or divorce of his or her parents. It's as though the foundations of his whole world are crumbling. Yet, it is amazing how many parents actually plan to "stay together for the sake of the kids, but as soon as they leave home, we're getting a divorce."

This is extraordinarily unwise. Not only is a teen's basic foundation crushed, but the blow occurs at the very time when he most needs support—a time when he is desperately trying to adjust to a new life, new friends, etc. In most cases, a young person will be burdened with heavy guilt. Regardless of how unreasonable it may sound, a young person feels that he is somehow responsible, either for the bad marriage or for the divorce. If a divorce is inevitable, it is far better that it take place long enough before the adolescent leaves home, so that he can work through the natural feelings of loss and grief with help of parents, friends, and minister, before he takes on the difficult task of leaving home for the first time.

I know one young man, John, who believed that his parents were happy in their marriage when he left for college. Within three months they were divorced. The mother remarried soon afterward and sold the family house. John seldom went home because it was so depressing for him. His base of security was destroyed. You can imagine what this did to his sense of well-being.

Another important factor as children leave is that they stay involved with sources of security, stability, and growth. One of these is the church. It is important not only to attend church regularly with our children and teenagers, but to do all we can to make the church experience pleasant for them. A good youth group is critical especially in the teen years. As our children move to college or work, we need to encourage them to become involved in church and Christian activities.

Spouse Selection

One of our priorities as parents was to make sure each of our children could identify the qualities that are desirable in a future spouse. It is not easy for a teenager to identify traits within a peer which indicate the ability to be a good spouse or parent. Because dating is a somewhat artificial situation, a young person often doesn't have much to go on other than how "good" he feels with that person. Of course, simply depending on such superficial feelings can be disastrous. Regularly, I counsel young people who have made that tragic mistake. They have depended on their feelings to decide whether to become involved or marry, rather than considering other far more important factors.

One of the first things Pat and I taught Carey about this

matter was to look at the character of a boy, as well as to consider the feelings he produced in her. We explained to her that the best indicator of how he will treat his wife after marriage is the way he presently treats persons whom he is not required to treat with consideration—those who are elderly, unpleasant, or helpless. We told her to observe how he treated people in service jobs, such as waiters and waitresses.

A third consideration, and the one Carey really latched on to, was to see how he treated and related to children, especially small ones. For you see, Carey had two younger brothers, providing a perfect litmus. Before we gave her these insights, she used to make sure David and Dale were out of sight before a date arrived. After our discussion, Carey would ask David and Dale to answer the door and talk with her date while she "got ready." It was interesting to watch Carey observe her date from a hidden place, to see how he did with her brothers. Our discussion truly helped Carey gain priceless insight into the boys she dated.

Carey certainly applied the valuable insights she learned from Pat and me. She married a few years ago. Her husband, Chris, is one of the finest young men Pat and I have known. We truly thank the Lord for Chris. He and Carey, by the way, have presented Pat and me with a wonderful granddaughter, Cami.

Another characteristic of a person who will be a good spouse or parent is his ability to reason. This is critical in marital and parent-child relationships; to be a reasonable person, one must be able to reason. If a person can reason, he usually has the ability to come to an agreement or compromise in family conflicts. In other words, the person can argue from his point of view but is able and willing to be proven wrong or to compromise, and to come to a mutual understanding with spouse or child. On the other hand, a person who cannot reason will almost invariably be unreasonable. He will be unable to argue, that is, explain his viewpoint in a conflict, and will probably demand his own way.

These traits, if looked for, can be identified after a short period of time, especially during a situation in which the person is angry. A person who *never* gets angry should be suspect. He could possibly be passive-aggressive, or he may not have the resources to develop a real emotional attachment to anyone. Either of these character types is difficult to live with. However, we must say that there are caring persons who simply are so low-keyed that they seldom are provoked to anger. I envy them. They *are* rare.

Another indicator, which is extremely important but difficult to discern, is a person's ability to manage ambivalence. Ambivalence is having opposite feelings toward the same person. Although ambivalence is difficult to detect, I think the best way to do so is to observe a person's tolerance of different kinds of people. For example, consider the person who has strong and uncompromising opinions about everything. To him, there is no gray area, no room for compromise about anything. He sees people as all right or all wrong, all good or all bad. This person cannot see that there is good and bad, pleasant and unpleasant, in everyone. We all have ambivalent feelings. Handling them well, on a conscious level, is an indicator of maturity. (See chapter 2 of *How to Really Love Your Child* for a deeper discussion of ambivalence.)

Another good way to determine what kind of spouse or parent a person will be is to watch how he gets along with his own parents, brothers, sisters, grandparents, other relatives, and long-time friends. This is an excellent indication of how he will treat his spouse and children in the future.

One problem in letting feelings have too much influence on one's choice of a spouse is that a young person will fail to ascertain the true character of his/her prospective mate. Character is not easy to define nor easy to discover in a person. Character is a person's underlying attitude toward him/herself in relation to others and his/her pattern of behavior.

Most people naturally put their "best foot forward" to make a good impression, especially during courtship. Eventually, however, their true character will emerge in all its good and bad aspects. It is *crucial* for a person to know all he or she can about a prospective spouse's character. Unfortunately, it takes a long time for a person's true character to emerge—especially the negative component. One of the most important truths I have tried to pass on to my children is that *you must know a person well for at least two years before you understand his/her true character.* This is one critical reason why the divorce rate is so high. Most people marry primarily on the basis of feeling, not understanding the character of the spouse, and hence marry too soon.

Be Optimistic

In our discussions about our young people, we have talked about some painful things. But we have also talked about how we *can and should* be optimistic and hopeful about our teenagers and their future. Yes, many of our youth have serious problems—some of them severe. But many are doing beautifully and are a real encouragement to me. Many times we have had the college students from our church come to our home for a get-together. What an uplifting time it was for me, with these warm, wholesome, mature, vivacious, and lovable young people. It reaffirmed for me that our efforts are worthwhile.

Dear parent, this book on teenagers was written expressly *for you* by another parent. My strongest desire was to see my children grow into strong, healthy, happy, and independent adults—and they did, thank God. I desire the same for your teenager. Some of the material in these chapters may be difficult to fully grasp on the first reading. I strongly suggest that you now reread the book, and let the material come together for you in your particular circumstances. We need to be continually reminded how to really love our teenagers.